Babies & Kids: in the City

www.babiesinthecity.co.uk

Jo Maxwell
Louise Taylor
Vanessa Redmond

Published by Babies in the City Limited
792 Wilmslow Road
Didsbury
Manchester
M20 6UG
Tel: +44 (0)161 438 2086
Email: info@babiesinthecity.co.uk
www.babiesinthecity.co.uk

Publisher: Jo Maxwell **Editor:** Louise Taylor
Illustrator: Vanessa Redmond
Authors: Louise Taylor, Jo Maxwell, Vanessa Redmond
Production Editor: Shelley White
Sub-Editor: Alan Rodney
Contributors: Caroline Blackburn, Laura Halls,
Fiona O'Sullivan, Nuala Slim and Kathy Whitaker
Junior Researcher: Rosie Collier

This edition is first published in Great Britain in 2010 by Babies in the City Ltd

ISBN: 978-0-9561215-1-6

A CIP Catalogue record for this book is available from the British Library

Printing and reprographics by Polestar Wheatons, Devon.

© Babies in the City Limited

Prices correct at the time of going to press. Where in operation, prices include a voluntary
10% gift aid donation. Many places listed are closed on Christmas Day and New Years Day.
Opening times may be different on bank holidays.

22

4

Contents

54

56

Contents

Harry, Oliver, Eleanor, Louise, Felix, Jo, Ted, Will, Vanessa and Sam.

Welcome

Six years ago, when my husband and I moved to Manchester, I didn't know a soul and was hopelessly clueless as to where to go and what to do with our baby son. I got there eventually of course but always thought some sort of mum's guidebook would have been handy. Meeting fellow mums Louise and Vanessa kick-started a day dream, and then, in 2009, my idea was realised as *Babies in the City* hit the presses for the first time.

We have been thrilled by the reception of the first edition of this book. The feedback has been tremendous and we have had some brilliant new recommendations. Like last year, we have continued to road test every single entry and it has been a great excuse to go back to all our favourite places. As well as updating our previous entries, we've introduced some exciting new content. I love our fab fresh café list and the addition of 'green-fingered mums' has been great fun too – who doesn't enjoy a potter round a garden centre! Shopping for the kids is a popular pastime for all of us, so it was a labour of love shaping that into a useful directory as well. And as you can imagine, researching our new 'Top Ten Pubs and Inns' section wasn't exactly a hardship!

This year I feel we have fine-tuned and improved the book; much of it as a result of the feedback from our readers. The biggest change is that during the course of our research, it occurred to us that our five toddlers were growing up a little and that we'd

naturally gravitated towards activities for older children also. Hence the addition of '& Kids' this year. However our fingers have remained firmly on the baby pulse too. Louise gave birth to her second child, Eleanor, at the start of last year whilst I had Ted, my third boy, just a few months ago. We're wondering when Vanessa will catch up…!

The *Babies in the City* website is up and running now, and over the next few months we'll be adding an up-to-date events list with child-friendly festivals, special exhibitions and shows, all suitable for families. We're also really excited about setting up our *Babies in the City* online swap shop where local parents can trade unwanted baby and toddler equipment. And hopefully we'll be updating our mums' blog a bit more frequently!

The great effect of writing this book is that we've come to realise what a fantastic place Manchester is to bring up children. The city has so many facilities and resources that there really is something for every type of child. Then of course, you only have to drive ten minutes or so to find the most amazing countryside and all that that offers. We believe we're incredibly lucky to be here and are delighted to be able to share that passion with you.

Jo Louise Vanessa

Museums and galleries

Manchester is superb for museums and galleries. Spanning all ages and tastes, it certainly gives London a run for its money. We've got several new entries this year north of the city, where the wealth of history is immense. So whether you're looking for a world-class destination like MOSI or a labour of love like the Fusiliers, there's little doubt you'll find what you want right here.

Museums and galleries

Bolton Museum, Aquarium and Archive

This museum houses a diverse collection where you can get to know a little bit about the history of Bolton as well as visiting displays of art, egyptology, archaeology, botany and zoology. There's even an aquarium on the basement level with around 18 tanks of exotic fish to have a look at!

We spent the majority of our time in the museum section on the first floor. Exhibits included Samuel Crompton's Spinning Mule, a horse-drawn manual fire engine and antique toys. Climbing up the stairs to the balcony section we found a great collection of stuffed animals including a kangaroo, an enormous African elephant head, monkeys and eagles. Access with buggies or wheelchairs is possible using a private lift so contact a member of staff. Back downstairs we whiled away time in the large children's area. It's got books, a Noah's Ark, a puppet theatre and lots of nostalgic wooden toys and games.

Plenty of pre-school activities are held throughout the year so do check the website. Unfortunately there is no café or any kind of refreshments in the museum but there are shops and amenities very close by. Baby changing is on the ground and first floor. Ask at reception for access.

Mon-Sat 9am-5pm. Admission free.
Bolton Museum, Le Mans Crescent, Bolton BL1 1SE
Tel: 01204 332211 www.boltonmuseums.org.uk

Bury Art Gallery, Museum and Archives

This art gallery was built to house the Wrigley Collection – more than 200 oil paintings, watercolours, prints and ceramics collected by local paper manufacturer Thomas Wrigley, which was donated to the town in 1897. It is set out over two floors and exhibits world-famous paintings such as Turner's 'Calais Sands' and Constable's 'Hampstead Heath' together with a changing contemporary exhibition. The museum is in the basement, which if you are visiting with a pram becomes your first port of call as there is a ramp down to it, avoiding the grand stone steps leading to the main entrance.

I remember when the museum was designed as an old-fashioned street you could walk along; on a recent visit with my boys I found this long gone, replaced by very modern glass boxes containing those original street items, which didn't engage my children. I think they would have preferred it the way it was before.

Upstairs in the art gallery Ollie and Felix immediately took an interest in a colourful totem pole and an embroidered book, before spotting an art table. Plenty of colourful paper, glue and colouring pens were set out so that the children could design feathers for a large bird mural. With feathers dutifully added to the mural, we then began a bit of dressing up. Brilliantly, the art gallery puts costumes similar to those in the paintings on a rail, so the children can dress up and then find themselves in the pictures. They've also created a game from laminated sheets showing eyes that you then have to spot in the paintings. These are two great ways to engage children in art and allowed me some time to look and appreciate the gallery. This is something of a work of art in itself, with fine mosaic floors and stained glass windows.

The children's activities that we experienced take place in school holidays and on Saturdays, and may have to be booked in advance. It is therefore worth contacting the gallery before your visit to find out what is on. The gallery provides picture bags bursting with activities and art materials at all times. So if you are already in Bury and fancy a bit of culture, it's definitely worth a visit. You could always combine it with a trip to the adjoining library, or the newly opened Fusiliers Museum opposite (see page 6). Just remember there is no café. A lift operates between floors and there are baby changing facilities available.

Tues-Fri 10am-5pm, Sat 10am-4.30pm. Admission free.
Bury Art Gallery, Moss Street, Bury, Lancashire BL9 0DR
Tel: 0161 253 5878 www.bury.gov.uk/arts

Catalyst Science Discovery Centre

Despite being only a 30-minute drive from South Manchester, Catalyst had never been on our radar. It does what it says on the tin – it is a science discovery centre, although quite honestly the science is probably a little out of the reach of the under fives (actually it was pretty out of my reach too!) However, Will, our four year old, was very, very taken with it and we ended up spending over an hour and a half mooching around the exhibits. On the wild and

OUT AND ABOUT

At Bury Art Gallery, children can dress up like characters from the paintings, which is a great way to engage them in art.

wet Sunday that we descended on Catalyst there were only three other people at the centre, so we had the run of the place. Will was most impressed with the rucksack he was handed on arrival (to borrow whilst you're at the centre), which contained a yellow safety tabard, helmet, torch and goggles – a great idea.

The ground floor is all interactive with one corner of the room called 'Mini Molecules' dedicated to younger children. Whilst Will and Daddy went to identify the magnetic quality of different metals, and pushed pucks along slippery surfaces, I let Ellie crawl round playing with building blocks and having a go on a little rocking horse. There are some excellent puzzles and games to try – my favourite was a giant fuzzy felt where you had to put together the parts of a flower. It's a great place to entertain younger children whilst the older ones check out how modern materials and chemicals are made using more than 30 hands-on exhibits.

The second gallery focuses on the history of the industrial revolution so is less interesting for the little ones. But the observatory on the top floor is excellent – the views are great and there is plenty to play with. The best for us were the child-friendly telescopes and the build a bridge activity, both of which kept our two entertained for ages. Another bonus was the Elements Café on the ground floor, which serves hot and cold meals and offers a children's menu.

My only niggles with the Catalyst Centre were that it is looking a bit faded, and the entrance price, which is maybe a little steep for those with young children who perhaps might not get as much out of it as older ones. That said, we did love it and it's always great to try something different!

Winter: Tues-Fri and Bank Holidays 10am-4pm, Weekends 11am-4pm. Summer: Tues-Fri, School and Bank Holidays 10am-5pm, Weekends 11am-5pm (last admission one hour before closing). Free car parking outside.
Adults £4.95, 5-16 years £3.95, under 5s free.
Catalyst Science Discovery Centre, Mersey Road, Widnes WA8 0DF
Tel: 0151 420 1121 www.catalyst.org.uk

Museums and galleries

Central Art Gallery

Located upstairs in Tameside Central Library with only two rooms displaying temporary exhibitions this gallery is small but friendly and welcoming. Noise and mess are encouraged and there is always a drawing table to create a piece of art. Regular children's activities for all ages are organised during the school holidays.

Unfortunately there is no café, but there is a drinks machine in the library and some tables to sit at. We needed to buy some lunch during our trip so we went to nearby award-winning café and cake makers, Trifles (see page 73).

So if you find yourself in Ashton-under-Lyne, perhaps visiting the market, and with time to spare, I would definitely suggest popping in.

Baby changing facilities are in the library.

Tues, Weds, Fri 10am-12.30pm/1-5pm,
Thurs 1-7.30pm, Sat 9am-12.30pm/1-4pm,
Mon and Sun closed. Admission free.
Central Art Gallery, Old Street, Ashton-under-Lyne OL6 7SG
Tel: 0161 342 2650 www.tameside.gov.uk/centralartgallery

Eureka!

Voted by *The Independent* as one of the top three family days out in the UK in 2007, Eureka! is well worth the journey. Billed as the UK's National Children's Museum, the thousands of 'must touch' exhibits are designed to inspire children to find out about themselves and the world around them.

We ventured here during the half-term break and it was inevitably crowded (the website actually advises quieter times to be term time mid-week, sunny days and weekends in school holidays). It took us a long time to get in but once we were, it was fantastic and definitely worth the wait. Designed over two floors, there are six main

The ground floor of the Catalyst Science Discovery Centre is completely interactive, with over 30 hands-on exhibits.

galleries aimed at 0-11 year olds and ranging from 'Me & My Body,' where you can find out what your skeleton looks like, to the 'Sound Garden', a giant sensory sound gallery for the really little ones with colourful singing flowers.

The favourite for our party was the 'Living & Working Together' section where the idea is that the children pretend they're grown-ups running the house and carrying out errands. You've got a scaled down Marks & Spencer store where the children shop with a little basket for their (fake) M&S food before scanning the products at a mini till; a Post Office where they can dress up in costumes and post various parcels and letters around the Town Square; a house with every room from the kitchen to bathroom, full of child-size props to explore; plus a fabulous Garage Workshop where there are miniature cars to sit in and steer, pumps to fill them with petrol, a car wash to manually operate and even a tyre changing bay.

The only snag came when we tried to get lunch. Lots of visitors meant the queues at the only café were enormous. Luckily one member of our group had had the presence of mind to pack a few snacks and drinks. So we took ourselves off to sit in the large heated railway carriage provided outside for those who bring their own lunch. That quickly filled up too, so, if you're struggling to find somewhere to plonk down, there are other seating spots on the second floor of the museum. Our advice is, if you are visiting at a busy time, take your own food.

Also worth noting are the pre-school activity room with arts and crafts for under fives and the large outdoor play area. Special events are held monthly at Eureka! in addition to the usual exhibition.

Daily 10am-4pm, Weekends and School Holidays Daily 10am-5pm.
Last admission one hour before closing.
Adult and child from 3 years £7.50, Child 1-2 years £2.50,
under 1s free.
Buggy parks/toilets/baby changing on both floors.
Baby feeding room on first floor. Pay and display car park.
Eureka! The Museum for Children, Discovery Road,
Halifax HX1 2NE Tel: 01422 330069 www.eureka.org.uk

The Fusilier Museum

Opened in 2009 and housed in a renovated and extended arts and crafts building, the Fusilier Museum is home to the collection of the XX Lancashire Fusiliers and the Royal Regiment of Fusiliers, commemorating over 300 years of history and heritage. It is a modern and vibrant addition to Greater Manchester's many excellent museums. I visited with my mum and boys and we got a parking space on a meter outside which had a

The children's area at the Fusilier Museum is fantastic. Felix and Ollie loved dressing up as soldiers and hiding in the camouflage.

particularly impressed by the sets of diagrams on the wall in this area, which enabled children to copy signals or salutes whilst looking at themselves in mirrors. After a quick trip to the toilet I came back to find Grandma being ordered around by two sergeant majors!

We ate lunch in Heroes café on the first floor, which has a mix of sofas, dining tables and bar stools as well as high chairs available. There was a good range of hot and cold meals, although we did find the café a little expensive. All in all we spent a very pleasant couple of hours in the museum and would definitely recommend it. With Bury Art Gallery and Museum directly opposite (see page 4) the two can be combined to make a full day out.

Daily 10am-4pm (last admission half an hour before closing).
Adult £2, Child £1, Family £5.
The Fusilier Museum, Moss Street, Bury BL9 0DF
Tel: 0161 763 8950 www.fusiliersmuseum-lancashire.org.uk

Greater Manchester Fire Service Museum

The Fire Museum is a treasure trove of old fire engines, photographs and uniforms. Laid out as a Victorian street scene, it's aimed at slightly older children, but there's still loads to look at, and never underestimate the appeal of a big red fire engine to a small child. Whilst you aren't really allowed on the engines, once you get chatting to the very friendly volunteers, they'll be happy to let you take a closer look (or at least they were with us).

Toilets and baby changing are available across the yard in the fire station. There is no café, but instead a coffee machine for 50p and crisps for 25p. Volunteers from the brigade have restored most of the exhibits and they also run the museum. It's only been open since January 2008 and already looks like it needs additional space. It's worth remembering that on the first Sunday of every month, the museum holds special events for families.

Parking wise, there is plenty on Richard Street, which is ideal as the entrance to the museum is here and not on Maclure Road. There is also a massive yard that they are happy for you to park in.

Every Fri and the first Sun of every month 10am-4pm.
Admission free.
Greater Manchester Fire Service Museum, Maclure Road, Rochdale OL11 1DN Tel: 01706 901 227
www.manchesterfire.gov.uk/about-us/fire-museum.aspx

Greater Manchester Police Museum

Tucked away in the Northern Quarter of Manchester city centre is the Police Museum. Voluntary run, it's only open on Tuesdays. For toddlers I don't think it is worth a special trip, but if you're in the area and have an hour this is a lovely museum and it's free.

In the Transport Gallery there is a police car and bike to look at, but unfortunately not touch. There

maximum two-hour stay. Alternatively there are plenty of public transport links a stone's throw away. The visit began with the boys getting very excited as they spotted an army jeep parked in a flowerbed in the pretty garden to the side of the museum, and insisted on having their photo taken next to it.

Once through the entrance doors into the new atrium, you are greeted by Bury's Tourist Information Office and a well-stocked gift shop. My boys love anything 'army' so they were immediately attracted to the toy soldiers and tanks on sale. Leading off from the atrium are the toilets and baby change, a lift and staircase to a café on the first floor and the museum itself.

The curators here have really made an effort to make the content appeal to children whilst at the same time respecting the subject matter. Throughout the museum are flaps, puzzles, life-sized fusiliers and interactive computer stations, which can be studied and messed with. In the replicated trench the boys howled with laughter as they dared each other to sniff the revolting smells of carbolic soap, trench sweat and 'poisonous gas' lurking in holes on the wall. One place perhaps where little ones should be reined in is the medal room, which houses six Victoria Crosses awarded to The Lancashire Fusiliers. Embarrassingly, one of the boys managed to set off a security alarm when he became a little too heavy handed here.

The highlight of our trip was a great children's area where the youngsters can dress as soldiers, hide in a camouflaged tent or just sit on beanbags reading books or play with toys provided. I was

Museums and galleries

are a lot of glass cases containing police equipment and uniforms and a case filled with toy cars, which is what my children were most interested in. There are loads of dressing up clothes and handling items like police helmets, which are good fun. You can see the original charge office and the Victorian cells with wooden pillows, which provides a taste of prison life. Upstairs is a beautiful wood-panelled Magistrates Court dating from 1895.

There is a lift and toilets but no baby changing facilities. No refreshments are available, but you're not far away from city centre cafés. There is no car park but meter parking is available outside.

Tues 10.30am-3.30pm.. Admission free.
GMP Museum and Archives, 57a Newton Street,
Manchester M1 1ET Tel: 0161 856 3287
www.gmp.police.uk/mainsite/pages/history.htm

Hat Works – The Museum of Hatting

Hat Works is the UK's only museum dedicated solely to the hatting industry, hats and headwear. Set out over three floors, the first floor is probably the one best suited to under fives. The hundreds of hats are displayed in glass cabinets and though their attention wasn't held for that long, our three-year-olds really surprised us by taking quite a bit of interest. They liked the airline pilots' caps, old-fashioned firemen's helmets, frilly bonnets and especially a native American head-dress. There's a large family fun area with hats to try on plus craft for the children to have a go at making their own – there are also puzzles, puppets and a garage and cars to play with.

On the ground level, you'll find the machinery gallery. It's a recreated factory floor where you can see the collection of working Victorian style hatting machines along with a hatter's cottage and working office. Level 2 houses the café, shop and toilets with baby changing. There's lift access throughout.

Café Pure (run by a not-for-profit Stockport social enterprise) was excellent value for money. Hot snacks for adults include beans on toast for £1.95, with children's lunch boxes starting at £2.10 for four items.

The main entrance to the museum is on the A6; we parked at Heaton Lane car park, which is just next to the viaduct – a 10-minute walk away. Hat Works is also right next door to the bus terminal.

Tues-Sat 10am-5pm, Sun and Bank Holidays 11am-5pm.
Admission free.
Hat Works Museum of Hatting, Wellington Mill, Wellington
Road South, Stockport SK3 0EU
Tel: 0161 355 7770 www.hatworks.org.uk

Imperial War Museum North

A morning trip to the Imperial War Museum lasted around an hour and a half, including a snack break. It is in a fabulous building and a great setting. The children loved the touchy feely action station and

The world-class Museum of Science and Industry – never fails to keep children entertained.

dressing up in the camouflage capes. The Time Stack interactive exhibits are probably more suited to older children, but staff are around to offer more information and take objects out for you to look at.

There are some fabulous large objects including a Harrier AV8 plane and a Russian tank outside (captured from Iraqi forces by the Royal Engineers in 2003), which of course the boys were desperate to climb on though unfortunately it's not allowed! I thought the Big Picture Show – the 360-degree film show projected on to the walls of the gallery – was excellent, but some children could be scared as the whole museum is thrown into darkness. They tend to run on the hour for about 15 minutes and they do give you a five-minute warning before it starts so that's the time to make a quick exit to the café.

There are also temporary exhibitions so check the website for the latest information.

The café is spacious with lovely views of the quay and a children's packed lunch costs £3.95. There are pens and paper available and the staff are happy to supply hot water to warm up milk or food. Toilets and baby changing facilities are downstairs, with the café and museum on the first floor (lift access throughout).

Car park £4. Admission free.
Mar-Oct Daily 10am-6pm, Nov-Feb Daily 10am-5pm.
Imperial War Museum North, The Quays, Trafford Wharf Road,
Trafford Park, Manchester M17 1TZ
Tel: 0161 836 4000 www.iwm.org.uk

We ate at the Terrace Restaurant and sat outside overlooking the Ship Canal and Imperial War Museum – it was an impressive setting (there's also a restaurant serving similar food and a coffee shop with kids' lunch boxes). There are highchairs and a children's menu with four choices of meals such as fish bites and chips or pasta. It costs £5.95 for a main, dessert and a drink. The adult menu is quite extensive but not particularly cheap! A sandwich or salad starts at £5.75.

Baby changing facilities are available directly below the entrance foyer in both the ladies and gents toilets and there is a vending machine selling nappy and wipe kits for £1. Bottle and food warming facilities are by the Tower Coffee Shop and at The Terrace Restaurant. There are sloping floors and lift access to all levels. Parking is in the Lowry Outlet Mall – it's free for four hours providing you make a purchase in the shops or restaurants – present your car park ticket at the till and staff will validate it.

Like many places, The Lowry offers lots of additional family activities aimed at pre-schoolers throughout the year, from dancing to messy art, so check the website for details.

Sun-Fri 11am-5pm, Sat 10am-5pm. Admission free.
Food available 12-3pm and 5pm – 45 minutes prior to curtain up.
The Lowry, Pier 8, Salford Quays, Manchester M50 3AZ
Tel: 0843 2086000 www.thelowry.com

Manchester Museum

'Explore the world and travel through the ages' is what the blurb for Manchester Museum claims and it definitely delivers. It's impossible to describe this museum in just a few lines because its 15 galleries have a bit of everything. There are skeletons galore, including a sperm whale, Stan the Tyrannosarus Rex and the recently introduced Maharaja, an elephant that once lived in Manchester. There's also an Egyptian room brimming with ancient art (including mummies) and the Darwin exhibition (running until August 2010), amongst millions of other items to look at.

The Lowry

Visiting The Lowry Galleries was a much more rewarding experience than I expected. First of all getting there – because it's slightly out of the centre and parking's all on site, it felt easy to access. There's also a bus service and the Metrolink tram drops you a 10-minute walk away. So we parked up and took a short stroll around the Salford Quays before arriving at the magnificent steel and glass clad Lowry building.

The feeling of space inside the brightly coloured foyer with its sloping blue floors is fantastic. We headed first for 'The Deck' and 'Family Corner', which are upstairs just to the left of the admissions desk. The Family Corner is aimed at the under fives and is a vibrant orange and red area full of mirrors, crayons and paper, magnet boards to stick things on and other games to play. The Deck area includes moving exhibitions. When we went there was a display of amazing pop-up designs where you could have a go at making your own, and a comfy sofa with children's pop-up books to pore over.

Next, to the main gallery. Again, it contains exhibitions that are continually changing throughout the year though there'll always be a collection of Lowry paintings on show. On our visit in the summer holidays the exhibition was, 'So you want to be an Artist?' and there happened to be lots of activities for children, which was great.

Sam and Freddie getting wet in the Living & Working Together gallery at Eureka!

Museums and galleries

Highlights from our visit were the small but perfectly formed Vivarium and Aquarium where the snakes, lizards and frogs entranced the children. We also got quite a lot out of the quaintly old-fashioned stuffed animal section, and the giant spider crab that welcomes you in the foyer is fantastic – it's over three foot high and nice and creepy! On the first floor, we found a small but colourful interactive area that has been created specifically with under fives in mind and there is plenty for them to investigate. Continue on to the third floor and there's the 'Play + Learn' space where children can read, draw and relax. Close by is the picnic area if you have a packed lunch or alternatively there is the museum café, which is excellent. There's a well-planned children's menu with choices such as sausage and mash or fish pie for £3.50 (they're generous portions so sharing's an option) or you can get a lunch box for £4.50. Highchairs are available and staff will help with bottle and food warming for babies. There are baby changing facilities throughout the museum.

Ultimately, it's a museum with a really nice feel and a wealth of exhibits. You can spend as little or as long as you like. Family orientated workshops are held regularly throughout the year so do check the website for details.
Tues-Sat 10am-5pm, Sun and Mon 11am-4pm. Admission free.
The Manchester Museum, The University of Manchester,
Oxford Road, Manchester M13 9PL
Tel: 0161 275 2648 www.manchester.ac.uk/museum

Manchester Regiment Museum and Setantii

The Manchester Regiment Museum is situated within the beautiful Town Hall in the main square of Ashton-under-Lyne. There are a number of steps leading up to the Victorian building but if you've got a pushchair there is side access with a lift. We went during the summer holidays and just chanced upon one of its regular art and craft sessions, every Wednesday during the school holidays between 11am and 3pm. The children loved making Nelson style hats, which went very well with the Sportacus outfits!

TOP FIVE MUSEUMS AND GALLERIES

MOSI
An outstanding museum reflecting Manchester's position as the birthplace of the Industrial Revolution – great fun for all ages. You never knew learning could be so much fun!

Museum of Transport
Buses win the popular vote from Babies in the City readers – we've had nothing but positive feedback. We love it.

Portland Basin Museum
A bit of a gem that's definitely worth discovering. With a fantastic changing programme of exhibitions, this is a real treat.

Eureka!
The UK's first and foremost children's museum and a truly unique experience. This is a centre of excellence definitely worth making the trip across the Pennines for.

The Fusilier Museum
A fabulous building with a magnificent collection celebrating a Regiment's heritage – loads to see and do for the whole family.

The museum tells the story of generations of Manchester Regiment soldiers from 1756 until 1958. There are lots of historical objects on display, including 1,800 medals of which five are Victoria Crosses. You'll also discover a few interactive exhibits and clothes from various eras to dress up in. In one section, there's a reconstruction of a First World War trench, which is actually a bit dark and quite scary for little Sportacuses.

Previously unknown to us, there is also another museum here called Setantii, which is the name of an ancient British tribe who lived in Tameside up to the time of the Roman conquest. This museum explores the history of Tameside from Celtic times to the present day. I actually preferred this museum; there are a lot more exhibits that appeal to small ones, including a 1940s kitchen and an air raid shelter complete with sound effects.

If you're local to Tameside, you can also trace your family tree at Tameside Family History Centre, which offers one-to-one help and advice, and is free.

Baby changing facilities can be found on the ground floor.
Manchester Regiment Museum Mon-Sat 10am-4pm, Sun closed. Setantii Mon-Fri 10am-4pm, Sat 10am-1pm, Sun closed. Admission to both museums is free.
Manchester Regiment Museum and Setantii, The Town Hall, Market Place, Ashton-under-Lyne OL6 6DL Tel: 0161 342 2254
www.tameside.gov.uk/museumsgalleries/

Manchester Museum's latest exhibit, Maharaja, who previously lived at Belle Vue Zoo is proving a hit.

The Clore Interactive Gallery gives children a chance to explore works of art through a range of hands-on activities.

Manchester Art Gallery

The Manchester Art Gallery was short-listed for the Guardian Family Friendly Museum Award in 2008. The gallery itself is of course stuffed with fabulous paintings by artists such as Adolphe Valette and Lowry, and while you're trying to check out the masterpieces there's a few dressing up clothes for the children to play with.

We tried to encourage our two-year-old to follow the drawing trail (cartoon-esque labels underneath some of the paintings by the children's illustrator Tony Ross) around the gallery and despite him being a bit young for it, we had mild success! Another feature are the story play bags that you collect at the information desk (free, but deposit required). The ones for children aged 3-6 years contain things like novelty cushions, paper and pencils, a magnifying glass and farmyard animals. Even better there's the Clore Interactive Gallery on the first floor where you get to explore real works of art through a range of hands-on activities. There are computer screens with headphones where you press a button to choose the character you want to see and hear; a game where you can race chariots; and magnetic boards where you stick on various items like sink plungers to create your own portrait. It's definitely worth a visit.

We had a lovely lunch in the ground floor café. The children's menu had two hot dishes (12-2.30pm) to choose from or a lunch box, all priced at £3.95. There are colouring packs and highchairs were available.

There are lifts to all floors or you can leave prams in the ground floor cloakroom. Baby changing is in both sets of toilets on the ground floor. There are various car parks all within five minutes of the gallery.

The Mini Family Art Club for under fives runs the second Friday of every month 10.15-11.15am and 11.30am-12.30pm. Advance booking is required. Other free family events run throughout the year.
Tues-Sun 10am-5pm. Closed Mon except Bank Holidays. Admission free.
Manchester Art Gallery, Mosley Street, Manchester M2 3JL
Tel: 0161 235 8888 www.manchestergalleries.org

MOSI (Museum of Science and Industry)

A world-class museum right on our doorstep – MOSI (Museum of Science and Industry) – never fails to keep my children entertained and when we have friends from out of town to stay, it is absolutely one of my favourite places to visit. I love the fact that you can dip in and out of this museum, that each time you go there'll be a different part that you probably didn't get around to seeing last time. With five major buildings – Main Building, 1830 Warehouse, Station Building, Power Hall, and Air and Space Hall – the sheer scale of the museum also means that the children can really enjoy having the space to run about and explore.

Due to the exciting redevelopment work currently taking place in the Main Building, which will see the removal of the central ramped staircase, the Xperiment gallery will be closed until summer 2010. This fantastic interactive area, where the whole family can get hands-on with science, will reopen after a major overhaul with several new exhibits to capture children's imaginations, plus putting the 'E' back in place at the start of its name. It will also retain old favourites such as 'Lift the Mini', where you can marvel at a real car that travels up and down a vertical wall using gears and chains; watch a tornado form – disturb it with your hand and watch it take shape again; and sample tubes to shout down or smell. Another excellent element of Xperiment that will be returning is the Under 5s area, with one corner of the room dedicated to babies.

One key change to the Main Building will be a stunning new gallery on the ground floor, 'Revolution Manchester', which will display iconic objects that tell the story of the city. From textile factories to Factory Records, the interactive gallery will celebrate Manchester's impressive industrial, technological and cultural heritage, as well as look to the city's future.

MOSi's Loft Café is currently on the second floor of the Main Building (a brand new relocated version is due to open in autumn 2010 as part of the redevelopment work). It is very popular and does tend to get busy in the school holidays so be warned. Children's portions of hot food start at £3.95 or you can purchase a sandwich lunchbox with five items for the same price. There are also separate picnic areas if you choose to bring your own food. Baby changing is located in the Main Building and in the 1830 Warehouse, although the number of spaces will be slightly reduced in the Main Building during the redevelopment work. If you ask, the staff will endeavour to find you a private room for breast-feeding.

The Museum of Transport is clearly a labour of love – and one that everyone should go to.

The Air and Space Hall is a big favourite. Located in the building just across the road from the main entrance, it is full of planes, cars and motorbikes as well as the fantastic motion simulator Morphis for the slightly older children. The Power Hall is another hit with youngsters – it has a superb range of trains on show as well as one of the largest collections of working steam mill engines in the world. MOSI also has a ride-on train – a replica of Stephenson's Planet steam locomotive, which operates at certain times during holidays and weekends. The train puffs up and down a short piece of track taking you past the world's oldest surviving passenger railway station (still on site!) and back again. The trip only lasts about 10 minutes but it is definitely worth it.

A visit to MOSI is a guaranteed success where kids are concerned. There's something for all ages and too much to cover in this entry – we didn't even get on to the Planetarium (minimum age advised is six years) or the Victorian Sewers – you'll just have to go!

Needless to say, MOSI runs lots of special family events throughout the year so do check the website.

Car park £7 before 9am, £5 after 9am, £3 after 3pm. Meter parking close by.

Daily 10am-5pm (except 24-26 Dec and 1 Jan).

Admission free to permanent galleries.

Train runs from February-September at weekends and during holidays 12-4pm. It can be cancelled at short notice so do check ahead before making a special trip.

MOSI (Museum of Science and Industry), Liverpool Road, Castlefield, Manchester M3 4FP

Tel: 0161 832 2244 www.mosi.org.uk

Museum of Transport

This is one that everyone should go to! The Museum of Transport is delightful. It's clearly a labour of love for all the volunteers that run it, and you can't help but be impressed by the enthusiasm behind it. Located within a genuine bus garage just off Cheetham Hill in Manchester, the museum features original transport offices preserved like time capsules from the past, complete with antique décor, furniture, old ticket machines and uniforms. Some of the collection was actually used in one of the Harry Potter films. There are over 70 restored buses, coaches and trams – honestly, when you first walk in, it's a sight to behold! You'll find yourself transported to a bygone age with vehicles dating from an elaborately painted Victorian open-top horse-drawn omnibus and a 1920s solid-tyred bus right up to the prototype for the modern trams that run in the city centre today, a few of which can even be climbed on.

Many of the buses are roadworthy and when the museum holds its frequent special event weekends (check the website), the classic buses are used to provide a free shuttle service, ferrying visitors to and from Victoria rail station or Heaton Park.

There is a café selling light refreshments including pies for £1.40 and a cup of tea for just 60p. They will provide hot water for heating up baby bottles. Baby changing is available in the disabled toilets and there is ramp access throughout the building.

Parking is on the road outside and we had no problems – one side has a yellow line so restrictions

Babies in the City 13

kidsunlimited
day nurseries

kidsunlimited has earned a reputatio
as a leader in top quality, progressiv
childcare.

kidsunlimited **offers:**

✔ warm, friendly and safe environments where
each child is encouraged to reach their full potenti

✔ boundless opportunities for children to learn
through imagination, creativity and play.

✔ parents the peace of mind that comes from
knowing their children couldn't be better cared for.

✔ experienced managers with care focused and
enthusiastic team.

✔ just one flat monthly fee. Our fees include all
the nappies, formula milk and later on, healthy,
balanced, nutritious meals.

We would be delighted to accompan
your child on their journey to explore
and discover the world.

Save £50
on your registration fee

◆ **Macintosh** (next to Oxford Road train station)
◆ **Didsbury** (Barlow Moor Road)
◆ **St Mary's** (off Princess Parkway)

To arrange a visit or for more informati
call **0845 365 298**

www.**kids**unlimited.co.u

Portland Basin is an immaculately kept museum designed with children in mind.

are in force weekdays and Saturdays until 12.30pm. The nearest car park is around five minutes' walk away at the Manchester Fort shopping centre.
Weds, Sat, Sun and Bank Holidays 10am-4.30pm. The museum isn't free and depends on donations. Adult £4, under 16s free.
Museum of Transport, Boyle Street, Cheetham Hill, Manchester M8 8UW Tel: 0161 205 2122 www.gmts.co.uk

Ordsall Hall

Ordsall Hall is a historic treasure – an amazing black and white half-timbered Tudor manor house located in the heart of Salford. It's a lovely place to visit with children as the exhibitions are very good, but it is presenly closed for a massive restoration project. It is due to re-open Easter 2011.
Ordsall Hall, Ordsall Lane, Ordsall, Salford M5 3AN
Tel: 0161 872 0251 www.salford.gov.uk/ordsallhall

People's History Museum

After two years of major refurbishment the new People's History Museum will now be based in one location, with a spectacular new extension.

This social history museum tells the story of democracy in this country and proves that ideals have always been worth fighting for. It is very much a family-friendly gallery with plenty of interactives for all ages throughout the building.

There is a café called The Left Bank as well as picnic areas on-site in the old engine hall. The new museum re-opens on Saturday 13 February 2010.
Daily 10am-5pm. Admission free.
People's History Museum, Left Bank, Spinningfields, Manchester M3 3ER Tel: 0161 838 9190 www.phm.org.uk

The Portland Basin Museum

This is a tad tricky to find if you're not familiar with the area but don't be put off – it is definitely worth finding. The main problem with locating the museum is that the boat signs that direct you to the Portland Basin disappear at what seems a crucial moment. For the record, coming from Manchester, when you hit the dual carriageway of Park Parade – on the opposite side is an industrial park with a large plumbing merchants visible – the museum is on the cobbles behind.

It is housed in a restored 19th century warehouse right next to the canal, hence the boat connection. Laid out over two floors, the ground floor contains the social history section whilst the one below is set aside for industrial history – it's an immaculately kept museum with lots to do with little ones. Downstairs, for example, there are displays of local crafts and industries with historic machines, a fun video game where you sit in the hull of a canal boat and have a go at steering it, and a 'Nuts and Bolts' educational play area for the under fives including costumes and props to play with. On the other floor is a brilliant mock-up of a 1920s street, with a school room and a fish and chip shop amongst others – all of which you can go in to. It's the perfect museum, with lots of buttons to press and flaps to open and it is easy for the children to run around too.

We spent a whole morning here very successfully

Museums and galleries

and then finished off with lunch at the Portland Bistro, where the food was great and the service exceptional. This is a lovely museum in a great setting and is definitely one to add to your list of must-see destinations!

Tues-Sun 10am-5pm. Admission free.
Portland Bistro 10.30am-4pm. Tel: 0161 344 2591
Portland Basin Museum, Portland Place, Ashton-under-Lyne
OL7 0QA Tel: 0161 343 2878
www.tameside.gov.uk/museumsgalleries/Portland

Salford Museum and Art Gallery

This small museum and gallery on the A6 approach to Manchester city centre seems surprisingly overlooked. We started with the ground floor (there are only two), which is more the museum bit. The main feature is Lark Hill Place, a recreation of a typical Salford street during Victorian times. On the way in there are a couple of clothes rails and a mirror, so plenty of fun can be had trying on flat caps and waistcoats! Once inside it is a fantastically dark, atmospheric experience crammed full of detail – toy shop windows, a cobblers, a Penny Farthing and lots more.

The art galleries are upstairs and the Victorian Gallery in particular contains plenty of activities to keep all ages amused whilst you take in some art. There is colouring, sculptures to touch, worksheets full of quizzes such as matching up the animals on the sheet with the animals in the paintings, and a box with hats in that again link in with the pictures. Most successful for us however were the colourful soft bags placed strategically around the room that contained various items relating to the paintings they were under. For example, the portrayal of Queen Victoria's arrival in Salford has a bag underneath containing crowns, books, a flag and a mini ermine and fur robe. It is a really well thought out idea.

The LifeTimes Gallery hosts changing exhibitions focusing on different aspects of Salford's history over

Salford Museum's main feature is Lark Hill Place, a recreation of a typical Salford street during Victorian times.

the last 200 years. One recent theme was music, when a corner of the room was dedicated to children with a miniature record shop (complete with till and vinyl singles) and small musical instruments to play on. A definite hit with the under fives.

We had a quick cup of tea in the Lark Hill Tea Shop (open Mon-Fri 10am-3.30pm) and although there's not a dedicated children's menu, we thought the food on offer sounded good value – sandwiches and toasties from £2. Highchairs are available and staff will heat up baby bottles and food. Baby changing is in the disabled toilet on the ground floor – you need to get the key from reception which is close by.

Salford offers additional family-friendly exhibitions throughout the school holidays. It also advertises 'Gallery Tots', a once-a-month story, singing, games and craft session for pre-schoolers.

Free parking is in front of the museum. Salford Crescent train station is a five-minute walk away.

Mon-Fri 10am-4.45pm, weekends 1-5pm. Admission free.
Salford Museum and Art Gallery, Peel Park, The Crescent, Salford
M5 4WU Tel: 0161 778 0800 www.salford.gov.uk/museums

Staircase House

This is a modern museum set in the oldest house in Stockport. It is a rare place indeed that actively encourages children to climb on the beds, touch everything and dress up in the various clothes dotted around, but that is exactly what's on offer.

On arrival children are handed a cloth activity pack with individual mini-bags numbered to match the relevant rooms. A word of advice though – do not get one for each child, it takes three people to manage this; one to hold the big bag, one to get the stuff out and the other to control the children! Inside there is also a laminated sheet which basically tells you the same thing; the packs are aimed at older ones but it is worth getting one just for the two glove puppets that are included.

In all the rooms bar the dining room children are encouraged to inspect, touch and play with the objects, which gives you time to have a good look around yourself. One of the favourites for the under fives is the counting room, where you can write with quill pens and literally get covered in ink. Another is the dressing up area – the only downside is that it is hard to drag them away.

Being linked to a modern building means that Staircase House has all the essentials, including a lift and baby changing facilities. The Stockport Story Museum is also housed in the modern section and gives a background to life in the town. It is a little bit dry for children but is definitely worth a look. There is a toy box at the bottom level that does gain you an extra 10 minutes while they have a root through.

Parking is fine on a Sunday as there are single yellow lines outside the building. During the rest of the week there is a pay and display car park nearby.

Staircase House: Tues-Sat 10am-5pm, Sun 11am-5pm.
Adult £3.95, Child £2.95, under 5s free.
The Stockport Story Museum: Mon-Sun 10am-5pm.
Admission free.
Staircase House, 30-31 Market Place, Stockport SK1 1ES.
Tel: 0161 480 1460 www.staircasehouse.org.uk

Stockport Air Raid Shelters

Stockport Air Raid Shelters is a network of tunnels nearly a mile long, dug out of the soft red sandstone hills on which Stockport town centre stands. We went on a Friday just after the last school trip of the day, so we had the tunnels to ourselves. We were specifically asked at reception if our three-year-old would be ok with the audiovisual display. They warned us it was quite loud. I thought he would be fine but he wasn't! The lights went down, the sirens started and Will freaked – we were back in the reception area within 30 seconds!

The labyrinth of tunnels are remarkable, authentically restored with props that give you a taste of daily life in 1940s war-torn Britain. The tour is very well illuminated and fully accessible for wheelchair users. The Air Raid Shelters are perhaps more suited to older children but it really does depend on the type of child you've got. There is no café or refreshments, no toilets or baby changing facilities, although there are public toilets directly across the road. There is some metered parking outside or Merseyway multi-storey car park a minute away.

Tues-Fri 1-5pm, Sat 10am-5pm, Sun and Bank Holidays 11am-5pm.
Adult £3.95, under 16s £2.95, under 5s free.
Stockport Air Raid Shelters, 61 Chestergate, Stockport SK1 1NE
Tel: 0161 474 1940 www.airraidshelters.org.uk

Stockport Art Gallery and War Memorial

Dating back to 1919, this gallery is found in a fabulously imposing neo-Classical building standing right next to the busy A6. Although not particularly one for the under fives, adults will enjoy the paintings and sculptures of local and national importance. Also of note is The Hall of Memory, a semicircular apse in the centre of which is a huge white marble sculpture depicting 'the sacrifice and devotion of the 2,200 men of Stockport who fell in the war'.

Tues-Fri 1-5pm, Sat 10am-5pm, Sun 11am-5pm.
Stockport Art Gallery, Wellington Road South, Stockport SK3 8AB
Tel: 0161 474 4453 www.stockport.gov.uk

Touchstones Rochdale

Based alongside the Tourist Information Centre in Rochdale, Touchstones is a modern, well laid out arts and heritage centre. It is ideal for under fives as there is just enough to keep their interest and I stayed much longer than I'd planned.

A guided tour in a Yellow Duckmarine is a superb sideshow for toddlers during a trip to the Tate Liverpool.

Tate Liverpool

The gallery itself, whilst terrific for adults, isn't geared for children. But if you can get an hour while your child is asleep in the pushchair, it's a lovely place to visit. The art is world class and the building is very pram friendly with ramps and lift access throughout.

The café has a selection of choices for the adults – exotic sandwiches, salads, pastas and dips. The children's menu has fish fingers, pasta or a cheese sandwich with cucumber and carrot sticks. This is topped off with fruit salad, chocolate brownie or banana split and washed down with fruit juice. It's a pretty good deal at £4 and that includes crayons and a colouring sheet. There are plenty of highchairs and a unisex baby changing facility in the basement below the café.

If you are visiting with toddlers this is an ideal trip to combine with The Yellow Duckmarine, otherwise known as the Wacker Quacker. This is a fleet of World War Two amphibious vehicles painted bright yellow and used to provide guided tours around the city. The tour guides are jokey and informal and the vehicle is unusual enough, what with its roll-up polythene windows etc to keep young minds and hands occupied. However, all of this pales into insignificance compared with the moment when children realise the bus is actually going to drive into the river. You hurtle down the gangplank arriving with a huge splash, and the tour finishes with a half-hour motor around the docks.

Tours depart approximately every hour, seven days a week from 10.30am till dusk (lasting around an hour). The ticket office opens at 9am. Children under two must sit on an adult's lap and only two babies are permitted on each tour. Prams and pushchairs can be left in the ticket office by the Albert Dock Visitor Information point.

The Yellow Duckmarine, 32 Anchor Courtyard, Albert Dock, Liverpool L3 4AS Tel: 0151 708 7799
www.theyellowduckmarine.co.uk
Adult £9.95, Child £7.95, under 2s free.
School and Bank Holidays, weekends Mar-Sept.
Adult £11.95, Child £9.95, under 2s free.
Tate Liverpool, Albert Dock, Liverpool L3 4BB
Tel: 0151 702 7400 www.tate.org.uk/liverpool
Sept-May Tues-Sun 10am-5.50pm (closed Mondays).
June-Aug Daily 10am-5.50pm.
Admission free apart from special exhibitions.

Museums and galleries

Although the museum is all in one room, the space is really well utilised as you keep noticing new things. There are loads of interesting objects accompanied by manageable amounts of text.

My three-year-old, after much persuading, enjoyed crawling through the coal pit tunnel and there were lots of hands-on activities in drawers including a bucket which smelt disgusting when you took the lid off, plus a lovely area with dressing up clothes and a large mirror.

There is a small but enticing café attached to the museum that offers good value options such as a bacon bap and cup of tea for £2. They also have heaps of cakes and do children's lunchboxes for £2.90. Baby changing is in both the ladies' and disabled toilets on the ground floor and there is lift access to the art gallery.

I left Touchstones with a real sense of times gone by in Rochdale; the staff were helpful and friendly and all told it was a thoroughly enjoyable visit. There is pay and display parking immediately outside and I'm glad I'd put in £1 for two hours instead of 70p for an hour.

Mon-Sat 10am-5pm, Sun and Bank Holidays 12-4.30pm.
Admission free.
Café: Mon-Fri 11am-4pm, Sat 11am-3pm.
Touchstones Rochdale, The Esplanade, Rochdale OL16 1AQ
Tel: 01706 924492 www.rochdale.gov.uk

Urbis

Since its arrival in 2002, Urbis has gone on to form an iconic part of Manchester's skyline. Sadly, from Saturday 27th February 2010, it will be closing to undergo transformation into the National Football Museum. It is due to re-open some time in 2011.
Urbis, Cathedral Gardens, Manchester M4 3BG
Tel: 0161 605 8200 www.urbis.org.uk

The Whitworth Art Gallery

Even with two little ones in tow, a visit to the Whitworth is still a favourite trip of mine. I find the gallery just so tranquil and inviting. Set over two floors and with plenty of ramps, it's easy to push prams around. The large airy spaces mean toddlers can enjoy a good waddle around too. At the entrance, you can pick up themed 'family bags' containing colouring paper and activities to entertain the children as you wander around and there's a couple of costume stations for them to try on outfits and amuse you with.

The Art Cart is now located near the wallpaper gallery. Here you'll find colourful beanbags for the kids to loll around on together with toys, books and activities such as jigsaws, floor shapes and stencils to get stuck into. Every Sunday from 1.30-3.30pm, the Whitworth runs 'Colourful Sundays' – a free

Even with little ones in tow, a visit to the Whitworth Art Gallery is still a favourite.

drop-in suitable for all ages where you can have a go at making things such as (pretend!) fireworks and sparklers, as on the day we went. Throughout the year, but particularly during the school holidays, the Whitworth is very proactive in putting on specific family events and art workshops for all age ranges, so it's worth checking the website or calling in for a leaflet to see what's coming up.

We always enjoy eating at the award-winning Gallery Café. It's not especially cheap but the menu's nice and seasonal and the food is freshly prepared. A children's option is always available, at a cost of £5.50 including a choice of pudding and a drink. Staff at the café are also more than happy to provide hot water to heat up jars and bottles. Baby changing facilities are available in the unisex disabled toilet on the ground floor. If you want to take a packed lunch there are picnic tables and a large grassy area outside as well as Whitworth Park next door.

My final tip is that as the gallery's positioned on a busy bus route, you may want to think about combining a visit with a bus trip. If you're driving, it is worth trying to grab a free place on Denmark Road next to the gallery, although there is a two-hour time limit. Otherwise there's a couple of car parks signposted just across the road.

Mon-Sat 10am–5pm, Sun 12-4pm. Admission free.
The Gallery Café at The Whitworth serves breakfast
Mon-Sat 10-11.30am, lunch 11.30am-3.30pm, Sun 12-3.30pm.
The Whitworth Art Gallery, The University of Manchester, Oxford Road, Manchester M15 6ER
Tel: 0161 275 7450 www.manchester.ac.uk/whitworth

Parks, woods and walks

Don't be deceived by the relative lack of city centre parks in Manchester. You're within easy reach of the grandeur of the Peaks and Pennines, the wildlife and woodlands along the Mersey Valley and the faded Victorian glamour of Heaton and Vernon Parks. So unpack your wellies and take to the great outdoors.

Parks, woods and walks

OUT AND ABOUT

Alderley Edge

Alderley Edge is a National Trust woodland with an impressive sandstone escarpment (the Edge!) and spectacular views over Cheshire countryside to the Peak District. It's a place steeped in mystical folklore and the area is strongly associated with a wizard thought to be Merlin.

We always have fun at Alderley Edge, with plenty of woodland tracks to explore and tree trunks to climb it's not surprising. We usually follow the wizard's walk, a 3.5-mile route taking in a number of landmarks featured in the legend of the wizard. Not for the faint-hearted is the 'thieves' hole' – a very deep unlit circular cave dug into the red sandstone high enough to walk into. Elsewhere you'll find a water pump to mess with; a tiny wizard's house (a stone hut!) and the Beacon marking the highest point of the Edge. Whilst this is great to climb up to, some of the paths are a bit steep – we've managed with a pushchair but you can avoid them if you wish.

If you are stuck for something to do on those perpetual rainy days but feel like getting some fresh air, then try Alderley Edge. The woodland canopy is dense enough to provide shelter from the rain during the spring and summer months.

There's also a tea room and a small enclosed wooded picnic area with tables, or alternatively you're not too far from The Wizard Inn if you fancy something a little stronger. There is an information office selling maps of walks and children's quizzes/trails. Public toilets are in the car park but provide no baby changing.

Access to the Edge: Winter 8am-5.30pm, Summer 8am-6pm.
Tea-room: Weekends Winter 10am-5pm,
Summer 10am-6pm and Bank Holidays. Admission free. The car park is pay and display, but is free to NT members.
Alderley Edge, situated on the B5087 at Nether Alderley, Macclesfield, Cheshire SK10 4UB Tel: 01625 584412 www.nationaltrust.org.uk

TOP FIVE PARKS

Lymm Dam
Gorgeous woodlands, a tranquil lake and an amazing rock feature. A haven to escape to.

Roman Lakes
Peaceful, beautiful and picturesque. Perfect for a stroll and a pot noodle!?

Heaton Park
A vast, beautifully landscaped park. Go for boating, farm animals, the land train and donkey rides.

Smithills Country Park
On the edge of the West Pennine Moors with superb views across Bolton, this is a great estate to explore. Take a picnic and enjoy.

Walton Hall and Gardens
An award-winning park with a zoo, playground and heritage centre. This is the ideal place for a family day out.

Boggart Hole Clough

Boggart Hole Clough is an ancient, densely wooded park three miles north of Manchester city centre. Park in the free Charlestown Road car park and set off in the direction of the lake but one word of warning – the park is anything but flat! As the name indicates it's in a clough – which means a ravine. In former times, the clough was said to be haunted by the Boggart, a mischievous goblin or phantom.

We were a bunch of one pram containing a baby, one toddler walking and three on scooters. So the scooters were whizzing perilously down hills, the mum with the pram was puffing up hills and amazingly the toddler just kept on walking regardless! We found the lake and had a walk round – it's nice enough but a bit neglected. You could imagine how it was in its glory days. We then headed further downhill into a more densely wooded section which made for a picturesque walk (there are tarmac pathways throughout so prams aren't a problem if you can cope with the ups and downs). We were aiming for the playground at the Rochdale Road end of the park, which was probably about a half-hour child's walk from the lake. But when we got there it was in fact a bit bleak – you'd be better going to the one close to Charlestown Road car park, which is relatively new and has swings, a climbing activity train and a roundabout.

The Lakeside café is now open in the old boathouse, serving hot drinks and food, where you'll also find toilets and baby changing. There are further toilets in the main car park, accessed by a key kept in the adjacent visitor centre.

Lakeside Café: Tues-Thur, Sun 11.30am-3pm.
Visitor Centre: Mon-Fri 8.30am-4.30pm, weekends warden dependent.
Boggart Hole Clough, Charlestown Road, Blackley, Manchester M9 7DF
Tel: 0161 795 2650 www.manchester.gov.uk/leisure

Kids love Alderley Edge, with plenty of woodland tracks to explore and tree trunks to climb it's not surprising.

Bruntwood Park

The best reason for visiting Bruntwood is its modern and well-equipped playground. There are three areas side by side, each aimed at different age groups. All the usual swings, slides and roundabouts are present, but there is also a really big climbing frame with lots of interesting features and one of our favourites, the giant ball catcher – where you hurl your ball into a large metal bucket on a seven-foot high pole and wait for it to drop out of one of four holes.

The different play areas are linked by gentle slopes which are perfect for children learning to ride a bike. In season and during most school holidays there's an inflatable bouncy castle (you do have to pay though). There's also vast expanses of green grass, mature woodland, ponds (with ducks) and wetland areas to explore.

Attached to Bruntwood Hall (not open to the public), in the original Victorian conservatory, there's The Vinery restaurant. It's very child-friendly (lots of highchairs and they will heat bottles and jars). For children you can choose things like pasta, sausages, fish fingers or sandwiches, which with a drink and ice cream costs £3.20-£3.50. They also serve breakfast, which is handy for early risers! Baby-changing facilities are in both the men's and ladies' toilets.

Back in the park, there's outside seating and a refreshment kiosk open during weekends and holidays. There is a baby-changing room in the toilet block close to the kiosk.

Pay and display car park.
The Vinery: Winter 10am-4pm, Easter onwards 10am-5pm .
Tel: 0161 491 0531
Bruntwood Park, Bruntwood Lane, Cheadle, Stockport SK8 1HX
Tel: 0161 428 5391 www.stockport.gov.uk

Clifton Country Park

Clifton Country Park boasts over 50 hectares of perfect meadows, woods, ponds and lakes and is an appealing tranquil setting. The main car park is by the visitor centre with a children's playground on the left-hand side just before you reach the water's edge. The play area is suitable for 3-11 year olds with the usual swings, slides, rope bridge and climbing frame. There is also an equestrian centre close by so there are plenty of horses in the fields to look at.

The main lake is huge, with geese and swans eagerly waiting to be fed and a purpose-built jetty to get to them. It's surrounded by buggy-friendly paths and took me about 40 minutes to walk round. It's mostly flat with lots of benches for resting and is well maintained. There's no café, but often a van sells refreshments in summer. Baby-changing is available in the toilets situated in the visitor centre but this isn't open all the time.

'Buggy walks' and various children's activities are held regularly, so do get in touch with the visitor centre for details. What appealed to me was the Tree Trail – some very user-friendly leaflets (pick up at the centre) with clear photographs of assorted leaves and the name of their respective trees for the older children to spot along the way.

Visitor centre: Mon-Tues 1-5pm, Fri 10am-5pm, Sun 10am-5pm, (these hours can be slightly unreliable during the winter).
Clifton Country Park, Clifton House Road, Clifton, Salford M27 6NG
Tel: 0161 793 4219 www.salford.gov.uk/cliftoncountrypark

Daisy Nook Country Park

Daisy Nook is an area of the Medlock Valley between Oldham, Failsworth and Ashton-under-Lyne. Despite us missing the turning it is actually quite easy to find (follow the sign to Daisy Nook Garden Centre)

Parks, woods and walks

Chorlton Water Park, Chorlton Ees and Ivy Green

Tucked away, not far from Princess Parkway, you'll find this great all-round park. It is a very easy one-mile walk round the lake and with flat paths it is perfect for pushchairs or bikes. There are a couple of gentle sandy slopes down to the water, ideal for feeding the ducks or poking around in the mud with a stick.

Take detours off the path and you'll find blackberry bushes and almost directly across the lake from the main entrance, over the bridge, you'll discover a path on your left leading to Kenworthy Woods – essentially a secret orchard, where you can help yourself to apples, plums and pears.

The playground is a bit basic – in truth it's probably due a revamp but to the right, through the trees, is an education pond with a boardwalk.

There is no café but on fine days there is an ice cream van that does a great trade. If you fancy a more strenuous walk then you can continue along the River Mersey that runs parallel to the far side of the lake and stop off at Jackson's Boat pub or continue through Chorlton Ees to Sale Water Park (see page 30) for a coffee.

Chorlton Ees and Ivy Green are a network of pathways, woodland and open fields (mostly pram-friendly), which can be accessed from several entrances, including a car park on Brookburn Road, Chorltonville, Chorlton. As there are several pathways it is a case of taking your pick and having a bit of an explore, but we usually take the far left path out of the car park along the stream until you come to a red bridge on your left. If you continue straight, you will eventually reach some playing fields that are great for kite flying. There is no café or toilets although there is a pub opposite the car park and you are only a stone's throw from Beech Road, Chorlton Green where you will find a plethora of places to eat.

Toilets for Chorlton Water Park are in the car park. The disabled toilet does have baby-changing facilities but you need to get the key from the office. The office is open during normal working hours and at the weekend there is an information desk open 9.30am-12.

Chorlton Water Park, Maitland Avenue, Chorlton, Manchester M21 7WH. Tel: 0161 881 5639 www.merseyvalley.org.uk

and is only five minutes from the motorway and Ikea. At the bottom of the hill is a free car park and The John Howarth Countryside Centre, a friendly café with information leaflets and displays. They sell hot and cold snacks, including bacon barms, toasties, cups of tea and hot Vimto. Tables can be found inside but there's also an outdoor picnic area.

It is worth calling in here for maps of the park as you can do short walks or longer trails that link up with other areas. Despite being so close to the M60 the park is attractive and diverse, with woodland, ponds, canals, rivers and a meadow. Most of the walkways from the visitor centre, although nice and flat, are along waterways which are all unguarded, so take care with young children. It is also only when you look over the edge of the path that you realise you're actually on the old aqueduct 80 feet above the winding River Medlock.

In the summer, the river's a great spot for paddling. In June 2007, Lowry's 'Good Friday, Daisy Nook', sold at Christies for nearly £3.8 million, the highest price paid for the artist's work at auction. The Easter fair celebrated in this painting is still held at Daisy Nook every year.

Café: Mon-Fri 9.30am-4pm, Weekends 9am-5pm.
Toilets with baby changing.
Daisy Nook Country Park, Stannybrook Road, Failsworth, Manchester M35 9WJ
Tel: 0161 308 3909 www.oldhamparks.co.uk

Delamere Forest

At 2,300 acres, Delamere Forest is the largest area of woodland in Cheshire and, quite simply, stunning.

Lots of dry sandstone paths make it ideal for buggies and bikes. There are clearly signposted routes around the lake that vary in length and the terrain is generally flat (with just a few ups and downs). There is certainly a choice of easy-to-walk forest roads and trails ideal for families with children on foot. Though we didn't do this particular one, there's even a trail with musical instruments on it to entertain the children!

No glockenspiels on our route, but biking around the beautiful forest, we happily bumped into an ice cream van halfway around. After some more strenuous cycling, we settled in for a lovely lunch at the Delamere Café in the visitor centre, where you'll find a kids' corner with an eight foot long fish tank as well as books and toys. For those with babies, there is a microwave for warming bottles and food.

Whether learning to ride a bike or just being pulled along, the kids had a terrific time and enjoyed watching the more adventurous adults attempt the treetop zip wires and Tarzan swings of Go Ape also sited at Delamere. You can rent bikes for the older children and adults as well as child

The best reason for visiting Bruntwood Park is its modern and well-equipped playground.

seats and trailers. Several car parks are available costing £2-£3 per day, although those adjacent to the information centre can get very busy at weekends.

Delamere hosts a range of annual summer concerts, which are well worth checking out. See the website for details.

Linmere, Northwich and Delamere are the nearest towns or villages. The forest park is well signposted from the A54, A556 and B512.

Delamere Café: Summer 9am-5.30pm, Winter 9am-4pm.
Tel: 01606 882726 www.delamerecafe.com
Information Centre: Summer 10am-5pm, WInter 10am-4pm.
Car park: Summer 8am-8pm, Winter 8am-4pm.
Delamere Forest Park Visitor Centre, Forestry Commission,
Linmere, Delamere, Northwich CW8 2JD
Tel: 01606 889792 www.forestry.gov.uk

Etherow Country Park

With family staying for the weekend and feeling in the mood for a brisk country walk before lunch, we all headed to Etherow. One of Britain's first country parks, it's approximately 240 acres in the Etherow-Goyt Valley, rich with wildlife, fungi, waterways and plenty of child and pram-friendly pathways. We set

off from the pay and display car park in George Street, Compstall, near the visitor centre, where there are also toilets and a café. The visitor centre, which sells duck food, aims to be open daily 9am-5pm but they can't always man it so it's potluck.

There were hundreds of birds by the man-made lake at the start of the walk: pink-footed geese, swans and ducks amongst others. We took a pram-friendly pathway that led past a small garden centre up the Goyt Valley alongside the waterway through woodland. We walked over and past a few footbridges perfect for Pooh sticks. There were a couple of picnic tables overlooking the weir – a lovely place to eat on a summer's day. The circular walk to the weir and then round the lake took just over an hour and was very manageable for my 23-month-old who didn't get in his stroller once. After our walk, we spent some time watching the sailing boats on the lake before heading to the café, where highchairs and baby-change facilities are both available.

Cafe: Daily Summer 10am-5pm, Winter 10am-4pm.
Pay and display car park. Toilets Daily 9am-5pm
Etherow Country Park, Compstall, Stockport SK6 5HN
Tel: 0161 427 6937 www.stockport.gov.uk

Fletcher Moss Botanical Gardens

Whether in summer or winter, this park is beautiful. There is limited parking off Millgate Lane and on Stenner Lane, but beware of parking in the Didsbury Pub car park as there are clamping signs everywhere.

The café opens most weekends and daily through the summer months, as well as occasionally on a cold bright winter's day. There is a small visitor centre at the bottom of the building behind the café which is open Mon-Fri 8am-4pm, and at weekends if there is a warden. Toilets are usually open, but there are no baby-changing facilities.

If you manage to get past the café without being tempted by the cakes, the old bowling green is now a pergola garden with wooden arches and roses,

Fletcher Moss is a botanical treat – beautiful at any time of the year.

Parks, woods and walks

making it an ideal picnic spot as dogs aren't allowed. There is a beautiful sloping botanical garden that follows a small stream down to a clay pond at the bottom. If you can keep the children quiet for long enough, you can see terrapins sunbathing on the lily pads.

My kids love this park for scootering as the gentle slopes make it a bit more exciting than other places, although they do tend to shatter the peace and tranquillity as they fly down the hill! You can also continue on into Stenner Wood. Although often flooded in autumn, in spring it is full of bluebells and snowdrops, and if you carry straight on you reach the River Mersey.

There is a paved path that leads back to Stenner Lane, and across the road you'll find Parsonage Gardens. This is a lovely spot with rare trees and beautiful gardens. It also contains the original orchid house, which is open if the ranger is there. You'll find koi carp and goldfish in the pond inside.

Fletcher Moss Botanical Gardens, Wilmslow Road, Didsbury Manchester M20 2SW Tel: 0161 434 1877

Healey Dell Nature Reserve

It's quite some time since I've been on a walk where so many people have said hello! Healey Dell is a very friendly place indeed and I gleaned quite quickly that it is clearly a popular walking spot for those local to the area.

It's one of those places that I think if you live nearby would be wonderful to exploit – for us who'd travelled some way with a baby in a buggy and a toddler, we'd misjudged the terrain somewhat. Much of the beauty of this area comes from the fact that the River Spodden has carved its way through a steep-sided valley. It's a dramatic landscape with waterfalls and well-known sites such as 'Fairies Chapel' being at the bottom of a steep descent, so impossible to access with a pushchair. We saw one couple with their baby in a backpack nipping over a narrow stile – they clearly knew what they were

doing! Nonetheless, we had a pleasant enough walk on the route marked for wheelchair users. We followed a trail that included a section of the abandoned Rochdale to Bacup railway line and found ourselves on top of a 100-foot high viaduct gazing across the magnificent Spodden Valley. This beauty spot is quite remote in feel, despite the fact that there are houses and streets nearby, so it's definitely one to visit with a friend.

Healey Dell Ranger Office: Mon-Fri 9am-4.30pm.
Healey Dell Nature Reserve, signposted from A671 Rochdale-Bacup Road and from B6377 opposite Healey Hotel. Car parking at Broadley Wood Lodge, off Station Road (probably the best place to park) and at the Ranger Office.
Healey Dell Ranger Office, Healey Hall Mills, Dell Road, Shawclough, Rochdale OL12 6BG
Tel: 01706 350 459 www.healeydell.org.uk

Heaton Park

One of the largest publicly-owned parks in Europe (650 acres, Grade II listed) and just four miles north of the city centre, there is loads to see and do with little ones in beautiful Heaton Park. There are four car parks so look on a map before you go to work out which one's best.

First off we visited the Farm Centre – home to pigs, cows, sheep, rabbits and alpacas, although the animals were slightly upstaged by the tiny outside play area with its wooden tractor. Thankfully the lure of a donkey ride tempted them away. The donkeys from the farm are harnessed up most weekends to give children rides for £1 in a large meadow at the front of the buildings.

Next up was the land train, which runs every day through the summer and school holidays from 11am. It takes you on a generous circuit around the park for £2 each. Heaton Park isn't short on hills with its spectacular views over the Pennines, so the train is a perfect alternative to walking. It's easy to take a pram along as well – they have a couple of specially adapted carriages with built-in ramps so you can just push your buggy in and sit next to it.

There are two places to eat – The Stables Café near the farm and The Boathouse Pavilion in a gorgeous setting next to the lake. It's basically self-service though you can order a selection of hot platters. Highchairs and bottle warming facilities are available and there is baby-changing in the toilets.

After lunch we hit the playgrounds – there are two large children's areas providing a range of activities for 3-14 year olds. Also worth mentioning are the rowing boats, which can be hired daily during the summer and out of season at weekends. They cost £8.50 for up to four people for 45 minutes.

There is so much to see and do at Heaton Park but one of the main attractions is the animals.

Holcombe Hill

As a child I lived at the foot of Holcombe Hill and therefore I'm rather fond of it, or more particularly of Peel Tower perched at the top. It was built to commemorate Sir Robert Peel, former prime minister and founder of the modern police force. I have since returned with my boys and we have enjoyed the spectacular views of Manchester and North Wales, whilst sat at the top of the hill eating a picnic.

On first assessment, there isn't anything particularly child-friendly about it – the paths are difficult for pushchairs and there are no toilets or places to eat. I therefore wouldn't recommend it for people who would struggle carrying children some of the way. But it is an achievable walk for older toddlers and for parents carrying children in a papoose or back carrier. There is a village and pub close by offering refreshments and toilets, so for that reason I would recommend it as a place for a good family walk. My three-year-old certainly demonstrated a sense of achievement at reaching the top of the hill and, after our picnic, enjoyed rolling back down parts of it again.

The tower is open on various days of the year, so if you can manage a further 150 steps after the hill climb, try and coincide your visit with an open day. On Good Friday morning it is traditional to roll eggs down the hill, and you will usually find children of all ages taking part.

Car parking available on Lumb Carr Road.

Holcombe Hill, Accessible from Lumb Carr Road, Holcombe Village, Bury www.bury.gov.uk

Holcombe Hill may be a stiff climb but Ollie and Felix relished the challenge.

Vintage tram rides operate on selected Sundays and most Bank Holidays (with limited winter opening times so check first). They run along a small length of track between the depot and the lakeside (the price may change but currently an all day ticket is £2). During most school holidays you're likely to find a fairground alongside the boating lake.

Also at the park are Heaton Hall (a Grade I listed country house, open 3rd Apr-29th Aug 11am-5.30pm Thurs-Sun and Bank Holidays), the wildlife garden and pond, a tram museum, orangery, 18-hole 'to scale' pitch and putt, horse riding and a garden centre.

Animal Centre open daily Easter-Sept 10.30am-6.30pm (in school holidays) and 10.30am-4.30pm (during term time); Sept-Mar 10.30am-3.30pm.

Stables Café open daily Summer 11am-5pm, Winter 11am-3.30pm.

The Boathouse Pavilion open daily Summer 8.30am-4.30pm, Winter 8.30am-3pm.

Heaton Park, Junction 18 or 19 of the M60, Off Middleton Road (A576), Prestwich, Manchester M25 2SW Tel: 0161 773 1085 www.heatonpark.org.uk

Hollingworth Lake Country Park

The two and a quarter mile flat perimeter path around Hollingworth Lake offers a superb walk if you have toddlers and pushchairs in tow. The lake is man-made (dating back to 1800) but appears natural and has beautiful countryside surrounding it. On a clear autumn day I took my parents, a three-year-old and a baby. The three-year-old managed to walk almost the whole distance without stopping, and was kept entertained by muddy puddles, a bridge over a weir, plenty of wildlife (ducks to feed, birds, rabbits, domestic dogs), throwing pebbles in the lake (not at the wildlife) from the small beach, and if that was not enough there is a small children's playground at the end of the circular route. There are plenty of benches for those who want to sit and take it in or eat a picnic. That said, there's also a great fish and chip shop at the side of the lake.

Pay and display parking is available at the visitor centre on Rakewood Road, where there is a café, toilets with baby-changing facilities, and the playground. In the

Parks, woods and walks

summer, rowing boats are available for hire and there is a ferry service across the lake. There is a vast network of paths and woodland (not suitable for pushchairs), which connect to the perimeter walk. These are great for toddlers who are good at walking or if you are using a papoose. A couple of lovely pubs overlook Hollingworth Lake, which offer meals and bar snacks, making a Sunday walk followed by a pub lunch a particularly attractive option.

Visitor Centre Apr-Oct Daily 9.30am-5pm, Nov-Mar Mon-Fri 11am-4pm, Weekends 10.30am-5pm.
Café Apr-Oct Daily 10am-4pm, Nov-Mar Mon-Fri 11.30am-3.30pm, Weekends 11am-4.30pm.
Alice Ferry: weather permitting Apr-Oct Weekends 1-5pm, school summer holidays Mon-Sun 1-5pm.
Crossing: Adult £1.50, Child £1.
Circle of Lake: Adult £2.50, Child £1.50.
Rowing boats: weather permitting Apr-Oct all day but no life preserves available.
Hollingworth Lake, Rakewood Road, Littleborough, Rochdale OL15 0AQ Tel: 01706 373421 www.rochdale.gov.uk

Longford Park

Despite the fact that between us we've lived in Didsbury and Chorlton for donkeys years, neither myself nor my friend Caroline had ever visited Longford Park, just a mile or so down the road in Stretford. So it was good to spend a couple of hours here exploring with our four children.

The park dates back to 1850 and still contains the historic coach house and stable buildings, though unfortunately the original house constructed by John Rylands, the famous cotton merchant, has been flattened. We strolled around the pretty gardens and although in some places you could see money needs to be spent (The Friends of Longford Park group is battling to raise funds), it was a lovely

place to wander. There are two children's play areas – one, for the slightly older children, had us rapt for ages because it had the most fantastic see-saw swing contraption (see above). The other playground is near Pet's Corner, with baby swings, slides and a sit-on roundabout. Pet's Corner itself is small but a bonus; there are hundreds of birds to look at together with rabbits and Horace the 12-year-old goat! There is no café (not a problem when you are only a stone's throw away from the amenities of Chorlton) but there are public toilets.

Longford Park, Edge Lane, Stretford, Manchester M32 8PX
www.friendsoflongfordpark.org.uk

Lymm Dam

Driving around Cheshire one day we passed a sign for Lymm Dam so decided to take a detour. We parked on the road over the dam itself, although later we learned there was a car park just behind the church that overlooks the lake.

LOVE — Babies in the City

There are two paths that take you on the mile or so circular route around the lake, one of which is wheelchair-friendly. We opted for the other one, which was perfectly easy going with three-year-old Max and five-year-old Lucas. If we'd had a pram, bar a few steps, I still think it would have been fine. As you walk, there are various diversions to keep the children happy. There are fishing platforms jutting out that they can climb down to (under strict

Clambering over the rocky outcrop formed millions of years ago at Lymm Dam is by far the favourite part of the walk.

Longford Park has two excellent children's play areas, one of which has the most fantastic see-saw style swing feature.

supervision) and throw sticks into the water. The path winds through some attractive beech woodland to the wishing bridge, a small hump-backed stone bridge under which the water rushes into the main lake – the children were fascinated by the two different water levels on either side. A little further on is another, smaller bridge, over the drain – this sluice is made of cement and with wellies on, the boys were able to walk down and paddle at the edge of the water. We continued on, finding a couple of rope swings, and just as Max began to complain of being tired we reached the church, situated close to the road where we parked. Before we reached the road, however, we came across a sort of rocky outcrop. Formed millions of years ago, this significant geological feature known as the 'bluff' provided the most fun, as the boys clambered up and down the red sandstone. It was far and away their favourite part of the walk. There is a paying public toilet on the road (although I couldn't get it to work when I tried it.) Or there is always the pub next to the church if you're desperate.

With plenty of benches and some picnic tables dotted all the way around, as well as the buggy-friendly path, Lymm Dam made for a really pleasant, easy walk.

Lymm Dam, South of Lymm Village on the A56, Lymm, Cheshire WA13.
Ranger: Tel 01925 758 195 www.warrington.gov.uk

Moses Gate Country Park

Restored from an old industrial site, this beautiful 305-hectare park is a place of national scientific interest due to its unique wildlife. It's easy to find and there's plenty of free parking – we parked at the bottom car park, which brings you virtually straight into the excellent children's playground and the Rock Hall Visitor Centre.

Moses Gate is centred on three lakes with miles of scenic parkland to take a walk in. There are pathways and seating everywhere, and the area we ambled around was nice and flat so access with a pram is easy. There's no café but plenty of well-maintained picnic areas. There are also lots of fun sounding 'Toddler Walks' with the ranger each month aimed at pre-school children and their families, so phone ahead to find out what's coming up.
Baby-changing in the visitor centre toilets.
Visitor centre Mon-Sun 9.30am-4.30pm
Moses Gate Country Park, Rock Hall Visitor Centre, Hall Lane, Farnworth, Bolton BL4 7QN
Tel: 01204 334343 www.boltonlife.org.uk

Moss Bank Park

In the summer holidays Moss Bank Park has an assortment of fun fair rides and activities, including a bouncy castle, an enormous inflatable slide and a carousel. In winter it is a much more sedate park but that is how I prefer it.

Moss Bank is also home to Animal World, which sounds quite grand and raises your expectations. Grand it isn't, but this is a free attraction and it is definitely worth a visit. You enter via the Butterfly House, which is actually pretty good, with wooden walkways over a running stream where you can see lots of fish, and butterflies are flying overhead in the tropical environment. You then move outside to a selection of animals and birds with peacocks roaming freely, as well as guinea pigs and farm animals, plus some lovely chipmunks.

Children love getting stuck in at Moss Bank Park, there's no shortage of things to do here.

Parks, woods and walks

The play area is comprehensive, with large slides and climbing frames as well as two huge sandpits, although in the summer it can get very busy at weekends. There is also a miniature steam railway running on Sundays throughout the year and more frequently during the summer.

Parking is free. Park in the bottom main car park as the small one at the top is for blue badge holders only. There are toilets in the car park but they tend to be open only in summer. The toilets by Animal World are always open but unfortunately there are no baby-changing facilities in either block.

There is a small café (open during the summer and at weekends in winter) doing a great trade in tea and ice creams, but what I liked was the hot Vimto for £1. Unfortunately they can't warm up baby bottles.

Animal World: Summer Daily 10am-4.30pm, Winter Mon-Thur 10am-3.30pm, Fri 10am-2.30pm, Weekends 10am-3.30pm. All times subject to change, so please phone ahead.
Animal World and Butterfly House, Moss Bank Park, Moss Bank Way, Bolton BL1 6NQ Animal World Tel: 01204 334050
Moss Bank Park Tel: 01204 334121 www.boltonlife.org.uk

Park Bridge

About five minutes away from that giant Ikea in Ashton, you'll find Park Bridge Nature Reserve. This side of Manchester is all pretty new to me, but if you look on a map you'll see that Daisy Nook,

Discover the history behind Park Bridge Nature Reserve. There are several nature trails and a lovely Heritage Centre.

Etherow County Park and Goyt Valley, amongst other open spaces, are all kind of joined up, and somewhere in the mix is Park Bridge. Once the site of one of the region's biggest iron works, this is now almost completely gone bar a few buildings and the area has been reclaimed as a nature reserve.

The Park Bridge Heritage Centre, set in the old stables, celebrates the local history. We started off by wandering around here reading the displays – for the children there's a small pretend coal tunnel to duck into, a touch and feel table and a couple of exhibits with buttons to push. Outside there are several trails around the area taking in the extensive history and geology of the district. We took some advice from the wardens there on which walk to tackle and opted for a fairly short circular route that bar a couple of gentle hills was nice and easy for us with the pram. We're looking forward to going back and tackling something a bit more challenging next time! Tearooms, light refreshments and toilets are all available.

Heritage Centre: May-Sep Tues-Thurs 11am-4pm, Weekends 11am-5pm, Bank Holidays 12-5pm; Oct-April Tues-Thurs 11am-4pm, Weekends 10am-4pm, Bank Holidays 11am-4pm.
Park Bridge Heritage Centre, The Stables, Park Bridge, Ashton-under-Lyne, Tameside OL6 8AQ
Tel: 0161 330 9613 www.tameside.gov.uk

Pennington Flash Country Park

With a huge lake as its focal point, Pennington Flash is a beautiful country park in Leigh. Clearly popular, there's a large pay and display car park by the water's edge.

We started our visit with the obvious favourite – the children's playground, which everyone loved. There was sand to play in, a large net-style circular swing, toddler swings and even a metal satellite dish style spinning ride – great equipment but I imagine on a busy weekend it may not be quite big enough.

Next we embarked on the walk. We checked the map first, did the toilets second (surprisingly clean – big tick there!) and then set off on what turned out to be a lovely hour-long stroll. The well-maintained paths were easy to navigate with scooters and prams and remained pretty much flat all the way around. There were a couple of bird hides strategically dotted about and the children enjoyed learning about what they were used for and then, of course, trying to spot some birds.

We ended up back at the car park tucking into ice creams from the van parked next to the lake. Make sure you take some bread, as there's plenty of ducks to feed along the way.

Pennington Flash Country Park, Off St. Helens Road, Leigh, Greater Manchester WN7 3PA Tel: 01942 605253 www.wlct.org

The bird hides at Pennington Flash Country Park are a brilliant feature that really capture children's imagination.

Philips Park

Opened in 1846, Philips Park is one of the world's first municipal parks. It's still crammed with original features including the carriage drive, serpentine paths and plantation, although its Victorian splendour has worn a little thin.

It's situated next to the City of Manchester Stadium and covers 31 acres of ground, with the River Medlock running through the middle. We found the best place to leave the car was on Stuart Street – the entrance there brings you straight in at the younger children's play area, then you can drop down towards the duck pond and have more of a walk around the bottom area of the park. It's all very accessible with plenty of footpaths and not overly steep. Toilets are in the lodge at the entrance close to the playground but they are only open when the warden is in residence.

Philips Park, Stuart Street, Manchester M11 4DQ
Tel: 0161 231 3090 www.philipspark.org.uk

Platt Fields Park

Although not the prettiest, Platt Fields has a lot to offer. There are two great playgrounds for small children, one specifically for under fives with lots of age-appropriate equipment and a central boating lake which is paved all around.

During the summer you can hire boats for around £5 for half-an-hour for up to four people. Through the rest of the park there are walking paths where you tend to stumble on some rather nice little mini-gardens such as the Shakespearean Garden and the Eco Arts Garden, the latter of which is great for exploring.

Toilets are in the Lakeside Centre, which is open every day, and there are baby-changing facilities in the disabled toilet. If you're driving, the car park isn't signposted and it's tucked down off Mabfield Road with a one-way system in operation.

Platt Fields Park, Wilmslow Road, Fallowfield,
Manchester M14 6LA Tel: 0161 224 2902 www.plattfields.org

Reddish Vale Country Park

Reddish Vale Country Park spans over 398 acres of green belt land along the River Tame in the heart of Stockport. Depending on where you think you might end up, you can either park at the bottom of the hill by the country park and walk up to Reddish Vale Farm and tea rooms or park by the farm and walk down to the country park. Either way parking is free and is less than a five-minute walk away.

To your left as you come to the bottom of the hill there is a little mill pond with great views of the viaduct and The Vale. To your right, past a small visitor centre, there is a wooded area heading down to another pond with a large wooden walkway enclosed by the river. There is also a large grassy area surrounded by a paved walk, which is the butterfly conservation park.

You can find baby-changing facilities in the toilets by the visitor centre and at Reddish Vale Farm (see page 47).

Tearooms at Reddish Vale Farm: Sat 9am-4pm,
Sun 9.30am-4pm. Open daily in school holidays
9.30am-4pm. Tel: 0161 480 1645.
Visitor Centre: Daily 1-4.30pm, closed Fridays.
Reddish Vale Country Park, Mill Lane, end of Reddish
Vale Road, Reddish, Stockport, SK5 7HE
Tel: 0161 477 5637 www.stockport.gov.uk

Parks, woods and walks

Roman Lakes Leisure Park

Less than 10 miles from the centre of Manchester you'll find the Roman Lakes – a real hidden gem. Though there is no tangible connection with the Romans, this was apparently a popular spot in Victorian and Edwardian times when excursion trains would ship visitors into nearby Marple Station.

It's a funny one to find if you're not in the know – a narrow, winding road eventually brings you out into the tranquil and beautiful valley in which sits the Main Lake. We took a gentle stroll around with prams and toddlers on foot – it got a bit boggy at times due to recent rainfall, but I think in sunny weather it would be fine.

There were many different birds to spot, from moorhens to herons, and we even saw a few fish. We ended back at the small refreshment hatch (open 8am-dusk) ordering coffee and ice cream – though they also do a magnificent range of pot noodles! We then sat outside enjoying the views of the grand Marple Aqueduct whilst the children were in the under eights play area. A very picturesque spot to spend an hour or two.

Roman Lakes Leisure Park, Lakes Road, Marple, Stockport SK6 7HB Tel: 0161 427 2039 www.romanlakes.co.uk

Sale Water Park and Broad Ees Dole Nature Reserve

The Mersey Valley is an important wildlife corridor running through the urban areas of Manchester and Trafford. It's a huge sector made up of wetlands, grasslands and woodlands.

Our walk started at the Mersey Valley Visitor Centre, where we parked the car. We set off down a pathway in the direction of Broad Ees Dole Nature Reserve, walking alongside Sale Water Park. The footpath was gentle and well surfaced and for the most part quite protected by tree canopies with gaps exposing views of the marshland and of course the lake. Despite it being a blustery day our three-year-old walked about a mile, which took us just into the Nature Reserve. Broad Ees Dole was formerly a flood meadow – the area now incorporates wetland, reed beds, meadow and woodland habitats. There are no footpaths leading through the Dole, they are around the perimeter but provide excellent viewpoints from which to watch the birds.

We headed back towards the car and decided to take refuge in Café Ark, which is adjacent to the visitor centre. It's a great little find, quite small – only six tables inside but several outside if the weather is fine. It's nicely individual, with paintings hanging on the walls, books and magazines to browse through and wonderful smells wafting out

Jo, with two-week old Ted in a sling and Laura, together with the boys enjoying the tranquility of the Roman Lakes.

of the kitchen. There's a large blackboard just underneath the serving counter and children are invited to draw. We didn't eat but the food, all vegetarian and made from scratch, looked great – lots of tempting dishes including cheese and onion pie for £5.50 or soup and a roll for £3.50. They are happy to provide water to heat up bottles and will blend any food for babies. There are also several highchairs available.

Toilets are located opposite the car park and are open seven days a week 10am-4pm.

Café Ark: Summer daily 11am-5pm, Winter Tues-Sun 11am-4pm, Tel: 0161 969 6775
Visitor Centre: Winter Tues-Fri 11am-4pm, weekends 1-4pm, Summer Tues-Fri 11am-5pm, weekends 1.30-5pm.
Mersey Valley Visitor Centre, Rifle Road, Sale Water Park, Sale, M33 2LX
Tel: 0161 905 1100 www.merseyvalley.org.uk

Smithills Country Park

Combining a walk in this country park with a trip to the adjacent Smithills Farm (see page 48) – and if you're up to it, a tour around the magnificent medieval hall – is a good way to pack a lot into a day trip to Bolton!

We started with a walk around the hall's gardens; they're neither sizeable nor grand, much more country garden style, but in full bloom they're charming – totally enhanced by the backdrop of Smithills Hall. After this we headed towards

the surrounding woodland following the shorter red-signposted route. A gravelled winding path led us down quite a steep descent to a bubbling stream then back up again towards the car park – all beneath a huge canopy of trees. It took around 30 minutes and bar a couple of steps was perfectly manageable with a pushchair and two toddlers on foot. The only hiccup for me was getting out at the other end as the wooden gate was a bit narrow for my pram, but one wheel off later and with a bit of persistence, we escaped!

For those with kiddies in backpacks you might want something a bit more challenging – Smithills actually comprises over 2,000 acres of woodland and grassland so I'm sure you'll find what you are looking for.

Toilet facilities are in Smithills Hall.
Smithills Hall: Summer Daily 12-4pm, closed Saturday.
Winter Fri and Sun 12-4pm. Adult £3, Child £2, under 5s free.
Smithills Country Park, Smithills Dean Road, Bolton, Lancashire BL1 7NP Tel: 01204 334010 www.boltonmuseums.org.uk

Stamford Park

This is a pretty big park, so big in fact that I made a fool of myself and drove through the open wrought iron gates instead of parking on the road outside!

The park boasts a small duck pond, large boating lake across the road (which operates seven days a week during the summer), a beautiful conservatory and a lovely wooded area known as The Dingle. The beds are beautifully kept and the bowling green

Parks, woods and walks

immaculate, but the park seemed to lack a bit of atmosphere. The aviary was missing the birds and the play area was a bit of a mish-mash. What looked like a water feature has been filled in to create a large sandpit and the café looked neglected and was closed.

Thankfully Tameside has realised what potential it has on its doorstep and £3.9 million has been granted by the Heritage Lottery Fund to dramatically improve the park. This will include overhauling the aviary and building a new pavilion to house a café, toilets and information centre. Renovations start in Spring 2010 and will be carried out over 18 months. Check the website for detailed information before setting out.

Stamford Park, Mellor Road, Stalybridge SK15 1QR
Tel: 0161 342 3348
www.tameside.gov.uk/consultation/stamfordpark

Tandle Hill Country Park

As you approach Tandle Hill Country Park, it has a really lovely feel. There is a wooden play area near the car park that is mainly aimed at older children but is very nicely designed and beautifully kept. There are a variety of walks of differing lengths, with an ideal two-kilometre circuit fully accessible with a pushchair. Once into the woods and across a small stream, there is a detour along a stone path to the highest point in the park, which provides fantastic views across to the Pennines, the Peak District and down into Greater Manchester. There are steps back down to the path, but if you're with a pushchair or bikes then you'll have to go back the way you came.

There's a café near the play area with plenty of tables as well as lots of grassy spots for a picnic. You'll find an information centre and toilets but unfortunately no baby-changing facilities.

Café: Weekends, School and Bank Holidays 11am-4pm.
Tandle Hill Country Park, Tandle Hill Road, Royton,
Oldham OL2 5UX Tel: 0161 627 2608
www.tameside.gov.uk/countryside/walk/health/tandle

Spinning around having some old-fashioned fun in Walton Park. As opposed to being on the wii!

Beautiful 'country style' gardens at Smithills, make this park in Bolton a must.

Vernon Park

Vernon Park is Stockport's oldest park, opened in 1858. It's a grand old place, typical of Victorian civic parks. Restored to its former glory in 2000 after decades of neglect, it's a beautiful open space overlooking the Goyt Valley and its river below.

In truth there's not a lot here for small children. There's no playground, nor any bespoke facilities. Not only that but Vernon Park is built into a steep hill and walking up with toddler and buggy is not for the faint-hearted. That said, for all its child-friendly flaws, this is a glorious park. There are lawns, fountains, cannons, sculptures and even a maze.

There's also a small café and slightly idiosyncratic (but tiny) museum containing artefacts of Stockport history with some Egyptian mummies thrown in for good measure, although there is no lift access. Both café and museum are run by Pure Innovations (a not-for-profit charity) and feel like a labour of love. A tots group runs every Thurs 10am-12noon (£2) but you need to phone and book. Baby-changing facilities are in the ladies' toilets downstairs.

Café and museum open weekdays 10am-4pm; weekends 11am-4pm (Bank Holidays and April-Sep until 5pm).
Vernon Park, Turncroft Lane, Stockport SK1 4AR
Tel: 0161 474 4460 www.stockport.gov.uk

Walton Park

Just off the Washway Road in Sale, where there is free parking, this is a lovely little park, with a couple of playgrounds and an enclosed area for the under fives.

Some of the playground facilities may be a little dated but this park has one special feature – a miniature railway. The quarter-mile, circular route is run by members of the Sale Area Model Engineering

Society and operates on Sundays between 12noon and 4pm. It's 30p a ride for both children and adults and has been running for more than 30 years.

Behind the park is the Bridgewater canal, which has a lovely towpath that is easily accessible for pushchairs and only a short walk from Sale.

Walton Park, Raglan Road, Sale M33 4AN
Tel: 0161 912 2000 www.trafford.gov.uk

Wythenshawe Park

This public park covering around 250 acres in south Manchester has a lot to offer – a working community farm, a playground, a sixteenth century hall and even a horticultural centre. It also has historic and ornamental woodlands, formal flowerbeds and beautiful wildflower meadows to explore.

The small farm (a registered charity) is always our main reason to visit. Because it's free and on the doorstep, it is easy to pop in for half-an-hour. There are cows, sheep, pigs, horses and chickens – the usual suspects. You can buy eggs here as well. If you're after a pleasant walk, a trip to a playground and a few animals, then Wythenshawe Park's definitely worth a look.

The Courtyard Tea Rooms are in the historic stables just behind the hall. The menu's reasonably priced, there are highchairs and the staff will provide hot water for baby bottles. Baby-changing is in the disabled toilets.

£1 car park charges apply Apr-Nov, weekends and Bank Holidays.
Farm: Daily 11.30am-3.30pm;
Glass Houses: Daily 10am-4pm (weather dependent)
Courtyard Tea Rooms: Daily 10am-3pm
Hall: April-Sept, weekends 10am-5pm.
Wythenshawe Park, Wythenshawe Road, Manchester M23 0AB
Tel: 0161 998 2117 www.manchester.gov.uk

Walton Hall and Gardens

On a cold and icy day between Christmas and New Year we decided to venture out and get some fresh air. We headed over Warrington way to Walton Hall and Gardens; entrance to the gardens and the children's zoo is free and it is open every day. After parking in the pay and display, you head into the park via a bridge over the Bridgewater Canal – a very picturesque start. Once in, head left and this brings you to the children's playground and then on to the zoo. The playground is large and could do with a bit of modernisation but it does have a couple of great pieces from the 1970s!

The zoo was excellent, particularly considering it was free. It is well kept and is centred around a large duck pond. It has a variety of birds and animals including red squirrels, miniature pot bellied pigs, peacocks, ducks and Shetland ponies. Feeding time is 2pm in summer and 1pm in winter. There is also a small visitor centre with an 'adopt an animal' scheme.

After this, you could try swinging a club around the crazy golf course or pitch and putt, but a jaunt in the park may be just as exhilarating. All paths are fully accessible with a pushchair and it is a pleasant circular walk. Beautiful formal gardens, a further duck pond and the impressive gothic Walton Hall complete the pretty setting (though unfortunately this is not open to the general public). The Heritage Centre contains a small exhibition including information on local author Lewis Carroll, who was born in nearby Daresbury Village, and it's certainly worth a quick look-in. There's a café serving the usual selection of sandwiches, teas and coffees, with a seating area in the old stable yard.

Zoo: Summer Daily 10.30am-5pm, Winter Daily 10.30am-4.15pm; Christmas and New Year's Day 10.30am-12, feeding time is 2pm in summer and 1pm in winter.
Café: Summer Weekends and school holidays 10.30am-5pm, Winter 10.30am-4.15pm.
Pay and display car park Mon-Fri £2.10; Sat, Sun and Bank Holidays £3.10.
Walton Hall and Gardens, Walton Lea Road, Higher Walton, Warrington, Cheshire WA4 6SN
Tel: 01925 262 908 www.warrington.gov.uk/waltongardens

Planes, trains and automobiles

As you'd expect from the cradle of the industrial revolution, Manchester is one great big opportunity to express your love of moving vehicles of every type. And let's face it, which small child doesn't thrill to a plane, a train or a Victorian hydraulic boat lift? They're all here and a lot more besides.

Planes, trains and automobiles

Abbotsfield Park Miniature Railway

Abbotsfield Park in Flixton looks at first sight like any other small park. It's a recreation ground the size of a couple of football pitches with a small children's play area. However, just as you're crossing the bridge to the entrance you're drawn to a plume of steam coming towards you at some speed. This is the Abbotsfield Park Miniature Railway and miniature is the word. It's the smallest locomotive you've ever seen outside of a domestic train set.

Our son watched rapt as this tiny engine thundered past with half-a-dozen people in tow. He couldn't wait to get on and do a couple of circuits of the park himself.

Arriving at the station, we discovered it was the HQ of the Urmston and District Model Engineering Society. This little railway is an absolute labour of love. It's been staffed by club members bringing delight to children since the late 1940s and is a local treasure. One to warm your heart.

Weather permitting, trains run Sundays and Bank Holidays from 11am-3.30pm in winter and 11am-4.30pm in summer.
Rides are 20p per person.
Abbotsfield Park and Urmston & District Model Engineering Society, Chassen Road, Flixton, Manchester M41 5DH
Tel: 0161 661 5439 www.udmes.co.uk

The Airport Hotel

From the front The Airport Hotel looks rather like an unassuming pub, but the rear sits just 50 feet from the final approach for Manchester Airport's Runway 23R, and the close-up views of aircraft landing are superb.

The car park at the pub is a small pay and display, but for £3 for one hour you get a £2 voucher redeemable against food or drink purchased inside; £5 for up to four hours' parking entitles you to a £4

voucher. A word of warning: do not park on the road as you're likely to end up with a £60 parking ticket.

At the back of the pub you'll find an enormous, safely enclosed beer garden with plenty of picnic tables and a large wooden climbing frame. On sunny days during the summer holidays, there is a bouncy castle and barbecue at weekends.

Planes land from your left-hand side, but quite often aircraft use the holding point on your right-hand side for take-off and the noise is tremendous.

The pub does a children's menu for £3 for fishfingers/burgers/nuggets and chips but there is a tomato and pasta option so is a little more varied than the 'everything with chips' first impression. And you can get a nice pint of real ale so it's not all for the kids. There is a dedicated family room open until 9pm. Baby-changing is in the ladies' toilet.
Mon-Sun 7.30am-9pm admission free.
The Airport Hotel, Ringway Road, Manchester M22 5WH
Tel: 0161 437 2551 www.theairporthotel.com

Anderton Boat Lift

The Anderton Boat Lift in Cheshire is a spectacular feat of Victorian engineering and was the first of its kind in the world when it was built in 1875. It's a 50-foot vertical link between two waterways – the River Weaver and the Trent and Mersey Canal. It's hard to describe and do it justice but it makes for a brilliantly different day trip.

You can choose a lift trip – where you sit on a large glass-topped boat that sails from its mooring into the lift cradle and you either go from top to bottom or vice versa. Alternatively you can take a river trip – a gentle one-hour cruise in the same glass-topped boat or you can combine the two. We opted for the 35-minute lift trip and to be honest our fidgety two-and-a-half year old got a bit restless even with that. It was worth it because it's such a lovely experience. Don't expect an Alton Towers style ride though – it's very slow – in fact you hardly notice you're moving.

We had an hour's wait but there's a good visitor centre (complete with gift shop and café) on site and the exhibition has a few children's activities such as a drawing table and dressing up area. The café is pretty basic with jacket potatoes, sandwiches and children's lunchboxes at £2.85. Baby-changing is in the ladies' toilets on the top floor and in the unisex downstairs in the exhibition.

The Anderton Boat Lift is a spectacular feat of engineering.

Watching aircraft take off and land in incredibly close proximity is an amazing experience, even if you're not a plane fanatic.

Outside there's a small park, a maze and a water toy structure called 'canal adventure'. This consists of four plastic loops filled with water where you push your boat along and into little lifts. There are also a couple of picnic areas with great views of the lift and river. The whole site is pushchair-friendly – you can even take them on the boats with you (maximum of two allowed per trip). In addition, if a family walk appeals, there's a large nature park next to the Boat Lift. The car park's located between the park and lift, but you do have to pay (£3 for all day).

Lift trip: Adult £7, Child £5; combined lift and river trip: Adult £11, Child £8. Under 5s free. 4th Feb-19th Mar Thurs-Sun 11am-4pm, lift open but no boat trip, 20th Mar-3rd Oct Daily 10am-5pm, 6th Oct-31st Oct Weds-Sun 11am-4pm, 3rd Nov-24th Dec 11am-4pm, lift open but no boat trip.
Anderton Boat Lift, Lift Lane, Anderton, Northwich, Cheshire CW9 6FW
Tel: 01606 786777 www.andertonboatlift.co.uk

The Aviation Viewing Park
A £5 note gains you entry to the large piece of grassy land adjacent to the runway at Manchester Airport that is always full of people with binoculars. It is somewhere I'd often wondered about as my plane came into land at the airport.

Summer 2009 saw the Aviation Viewing Park re-open after a £1 million facelift. All the facilities have been improved with a smart new restaurant offering meals (including a well-priced children's selection) throughout the day, a more casual take-out café where you can grab coffee, hot snacks and ice cream and a fun shop selling more aeroplane-related items than you could possibly imagine.

The most impressive feature on arrival is the swish new glass-fronted hangar housing Concorde – however, you have to pay extra to gain access to this area. Daily afternoon tours are usually held during the school holidays, cost £5 and don't require a reservation. At other times you have to book. Slightly disappointing is that if you don't do this tour you can't see much of Concorde by peering into the hangar. There are two further passenger airplanes outside but these can only be viewed as part of an organised tour. Without wishing to state the obvious, the main reason to visit this attraction is simply to stand next to a runway where on the three raised viewing mounds you can get a thrill from seeing aircraft take off and land pretty close.
Daily from 8.30am-dusk.
Cars including driver £5 each. Car passengers or pedestrians (aged 4 and above) £2 each – the day I went no cards were accepted.
Ringways Restaurant: Summer 10am-6pm, WInter 10am-3.30pm.
The Aviation Viewing Park, Sunbank Lane, Altrincham WA15 8XQ
Tel: 0161 489 3932 www.manchesterairport.co.uk/concorde

City Airport (Barton Aerodrome)
If you have driven over Barton Bridge on the M60 or visited The Trafford Centre you must have noticed the light aircraft coming in to land or taking off from City Airport, locally known as Barton Aerodrome.

One clear late Saturday afternoon, as we were driving this way, we decided to stop off for a closer look. Don't be put off by the security barrier and seemingly private nature of the airfield – it IS open

Planes, trains and automobiles

Brookside is a perfect venue for those mad about trains.

Brookside Miniature Railway

We always have a fun time here – in fact it's always a struggle to drag the kids (and their dad) away from it at the end of the day! Brookside, located at a garden centre, has five locomotives – three steam engines and two diesel. The trains are located at their very own station, Brookside Central, which is a replica West Country station with authentic buildings, sidings, turntable and original signage on the miniature platform.

Inside the waiting room (which doubles as a gift shop and museum), you purchase your ticket then it's all aboard! The train takes you on a half-mile circuit through tunnels (one of which is 65ft long), over streams and level crossings and around the perimeter of the centre. It costs £1.30 per person (free for under 2s) and lasts about eight minutes.

After several goes on the train we usually end up at the little children's play area, where there's a life-size static tank engine that you can climb a ladder and have a look at as well as several ride-on machines – Postman Pat, Thomas the Tank Engine and a kiddie tramway (where the children ride along a short track by themselves). Also on site is a children's pottery studio where you can paint your own pots. During summer months and school holidays you'll often find a small children's funfair at one end of the garden centre, which the train chugs round and makes a stop at for anyone wanting a quick game of hook-a-duck.

Food-wise there's two choices – a small coffee shop or the larger Romany Restaurant, which does have a children's menu available.

Baby-changing is in the disabled toilets in the main garden centre.

Brookside offers children's railway parties for those mad about trains, which is ideal as a novel birthday theme. *Weekends all year round 11am-4pm, also in addition Weds April-Sept and school and Bank Holidays. Closed Easter Sunday. Steam locomotives only run during weekends.* Brookside Garden Centre, Macclesfield Road (A523), Poynton, Cheshire SK12 1BY Tel: 01625 872919 www.brooksidegardencentre.com

to the public! Immediately on entering the airport's grounds you're up close and personal with the planes, as the airfield is slap bang next to the car park and although it is well fenced with a wooden picket fence, you're really near to the aircraft, which is just amazing. Parking was straightforward enough, although I understand the car park can get pretty busy on summer weekends.

We soon saw a helicopter coming in to land and could excitedly feel the breeze from the rotor blades as it touched down only metres away. You won't see Jumbo jets here, but I guarantee you will see lots of Cessnas and similar light aircraft taking off and landing. The Control Tower dates from 1930 and was the first to open in the country; it can be accessed via a short fenced walk, with plenty of parked aircraft and hangars to admire on route. A staircase takes you to a first-stage viewing platform (open air) so pushchairs would have to be left at the bottom. It's worth the climb, as it allows you a 360-degree view over the airport and beyond towards the rumbling motorways and the Pennines.

After about half-an-hour of pretending to be air traffic controllers we headed back towards the entrance and into 'Heather Melvin's Café Bar'. The décor is old-fashioned but it enjoys great views over the airfield, and the tables clothed in air maps are a talking point for little ones. This fully-licensed café also has a fenced garden with picnic tables to the front where it is great to enjoy an hour or so having a drink and watching the planes in the summer months. A children's menu is available and meals were in the region of £3. Baby-change is in the café's toilets.

The Barton Heritage Centre and Museum, situated in the car park, is open only on a selection of weekends and weekdays throughout the year. It's tiny – just a small portacabin – but has some really interesting plane memorabilia. *Mon-Sun 9am till sunset. Consideration must be given however to the weather conditions as light aircraft may not fly in heavy winds, snow etc. Heather Melvin's Café Bar, Daily from 10am, closing times vary throughout the year. Car parking: first half-hour free, £1 for 2hrs, £2 for 2-8 hours. Pay for your car park ticket in the Control Tower before leaving.* City Airport (Manchester Barton), Liverpool Road, Eccles, Manchester M30 7SA Tel: 0161 789 1362 www.cityairportltd.com

Dragon Miniature Railway

The Dragon Miniature Railway is located at a garden centre in Marple. There, just by the side of the car park, you'll find a little station with two trains (one diesel and one steam) running alternately on a half-mile track. For 70p each you'll be taken through a tunnel, alongside a river, via eccentric displays of garden gnomes and blow-up dinosaurs – you'll even get the chance to stop off at a small picnic and children's play area filled with Little Tikes style toys – open Mar-Oct.

The railway is run by enthusiasts and is a nice way to while away some time before popping into the garden centre for a mooch around the bedding plants. There's a selection of 20p ride-on machines next to the train station and also 'Tara the Tram', a little tram that self-propels up a short track where you can even ring a bell – all very sweet!

The garden centre itself has a fairly substantial café that offers a children's menu.

Weekends and school holidays (weather dependent) 11am-4.30pm. Dragon Miniature Railway, Wyevale Garden Centre, Otherspool, Dooley Lane, Marple, Stockport SK6 7HE Tel: 0774 8581160

East Lancashire Railway

Arriving at Bury's Bolton Street Station is like stepping back in time. There are traditional ticket booths, lovely signage and helpful staff. We decided to go from Bury to Ramsbottom but for a longer ride you can take the train from Heywood all the way to Rawtenstall. There is a pay and display car park at Bury Station which is free on Sundays.

At Bury Station The Trackside pub, situated on Platform 2, does children's meals at £2.25 for sausage or fishfingers with chips and beans, and they are will warm up bottles or baby food. Baby-changing is in the disabled toilets at the end of Platform 2, there are also facilities at Ramsbottom

Station. There are steps at Bury but staff are happy to help with pushchairs. Alternatively there is access to the platform by The Trackside and staff will accompany you across the track.

Ramsbottom is a 15-minute journey through some gorgeous countryside. We've travelled on both diesel and steam trains. Both are good, but I think the romance of the steam train wins. The boys loved it and had their heads pressed against the window for the entire journey. There is a buffet car on board as well as toilets. Ramsbottom station is only a five-minute walk away from shops and cafés, including the wonderfully indulgent Chocolate Café (see page 67), and there are plenty of picnic tables by the station, as well as a children's park. A traditional country market can be found every Saturday and on the second Sunday of each month a farmers' market.

Family days with Jimmy the Jinty run throughout the year and there are Santa Specials in December but pre-booking for the latter is essential. Bury Transport Museum is also due to re-open in April 2010 after a £3 million refurbishment.

1st Apr-10th Sep Wed-Sun plus Bank Holidays; 3rd Jan-5th Apr, 19th Sep-24th Dec Weekends; Santa Specials 27th Nov-24th Dec. The Trackside, food available Mon-Thurs 12-3pm, Fri 12-6pm, Sat 9am-5pm, Sun 10am-5pm.
Return fares from Bury to Ramsbottom: Adult £6.80, Child £4.60, Under 5s free.
Bolton Street Station, Bolton Street, Bury, Lancashire BL9 0EY
Tel: 0161 764 7790 www.east-lancs-rly.co.uk

If you want to get up close and personal with planes, Barton Aerodrome is the place to go.

Planes, trains and automobiles

Haigh Hall

See page 54.

The Heights of Abraham

If you fancy a trip in a cable car... well, it's not impossible, but it's a bit of a drive. An hour and a half south in fact, through the Peak District to Matlock Bath in Derbyshire. If it does take your fancy, it's a good trip, as it's through stunning countryside, taking in the likes of Buxton, Bakewell (try a tart – nothing like the shop-bought ones) and Chatsworth.

The Heights of Abraham was Britain's first alpine-style cable car when it opened in 1984. It's now a beautiful trip up over the Derwent Valley to Hilltop Park at the Heights. Once up there, as well as the fantastic views, you'll find caverns, woodlands, adventure playgrounds, a fossil factory, an amphitheatre which hosts special events and a café. A lovely way to while away a few hours on a clear day.

13th Feb-21st Feb, 4th Oct-31st Oct Daily 10am-4.30pm; 27th Feb-14th Mar Weekends 10am-4.30pm; 20th Mar-3rd Oct Daily 10am-5pm.
Adult £11.50, Child £8.50, Under 5s free.
The Heights of Abraham, Matlock Bath, Derbyshire DE4 3PD
Tel: 01629 582365 www.heightsofabraham.com

Hills Miniature Railway

Run by South Stockport Model Engineering Society, this delightful railway can be found at Hills Garden Centre, just south of Knutsford. There's an authentic station shop where you collect your £1 ticket (this doubles up as a gift shop selling toy trains and accessories) and the train puffs its way around the perimeter of the garden centre, taking in the odd tunnel along the way.

Also at Hills is a Toby Tram – a self-drive tram popular with younger children, and a nine-hole miniature golf course. There's a lovely café but it does get busy and isn't very big so get there early if you're intending to have lunch. A good selection of hot and cold food is on offer and there is a dedicated children's menu. If you've got a child who's fanatical about trains, Hills does offer private railway parties.

Weekends, School Holidays Daily, 11am-4pm (Weather dependent)
Hills Garden Centre, London Road, Allostock, Knutsford, Cheshire WA16 9LU
Tel: 01565 722567 www.hillsgardencentre.com

Manchester City Bus Tour

A beautiful sunny Saturday afternoon in September found me, partner, a three-and-a-half year old and a seven-month old running madly down Liverpool Street, bags flapping (not as much as me), waving frantically at one of Manchester's bright red sightseeing tour buses to stop and let us on... yep, we'd been waiting at the wrong bus stop near MOSI so rather than wait another 45 minutes for the next

Sitting on an open-topped double decker bus gives you a whole new perspective.

one, we decided to plead, and generously the driver allowed us to board. It was a bit of a kerfuffle – the pram wouldn't fit on without being collapsed and we really did have quite a lot of baby-associated bags hanging off it. No allowances were made and the bus set off quickly as I was swinging babe in arms up to the top deck, but we landed safely in some seats in the open-air back section.

The tour, which lasts about 90 minutes, takes in sights such as Old Trafford, Granada Television, and Manchester Cathedral. You can hop on and off as often as you like and the tickets are valid for 24 hours, but the price remains the same. Unfortunately, with the road works plaguing Manchester at the time of going to press, there were plenty of traffic snarl-ups, causing us to be stationary at several points.

The automated audio tour was not especially inspiring – outside House of Fraser on Deansgate we were informed that Dave Lee Travis was once a window dresser there.

The weather helped, as did the fact that the children loved bouncing along on the bus. Sitting on an open-topped double decker gives you a whole new perspective and there are some terrific buildings that we'd never noticed before. Verdict: bit pricey but a good thing to do if you have friends up from out of town.

At the time of going to press, City Sightseeing hadn't awarded the new contract so check website for times and availability.
Adult £7.50, 5-15 years £3.75, Under 5s free.
City Sightseeing Manchester starts at St Peter's Square.
www.city-sightseeing.com

Walton Park, Sale
See page 32.

The Wheel of Manchester
Every trip into Manchester city centre for the past 12 months has been dogged by our three-year-old pleading to go on the big wheel. As a vertigo sufferer, I've sought to avoid this, so he's been the beneficiary of a ridiculous number of bribes to divert attention. However, with friends to stay who were also desperate to go up, I found myself in a pod with another nervous father and two highly excitable toddlers.

Up we went, with the kids dashing from side to side, each outdoing the other spotting buses, trains and trams. My little boy started to point out places we'd been to and was fascinated by how different they looked 60 metres up. Amazingly, once our stomachs had settled a bit, we found we were enjoying it too – though we were playing pub spotting!

The Wheel's a brilliant addition to Manchester's attractions. It takes about 10 minutes to go round and getting a perspective from on high of this ultra-modern city nestling comfortably between Peaks to the south and Pennines to the north is a rare treat. You can't take buggies on, but there's a safe fenced area where they're kept at owner's risk. There are also plenty of staff on hand, most of whom will want to take your photo at a vastly inflated price. Although I wouldn't bother with this bit, my small son was quite right... it's definitely worth taking a turn on the Wheel.

Mon-Thurs 10am-10pm, Fri 10am-midnight, Sat 9am-midnight, Sun 10am-7pm.
Adult £6.50, Child 4-12yrs £4.50, 1-3yrs £1, Under 1s free, Family ticket £18 (book online for a 10% discount).
The Wheel of Manchester, Exchange Square, Manchester M3 1BD
Tel: 0161 831 9918 www.worldtouristattractions.co.uk

Windmill Farm
See page 49.

The Wheel is a brilliant addition to Manchester's attractions.

Animals, nature and wildlife

Little appeals to kids more than animals, and there's certainly no shortage of options – from zoos and wildlife parks to farms and nature reserves, you've got it all on the doorstep.

Animals, nature and wildlife

Blackpool Zoo

"We're all going to the zoo tomorrow, the zoo tomorrow, the zoo tomorrow...". Our household is always excited when we have a trip to the zoo planned. If you are thinking of a full day out, then Blackpool Zoo is a great choice as it has lots on offer but is just about the right size to get round in a day with little legs.

We visited on a chilly October day so the modern entrance, which contains the admission points, café, toilets and gift shop was ideal as it meant we could get the stressful toilet stop, paying, glove and hat applying done in the warmth. Once in, we were greeted by 'Darwin', an 85-year-old tortoise, and his chums. Darwin was surprisingly active and held the children's imagination for some time. We then headed through 'Dinosaur Safari', an attractively landscaped area, complete with a fiery volcano, where the dinosaurs live. But beware there are no cages and they may bite! The walkway took us on a journey through time from the Triassic to the Jurassic periods and the children were able to get face-to-face with a tyrannosaurus rex and scare him with their very loud roars.

We found the feeding times and events at the zoo well advertised and scheduled our next stop for the elephant talk and feed. This was a bit dry for my two-year-old but interested my five-year-old. Next to the elephant house is 'Amazonia', which includes monkeys that are free to roam and swing above you on ropes. We all found these delightful and were able to get very close to them, although we made a sharp exit when one of them dropped a present on us from above! Next on our agenda was the 'Creepy Crawly' experience, an opportunity to touch and feel things that make you go 'yuck', but unfortunately the room was full to capacity when we got there.

The zoo has plenty of picnic spots for lunch but due to the time of year we decided to eat at one of the two self-service cafés at the zoo. We opted to take a short walk back to the entrance coffee shop, as advised by the admissions staff, as the more centrally-located café can be busy. The coffee shop offered a range of sandwiches, toasties and jacket potatoes. With our batteries recharged we enjoyed an afternoon of animal antics, including wrestling lion cubs and speedy penguins. The two highlights of the day were the eight-day-old giraffe and the ring-tailed lemur enclosure. The multi-level viewing in the 'Giraffe Heights' enclosure allows you to look at the animals from both ground and eye-level so we were able to get a really great view of the new splayed legged, and doe-eyed beauty. The lemur enclosure allows the animals to roam freely and even climb on to you. We observed them for some time and my two-year-old was thrilled when one climbed on his shoulders. We couldn't help humming, 'you've got to move it, move it' until we got home.

We concluded the trip with the children going on the bouncy castle to burn off those last bits of energy and, of course, the customary visit to the gift shop, which you are channelled through on the way out. We went home a rubber snake and safari-jeep heavier. All in all, however, we thought it a great value-for-money day.

Daily 10 daily, closes 45 minutes after the last admission, check website for closing as times vary.
Adults £14.50, Child £10.25, under 3s free.
Blackpool Zoo, East Park Drive, Blackpool, Lancashire FY3 8PP
Tel: 01253 830 830 www.blackpoolzoo.org.uk

Go on safari with the dinosaurs at Blackpool zoo for a roaring time.

Blue Planet Aquarium

I went with a group of mums plus kids on a typical rainy day. The queue at the entrance was long but it did move fairly quickly. On bank holidays it would be wise to book ahead and fast track the queue. Entry is free for children under 95cm, otherwise a child price is £10.50, which does seem quite steep.

It is a big aquarium, laid out over two floors with the majority being below ground. There is lift access to both floors but this is quite small, although it's meant to take four pushchairs. The centre piece to Blue Planet is the fantastic Aquatunnel – 70 metres of underwater tunnels with sharks and manta rays floating only inches away. I lost count of how many times we went through it, until I realised the children had become more enthralled with the moving walkway! On busy days this section can be a nightmare with a pushchair. Halfway round the tunnel section in a separate 2,000 litre tank is the Caribbean reef. This is where the children get to see lots of Nemos!

The aquatheatre, a partially-seated auditorium with a massive picture window into the aquarium, gives you a sense of just how large the sharks really are. There is a regular show where divers get in to feed the fish.

All the children enjoyed the rock pools, where you can stroke the rays. There aren't many children who don't relish the opportunity of getting wet! This area does get very busy and you have to wait for someone to get bored so you can squeeze in. There are lots of sinks around for hand-washing afterwards.

The café area is large but very tightly packed with tables so it's difficult to manoeuvre your pushchair. Set out in a fast food chain style they offer hot and cold meal deals such as chicken nuggets and chips, a drink and fruit for around £3.95. The sandwich boxes had sold out when we got there. Baby-changing is in a separate room near the toilets by the restaurant.

We had brought a picnic and you're not allowed to eat this in the café, but there are tables outside and you can eat in the aquatheatre.

Outside is Octopus Island, a good play area where you'll also find the otters.

I don't think we missed much and including our lunch we were there for around three hours. You can go round the aquarium as many times as you like, but I didn't feel it's really a full day out.

Round every corner in Blue Planet there was something to spend money on, whether it's face painting, helium Nemos, photographs, vending machines or the enormous gift shop – all a nightmare for parents still reeling from the entry fee.

Mon-Fri 10am-5pm, weekends and school holidays 10am-6pm. Adult £14.75, Child £10.75, Family £49, Groovy Grandparent Ticket £45, Child under 95cm free. Free car park.
Blue Planet, Ellesmere Port, Cheshire CH65 9LF
Tel: 0151 357 8804 www.blueplanetaquarium.com

Bowland Wild Boar Park

It was a fantastic sunny autumn day when we visited the Forest of Bowland and the Wild Boar Park. Being surrounded by trees, the scenery was beautiful. I had to do a quick feed with the baby when we arrived so got to sample the homemade food very early on – the flapjacks in particular were great. All the food was very reasonably priced and included wild boar sausages as a speciality. Behind the café they've rigged up a massive branch with loads of bird feeders. As well as being able to enjoy watching native birds there were peacocks vying for food.

Despite the fact there were lots of animals to see, my boys were thrilled with the wooden play area. All the usual swings and slides, plus a great zip wire and tractors to climb on – they particularly liked the rabbit warren, a tunnel running from one end of a small hill to the other. A good excuse to crawl around and get nice and dirty.

The Wild Boar Park is set in 60 acres of woodland where children can wander, stroke rabbits and

chicks and feed deer with food costing 25p a bag. We did a great circuit alongside the river around the edge of the park. It's approximately one kilometre and probably took us about half-an-hour. It is pushchair-friendly but could get muddy (we were all wearing wellies). The walk took us past meerkats, owls, prairie dogs, wallabies and of course the wild boars. You'll also find wonderful wood carvings of animals and birds dotted around. There are loads of other walks into the woodland behind the park, perhaps more suited to older children, although during the summer you can hitch a ride with a tractor and trailer. We'd planned a visit to the Inn at Whitewell nearby (see pub guide on page 88), although you can picnic at any of the tables placed around the park.

Summer: Easter-31st October Daily 10.30am-5pm.
Winter: 1st November-Easter Daily 11am-4pm.
Café open daily during the summer and holidays, Fri-Mon during the winter.
Summer: Adult £4.50, Child £4, under 2s free, Family Ticket £15.
Winter: £3.50 for everyone over 2 years old.
There is an 'Honesty Box' if no one is in attendance on the gate.
Bowland Wild Boar Park, Chipping, Preston PR3 2QT
Tel: 01995 61554 www.wildboarpark.co.uk

Bowland Wild Boar Park is set in 60 acres of woodland. In summer you can hitch a ride with a tractor and trailer.

Chester Zoo

An easy drive to Chester from Manchester and lots of parking made a good start to the day. We were visiting mid-week, during term time and over winter, so it wasn't busy. There is so much to see over such a vast area, that you could easily come back for a second visit. In the summer months it does get very busy and unlike the unlimited viewing of the orangutans that we had, it can be a slow moving walk past with no opportunity to stop and admire.

We had taken a packed lunch and happened to stumble on the Arara Picnic Lodge by the jaguar enclosure just as it started raining, which was perfect timing. Although not heated it did keep us warm and dry. Children's meals are available at all the restaurants, staff are happy to heat up bottles and there is a microwave available at Café Tsavo, which is located near the main entrance.

Highlights of our visit included the orangutans – they really appeared to try and communicate with

us. The jaguars were gorgeous too – in the middle of the Jaguar House there was what looked like a branch, which I thought was to add ambience; it took a three-year-old to point out that in fact leafcutter ants were busy working away carrying leaves – absolutely hypnotic.

My children did get excited at one particular sighting... pointing eagerly as a big yellow JCB digger dug a hole. Honestly, I felt like shoving them all in the car there and then!

I really liked the Twilight Zone. I couldn't get my friend to come in with me as she was terrified, so I went in with all the kids. It is a bit surreal – a big open enclosure with bats flying around. You can feel the movement of the air as they brush past your ear. There were overhanging rocks to walk under and by the end of it even I was spooked! Also well planned was the monkey area. With no cages, it is all set on an island with a small moat and you feel you could just hop over.

The children's play area, Fun Ark, is great for a bit of time out for parents so you can grab a cup of tea. There is also face-painting for £4 and a pottery painting studio.

The zoo is a massive 110 acres, a big area to cover and often a long walk between enclosures so I would recommend taking your pushchair with you. Everywhere is accessible and if you forget yours you can hire one from Zoo Mobility at the main entrance for £5 plus

TOP FIVE ANIMAL ATTRACTIONS

Blackpool Zoo
"Move it, move it" to experience one to ones with the crazy lemurs at this excellent zoo.

Bowland Wild Boar Park
Enjoy the wildlife in this stunning setting. Feeding llamas, deer, goats and lambs make this a special day.

The Chestnut Centre
A unique wildlife park which contains one of Europe's largest groups of otters and owls. Well worth a visit.

Martin Mere
A fantastic wildfowl and wetlands reserve right on the doorstep – a brilliant introduction to bird life.

Reddish Vale
The perfect farm for the nought to five age group – there's certainly no shortage of animals here!

a £10 refundable deposit. You can also pre-book a pushchair by calling 01244 389482.

Separate baby-changing facilities are available at all toilets, which tend to be near the café areas and the main entrance. You can buy nappies from guest services or from vending machines at the loos.

A waterbus runs from Easter until autumn though only at weekends during term time. It's a 15-minute trip allowing close-up views of some of the animal enclosures; it costs £2 for adults and £1.50 for over threes. You can't take pushchairs on but there is a place to store them.

Lastly, to get the children out of the zoo we promised them a trip on the Zoofari monorail; it costs £1.50 for adults and £1 for over threes and you buy tickets at the machine. If you go from Jubilee Station at the furthest end of the zoo, you whiz back to the entrance and the kids get a last look at the animals. You can't however do a round trip as you must split your journey. It is no problem taking your pushchair on.

Winter 10am-4pm, Summer 10am-5pm,
Summer holidays 10am-6pm. Last admission is one hour before closing. Check website for details. Free parking.
High Season: Adult £15.35, Child £11.30, Family Ticket £50.
Mid Season Adult £14.50; Child £9.95, Family Ticket £45.
Low Season Adult £12.35, Child £9, Family Ticket £37.70.
Chester Zoo, Cedar House, Caughall Road, Upton-by-Chester, Chester CH2 1LH Tel: 01244 380 280 www.chesterzoo.org

The Chestnut Centre Otter, Owl and Wildlife Park

If you fancy a little run out, this delightful park on the Manchester edge of the Peak District is a perfect place to visit. Our two-year-old was really taken with it and has not stopped 'twit twooing' ever since!

The conservation park is made up primarily of lots of otters (it houses Europe's largest collection

A highlight for any horse-mad child is a visit to the Cotebrook Shire Horse Centre.

Animals, nature and wildlife

of multi-species otters) and then also 16 types of owls along with buzzards, pine martens, polecats, foxes, Scottish wildcats and deer.

A special highlight is Manoki, the UK's only giant otter – he's around 1.5 metres long. Rather brilliantly you get a great view in to his enclosure via a glass wall and he does seem to love performing to a crowd when he's fishing. New in 2009 was the arrival of Panambi, a mate for Manoki.

Your tour round the park and its animals (which took us about two-and-a-half hours) is via a very picturesque woodland trail dotted with information boards about what you're seeing. The enclosures are well designed so you get to see the animals close up and the otters are clearly very happy in their environment. We actually took a pram round (the centre describes itself as wheelchair access manageable with fit helpers only) and that was fine because there were two of us to negotiate some awkward areas where there were steps. But be warned, the final leg of the trail back up to the car park is a relatively steep walk through a path in a field!

The café sells simple but delicious food – jacket potatoes, sandwiches or soup. Children's lunch boxes were £2.25, which were good value. Highchairs are available and the café will provide hot water for bottles.

Daily in Autumn and Winter (weekends only in January)
10.30am-dusk, Daily in Spring and Summer 10.30am-5.30pm.
Adult £7, Child £5, under 2s free, Family Ticket £21.50.
Baby-changing facilities are in the ladies toilets.
Chestnut Centre, Chapel-en-le-Frith, High Peak,
Derbyshire SK23 0QS
Tel: 01298 814099 www.chestnutcentre.co.uk

Cotebrook Shire Horse Centre and Country Park

Cotebrook is located in the heart of Cheshire countryside – so the drive out alone is a pleasure. Winner of a best visitor attraction award in 2008, Cotebrook Shire Horse Centre is well-organised. There's plenty of parking at the front and after paying your entrance fee, signposts guide you during your visit.

Firstly you come to the farmyard, stabling some of the 30 or so magnificent stallions, mares and foals together with other animals such as black pigs, sheep and hens. You can't feed the horses, but you can stroke them. Walking on further there are paddocks and then larger fields with more Shire horses and a nature trail. This includes owls, badger setts and an otter pool. It was a sunny day so we decided to go for a bit of a walk round this area with a newborn in the pram and a three-year-old on a buggy

Home Farm is a working farm where children can get hands on with a host of different animals.

board behind. It was a little hard going in parts (I'd imagine in wet weather it would be too difficult with a pram and you would definitely need your wellies) but in the main fine. We had a bit of a moment at one of the furthest points away from the farm where a young horse had managed to escape his enclosure and was trotting around looking more than a little enormous, but hey, it all added to the feeling of escaping the city!

We ended our trip with an enjoyable lunch at the Lakeside Café, which has outside seating overlooking the lake. There's a children's menu which includes jam sandwiches and beans on toast. You're also welcome to bring your own picnic and plonk down next to the duck pond.

Daily 10am-5pm (last entry 4pm).
Adults £7, Children £5, under 5s free, Family Ticket £22.55.
Welly Hire service available! Toilets and baby-changing.
Cotebrook Shire Horse Centre and Country Park, Cotebrook,
Tarporley, Cheshire CW6 9DS
Tel: 01829 760 506 www.cotebrookshirehorses.co.uk

Farmer Ted's

They are always busy at Farmer Ted's, and after changes made last summer this already great farm attraction is an even better place to visit. In addition to the large animal barn with cows, pigs, llamas and ferrets (organised ferret racing sessions are held throughout the day), a new bug and reptile centre has been added which features snakes, scorpions, huge millipedes and frogs. Whilst this is a terrific attraction for the boys, my six-year-old girl Lauren wasn't overly fussed!

What is so nice at Farmer Ted's is that there are organised activities throughout the day, which keeps everyone occupied. The farm allows children to see and take part in demonstrations ranging from milking cows and handling guinea pigs to grooming ponies – much more Lauren's cup of tea!

Animals, nature and wildlife

The play areas are as extensive as before, with an outdoor adventure playground zoned for the over and under threes, a pedal tractor park, an excellent indoor sand pit, tractor barrel rides (£1 extra and weather dependent) and a go-kart circuit. I was a bit disappointed that the hay barn had been converted into a climbing frame area, but the kids did not seem to mind – and they didn't come out itching this time!

We ate at the café, where the food on offer was lovely. There are also plenty of benches outside as well as in covered areas for picnicking. We left the farm exhausted – but not before having a trip to the farm shop to buy a hearty tea for when we got home.

Daily 10am-6pm (closed Tuesdays during term time).
Mon-Fri Adult £2.50, Child £4.50, under 3s £3.50, under 1s free.
Weekends, School Holidays and June-Sept Adult £4.50,
Child £6.50, under 3s £4, under 1s free, Family Ticket £20.50.
Farmer Ted's Farm Park, Flatman's Lane, Downholland,
Ormskirk L39 7HW Tel: 0151 526 0002 www.farmerteds.com

Heaton Park Farm
See Heaton Park on page 24.

Home Farm at Tatton Park
With a neo-classical mansion and acres of stunning landscaped parkland as its backdrop, this pretty farm probably wins the award for best setting! There's a car park within Tatton Park grounds (charge for car entry to Tatton £4.50) and from here, the farm's about a five-minute walk. During most weekends and school holidays there's a Land Train running between the two.

At the working farm children can feed the goats and hens, meet the pigs, cows, horses and donkeys, and take a peek inside a 1930s' cottage. It's not huge but very sweet and food is available to buy in the shop (30p for a bag of corn). Another highlight was seeing the adorable baby piglets – children can get a great view of the pigs and piglets through the new glass viewing panels. Home Farm has an impressive pig herd comprising six rare breeds and as they farrow twice a year it is possible to see a newborn litter each month. Much of the farm is cobbled with uneven stones but we were absolutely fine with our pram.

The farm has toilets and there are baby-changing facilities. A tuck shop serving ice cream and refreshments is open during high season. The nearest restaurant is back near the car park.

Events do run through the year, and one to look out for is lambing weekend, so keep an eye on the website.

Low Season: Oct-March, Weekends 11am-4pm (last entry 3pm).
High Season: March-Oct, Tues-Sun 12-5pm (last entry 4pm).
Low Season: Adult £4, Child £2, under 4s free, Family Ticket £10.
High Season: Adult £4.50, Child £2.50, under 4s free, Family
Ticket £11.50. Totally Tatton Family Ticket (£17) allows entry to the
mansion, garden and farm. You can use this ticket on another
day if one or more of those attractions aren't visited (car entry
must be paid again).
Tatton Park, Knutsford, Cheshire WA16 6QN
Tel: 01625 374435 www.tattonpark.org.uk

Knowsley Safari Park
The safari park driving route snakes for five miles through various open animal enclosures. If it's a quiet day, you can do this at your own pace, and spend time observing the animals. On our trip, we actually drove round the route twice at my children's insistence. However, a friend who ventured there on a Bank Holiday said that her tour of the park was one long traffic jam in the heat and her brood got very restless. So it is probably best to choose your day to visit carefully if you have young children who may need a toilet break. Once you are in your car and on the route, you can't get out, and whilst throwing yourself to the lions may seem preferential to sitting in a hot car with screaming children, it really isn't an option.

As anyone who has ever been to a safari park will testify, the best part is the monkey enclosure. The monkeys can be avoided if you are the car polishing type, but this definitely precludes us, so we headed in. The animals' antics sent my children into a mixture of laughter and tears. A large baboon's bottom in your car window can be funny but a monkey's head suddenly popping into view just an inch from your face can be a bit scary for a two-year-old.

Once out of the car there are still more animals to see on foot including otters and elephants, which can be viewed at reasonably close proximity. There are sea-lions who at regular times throughout the day put on a show of diving through hoops. There is also a small but well stocked farm

with all the usual suspects plus a few llamas and a bug house, so all in all animal wise Knowsley has it pretty well covered.

We then headed on to the amusement park, which was great for under fives. One thing to note: the rides are not included in the entrance price – you have to buy a book of tickets from one of several booths dotted around the place. Particularly enjoyable was the little train that took us on a lengthy circular tour and allowed views of some of the animals.

The restaurant serves a variety of food and drinks at reasonable prices. Alternatively you can take a picnic to eat at one of the tables by the otter enclosure.

Admission to Knowsley Safari Park isn't cheap and when you add on the cost of the amusement rides and ice creams it does mount up. But there is a good mixture of things to do so all in all it is reasonable value for money. It's a nice treat.

Baby-change facilities available.
Summer: Daily 10am. Last entry to Safari Drive 4pm.
Winter: Daily 10.30am. Last entry to Safari Drive 3pm.
If the weather is very icy or snowy it is closed for safety reasons.
Adult £14, Child £10, Pedestrians £8 (but you might get eaten!), under 3s free.
Amusement rides: £1.50 per ticket, £1 per ticket for 50 or more (but you would have to be insane!) Wristbands for amusement park £9. The amusement park is closed in Winter for maintenance.
Knowsley Safari Park, Prescot, Merseyside L34 4AN
Tel: 0151 430 9009 www.knowsley.com

Felix and his Grandad hopping over the stepping stones in the oriental section at Martin Mere.

Martin Mere Wetland Centre

Martin Mere is a wildfowl and wetlands reserve allowing visitors' access to animals in a natural and tranquil environment. I went with my 22-month-old son in November and later learnt that this is one of the more exciting times of year in the bird watching calendar as it is when migratory birds depart and arrive for winter.

The distance between the M61 exit and the centre was a little longer than I had anticipated but it was a scenic drive, and very well signposted. Entry was via a visitor centre which also houses a restaurant, gift shop and toilets. We had a quick tea and juice stop in the restaurant, where we bought a bag of crusty bread duck food for 50p, before exploring the wetlands.

The wetlands are initially set out in a series of fenced areas, linked by a circular paved route, with birds from different continents of the world. My son toddled between the continents poking his crusty bread at the birds and was particularly taken by the magpie geese from Australasia, which tickled his fingers, as well as the stepping stones across the pond of the Oriental section. Also in this part of the centre is the beaver hide. Unfortunately we didn't see any beavers on this visit – this may have been because my son scared them off shouting 'beefers' at the top of his voice. Fortunately a pre-recorded web cam of the beavers can be watched in the hide to avoid any disappointment.

On the periphery is the mere and the reed beds, which are overlooked by a series of hides, the most impressive of which is the harrier hide. This is built in wood to look like a harrier bird, with an interesting history of the wetlands on the pathway, and floor to ceiling windows inside. The spectacle and sound of flocks of birds and the pairs of honking whooper swans gliding on to the still mere were both beautiful and moreover fascinating to my little boy. He was quite content sat on a stool watching and pointing for well over 30 minutes. I only wished I'd packed a pair of binoculars.

We ate lunch at the restaurant, where hot food is served from 11.45am-2.30pm. I settled for a bacon butty which was delicious and my son had a child's lunch box, which consisted of a sandwich, fruit, juice and some crisps for £3.50. A hot children's meal was available for the same price.

We ended the visit in the play area, which was an added bonus. It's accessed via a tunnel and divided into two parts dependent on age, both of which have a good range of equipment. There are also plenty of benches so you can comfortably sit and watch.

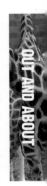

Harry loved feeding the donkeys from his bucket of carrots at Reddish Vale Farm.

In the spring a hatchery/nursery is open and baby chicks can be viewed up close, which we'll definitely go back to see!

Unisex baby-change facilities are available. There are highchairs in the restaurant and staff are happy to heat baby food and milk.

Nov-Feb Daily 9.30am-5pm (last admission 4pm). Mar-Oct Daily 9.30am-5.30pm (last admission 5pm). Adult £8.45, Child £4.14, under 4s free. Family Ticket £22.64. Car parking free.
WWT Martin Mere Wetland Centre, Fish Lane, Burscough, Lancashire L40 0TA Tel: 01704 895181 www.wwt.org.uk

Reddish Vale Farm

From the outside Reddish Vale Farm looks quite small, but this is why I liked it. For the nought to five age group it is the perfect farm. Because of its size it feels very safe – nobody can wander off and get lost. There are plenty of farmyard animals, ducks, pigs, horses, sheep, donkeys and goats plus a lovely petting area with guinea pigs and rabbits. All the animals are easy to see and they even have low windows in the pigsty. Buckets of carrots to feed the animals are 50p.

For a final workout there is a bouncy castle and a bouncy slide, also 50p. Plus there is a selection of free ride-on tractors and trailers. On Sundays from 1-3pm there are pony rides for £2.

The tearooms are open every weekend throughout the year. Children's meals are available from £2.50 for either a burger, chicken nuggets or hot dog and chips. A bottle warmer and highchairs are available. Baby-changing is in the disabled toilet by the entrance to the farm. See page 29 for information on Reddish Vale Country Park.

Feb-Oct and Dec, Weekends 11am-4pm; school holidays and Bank Holidays Daily 11am-4pm.
Adult £3, Child £2.50, under 3s free. Cash only.
Tearooms: Sat 9am-4pm, Sun 9.30am-4pm. Open daily in school holidays 9.30am-4pm. Tel: 0161 480 1645.
Reddish Vale Farm, Reddish Vale Road, Reddish, Stockport SK5 7HE Tel: 0161 480 1645 www.reddishvalefarm.co.uk

Sea Life

Worth a visit is the Sea Life centre on Blackpool's Golden Mile. We went out of season which made for a relaxing trip with no fighting for a glimpse of the fishies. It's not massive and it takes about an hour to potter round.

First up is the touch pool – an open rock pool filled with various sea creatures. We thought the staff here were excellent. A young woman completely engaged with Will and Sam as she helped them hold a starfish. From there it's on to the aquarium itself. The 50-odd tanks are all at a good height for little ones. Our boys were soon counting sharks, rays, seahorses and piranhas.

They loved walking over the pool on the walkway above the rays, it gives you a great view of the fish being fed by staff. The only bit not to meet with full approval was the talking pirate hologram by the aquatheatre. This was deemed 'a bit scary'.

The café is quite small and has no outside space. It does however have a mini soft play area and ball pit, which kept our lot happy for a good half-hour. When the café is quiet, you're welcome to eat your packed lunch there. A meal deal including sandwich, crisps and drink costs £3.95. There are highchairs and the café will readily heat up bottles. The only toilets are near the ray pool and baby-changing facilities are found in the disabled cubicle.

If you have a pram, you'll need to walk back to the beginning of the tour to use the lift. Otherwise you'll be faced with a huge flight of stairs at the end.

Sea Life frequently offers promotional discounts so check the internet or contact the tourist office first. Nearest parking is on Bonny Street, behind the centre.
Mon-Fri 10am-4pm, Weekends 10am-5pm.
Adult £13.79, Child £10.79, under 3s free.
Sea Life, Blackpool Promenade, Blackpool, Lancashire FY1 5AA Tel: 01253 621258 www.sealifeeurope.com

Animals, nature and wildlife

Smithills Open Farm

The main attraction at Smithills Farm is the big barn – inside the noise is incredible and the smell is pretty overwhelming too! You can buy bags of animal feed for 50p, which is a must as literally every type of farm animal is available for you to stroke, feed and pet. We saw cows, calves, pigs, sheep, chickens, plus some overzealous goats that managed to grab the food bag and eat the whole lot!

Thankfully, in the same barn and perfect for a quick distraction, there's a seated pets corner, probably our children's favourite bit. They loved holding baby rabbits, guinea pigs and even tiny chicks – I was trying to look calm, fully expecting a child to drop one or accidentally squeeze the poor thing a bit hard, but staff are on hand to help with the squirming animals.

Outside and up in the top fields there are plenty of other animals still to see and friendly pigs trot along after you as you visit llamas, alpacas and deer. There is a large adventure playground for older children, an old tractor to climb on plus some ride-on tractors. A smaller play area for toddlers is by the main entrance. Donkey rides are available every day for £1 a go. Plus in the summer and weekends during winter, tractor-trailer rides are £1 per person. There are two bouncy castles inside which are free with no time restrictions.

There is a good size café with highchairs and children's meals are £2 for chicken nuggets/fish fingers/sausages with chips. They are happy to warm up milk or baby food. You are welcome to bring a picnic – there are plenty of tables outside, and if it is raining there are some indoors too.

Baby-changing is in the disabled toilet, which could do with a bit of an upgrade.

A visit to Stockley Farm starts the minute you park your car. The difficulty is dragging the children away at the end of the day.

Every day at 1pm you can watch the cows being milked in the main barn although it does get a bit smelly! During the summer and at weekends you can help feed the lambs.

Lastly there is a small vivarium, which if you don't like snakes you can easily avoid. The snakes are only brought out for demonstrations but if you really want to hold one you can ask a member of staff and they are happy to oblige.

Mon-Sun 10am-5pm. Adult £5, Child £4, under 2s free.
Smithills Open Farm, Smithills Dean Road, Bolton, Lancashire BL1 7NS Tel: 01204 595765 www.smithillsopenfarm.co.uk

Stockley Farm

A visit to Stockley Farm starts from the moment you park your car. A tractor and trailer are waiting in the car park to transport you down to the farm. The drivers are happy to help you with a pushchair, and your little ones clamber up to sit on bales of hay.

First off we hit the sheds to see the cows and calves, pigs, goats and lambs. We then moved on to the pets corner, where the boys enjoyed stroking baby rabbits, guinea pigs and chicks – I was amazed at how gentle they were.

There is a brilliant sand pit with at least half a dozen mechanical diggers and loads of toys. There's also an old tractor, a climbing frame and slide. In the large barn there is another sand pit with a cement mixer, a small soft play area, ride-on pedal tractors, a bouncy castle and the boys' favourite – enormous hay bales to roll around in.

Throughout the day there are opportunities to feed the animals. This is very popular and does get busy. In the summer, sheep races are held plus at weekends there are bird of prey displays.

For lunch there is a spacious café with loads of highchairs offering home-made cakes and sandwich boxes for children. There is a microwave and bottle warmer for baby food and bottles. We'd brought a picnic and you'll find plenty of tables either outside in the play area or inside the barn.

The disabled toilet has a pull down changing table and a nappy dispensing machine. There is also a heated mother and baby room with a changing mat and a comfy chair for breastfeeding.

At 3.30pm every day you can watch the cows being milked via a special viewing gallery. When it was time to leave, the only way to get mine out was the promise of another tractor ride back to the car.

14th Mar-31st Oct Weekends 11am-5pm, Weds 1-5pm, school holidays Daily 11am-5pm, Dec Weekends 11am-5pm.
Adult £8, Child £7, under 2s free, Family Ticket £28.
Joint Tickets for Stockley Farm and Arley Hall and Gardens are also available.
Stockley Working Farm, Stockley Farm, Arley, Northwich, Cheshire CW9 6LZ Tel: 01565 777323 www.stockleyfarm.co.uk

One of Windmill Farm's best features is its miniature railway, which is more than a mile long.

Windmill Animal Farm

A group of us took a trip to Windmill Animal Farm near Burscough during the spring half-term. Driving in convoy, we found it fairly easily, located very near Martin Mere Wetlands. It is a great place to take six giddy children.

The outdoor play area is enormous, with a huge wooden climbing frame, along with a zip wire and a big basket swing. Even in wet weather Windmill Farm is good – its indoor soft play area is the largest I've seen on a farm. Here you'll also find the café serving the usual selection of hot and cold food. Children's meals are £2.99 for sandwiches, crisps and a drink. There are a number of benches both indoors by the play area and outside, and you are very welcome to bring your own picnic.

Along with all the farm animals, there are also pedal tractors and one of Windmill's best features, its own miniature railway! Both steam and diesel engines run on the 15-inch gauge track that crosses the farm and it is more than a mile long. The train stops half way round at Lake View and there are more picnic tables if you want to have your lunch here. To occupy the children while you wait for the next train you'll find a small wooden climbing frame. The railway station here is actually an original wooden ticket office from Lancaster Railway station, inside you'll find an electric train whizzing round a Playmobil cowboy and indian themed scene. If you've got a range of ages Windmill Farm caters for all of them.

6th Feb-Easter Weekends and half term daily 10am-5pm, Easter-end of Sept Daily 10am-5pm, Sept-Christmas Weekends 10am-5pm
Adult £5.50, Child £4.50, under 2s free, Family Ticket £16.
The train runs 11am-4.30pm every day the farm is open.
Santa train specials in December
The Windmill Animal Farm, Red Cat Lane, Burscough, Lancs L40 1UQ
Tel: 01704 892 282 www.windmillanimalfarm.co.uk

Wythenshawe Farm

See Wythenshawe Park on page 33.

Estates, Castles and Ruins

Step back in time and lose yourself in the splendour of North West past. Gorgeous grounds, romantic houses and splendid deer parks – a stunning escape from city life.

Estates, Castles and Ruins

Arley Hall and Gardens

This is a great place to go with young children if you are a garden lover. We have visited both in summer and at Christmas and have found Arley a treasure trove for young and old alike. With the car parked, it's a short stroll along an impressive tree-lined avenue. On entering the estate via the gift shop, you'll find a cobbled stable yard bordered by the restaurant and toilet facilities. In the warmer months several tables are set out for eating here. The cobbles are a bit awkward with a pram but the rest of Arley is very accessible. Passing under the clock tower, which houses a bell that to the delight of the children is rung regularly, you are greeted with the splendid hall. The hall itself, whilst beautiful, is probably a bit dull for little ones; but it isn't large and sprawling so a tour round can be short if you wish. At Christmas the hall comes to life with floral displays and activities for children. My three-year-old son made a beautiful floral table display last year that we proudly used on Christmas Day, and we all learnt about Victorian Christmas food in the kitchens.

The gardens are magnificent. Clearly a lot of love and care has gone into their design and maintenance. For under fives they are as much fun as you want to make them. Separated into 'rooms' of colour or design there are plenty of pathways and hidey-holes for playing chase or hide and seek. Situated in the gardens and surrounded by shrub roses is a little half-timbered cottage, built in the mid-19th Century, as a place for the family living at Arley at the time to enjoy afternoon tea. Today it is open to go inside, and with its tiny proportions makes a perfect place to play house.

The children also love watching the fish in the fish garden and try their best to get wet in the several fountains dotted about. There are plenty of open spaces where they can run and jump, and with the grass being manicured and dog poop free it makes a perfect place to roll around or kick a ball. If you are looking for something a bit more rugged, there is a woodland walk on the other side of the hall, which we found manageable with slow walkers and prams.

The restaurant is housed in The Tudor Barn, a terrific building which between 11am and 5pm serves a good selection of food. The kids menu includes cheese sandwiches for £3 or pizza for £3.95. There weren't many highchairs when we went but apparently plans are afoot to change this. The staff will happily heat up baby jars and bottles. Alternatively, if you want to take your own food there is a pleasant picnic area situated round a new and well-designed playhouse. This doubles as a climbing frame and incorporates, among other things, noughts and crosses, and a long rope to thread in and out of many different holes. It certainly captured my children's imagination.

Baby-changing facilities are available.
Gardens, chapel, grounds and plant nursery: 2nd Apr-31st Oct Tues-Sun and Bank Holidays, Nov Weekends, 11am-5pm.
Hall: 2nd Apr-31st Oct Tues, Sun and Bank Holidays, Nov Sunday, 12-5pm. Parking free.
Adult £6.60 for Gardens, £2.50 for Hall; under 16s £2 for Gardens, £1 for Hall; under 5s free, Family Ticket £14 for Gardens, £7 for Hall. Joint tickets available with Stockley Farm (see page 48).
Arley Hall and Gardens, Northwich, Cheshire CW9 6NA
Tel: 01565 777353 www.arleyhallandgardens.com

Bramall Hall Park

Just outside Bramhall village near Cheadle Hulme, Bramall Hall Park is 70 acres of breathtaking parkland surrounding one of Cheshire's grandest black and white timber-framed buildings. There is a pay and display car park, 70p for one hour, £1 for two hours, but entrance to the parkland is free.

Designed in the style of Capability Brown, the park offers magnificent vistas from the Hall, which is perched on the brow of a hill. Grass terraces lead downhill to three substantial man-made ponds and the diverted River Ladybrook, which snakes its way through the grounds. The ponds contain islands designed to resemble a Himalayan wilderness. I'm not so sure they are that, but they certainly create a stunning landscape.

Well-marked, tarmac paths run through the formal gardens near the Hall and the woodlands beyond, so it's pretty pram-friendly. There are three main bridges so crossing between the sides of the river is easy and a leisurely stroll takes less than an hour. The park's full of good climbing trees and the river itself has safe shelving banks so children can play at the water's edge as well as cross to parts of the 'Himalayan islands'. Wellies are definitely strongly recommended!

TO FIND OUT ABOUT BUS, TRAIN AND TRAM SERVICES TO EACH VENUE PHONE TRAVELINE ON 0871 200 22 33

The garden's at Arley are magnificent, take a peek inside the 19th century little half-timbered cottage.

Back up at the main house there is a large gated children's playground, aimed at the under eights, plus four climbing frames on a grassed area for the older ones. There is also a grassed slope down to the water that is great for 'rolling'! The Hall is open for guided tours only. We didn't go in, but it looked beautiful from the outside.

There is a lovely café in the courtyard by the Hall, which has an enclosed outer seating area as well as an indoor section. It offers a reasonably priced selection of hot food and snacks as well as a lunchbox for children with a choice of what's included (£2.10 for four items or £2.50 for five).

There are toilets within the park grounds close to the car park, in the café and in the Hall. Baby-changing is in the disabled toilets in the café.

Bramall Hall: Summer 1st Apr-31st Oct Tues-Thurs 1-4pm, Fri-Sun 1-5pm, Winter 1st Nov-31st Mar Weekends 1-4pm.
Café: Summer Daily 10am-5pm, Winter Daily 10am-4pm.
Adult £3.95, Child £2.95, under 5s free.
Tickets can be bought in conjunction with Staircase House and Stockport Air Raid Shelters (see page 16).
Bramall Hall, Bramall Park, off Hall Road, Bramhall, Stockport SK7 3NX
Tel: 0161 485 3708 www.bramallhall.org.uk

Chatsworth House

Whilst the road from Manchester and particularly North Manchester may be a long and winding route, it is definitely worth making a day trip to Chatsworth. I have been with my boys in both summer and winter and each trip has been a huge success.

The farmyard and adventure playground are superb. These two features alone make it worth the trip. At the farmyard you can stroke the guinea pigs, watch the cows being milked, sit on a tractor, and see, among other favourites, the shire horses, piglets and goats. The adventure playground can be accessed by a child-sized tunnel and ladder.

Water and sand are always a winning combination for children and the playground at Chatsworth does it brilliantly. Water can be drawn from a passing stream by turning a large metal corkscrew which then empties into a series of channels, cogs and funnels, before seeping out into troughs dug by children in the sand. On a summer visit my boys spent at least an hour in the sandpit, digging, paddling, splashing, turning and damming. There are also sit-on diggers which scoop out the sand and buckets on chains to hoist it up to a wooden platform. There were buckets and spades available to use on our visits but it may be worth taking a set with you, along with a pair of wellies and a change of clothes.

The rest of the playground is set in the woods and is divided into age appropriate sections with wooden rope bridges, slides, nets and trampolines. There are picnic tables in both the playground and farmyard areas. There is also a simple café set over a well-stocked gift shop selling pasties, sandwiches, ice creams and drinks etc. The whole area is easily accessible for pushchairs and wheelchairs. Look out for family activity and seasonal days at the farm.

Chatsworth House is not purely for the children – it caters for the parents as well. Visitors can treat themselves to afternoon tea in the stables or browse around the gift and garden shops. If that doesn't appeal, then there are beautiful gardens and of course the magnificent Chatsworth House itself. Alternatively try and coincide your trip with one of the many visiting events such as the Sculpture Exhibition. Hoping to run again in 2010, it hosts works from artists as celebrated as Henry Moore. Chatsworth also lays on seasonal events, for example during Christmas there was carol singing, a brass band and a tour of the festively decorated house. Look out in 2010 for 90th Birthday events on the website.

Food outlets, cafés, toilets and paid parking are all available, and there are baby-changing facilities throughout the estate.

Park open all year. House, Gardens and Farmyard open 14th March-23rd Dec (car park shut during closed season).
House and shops open 11am-5.30pm; Garden open 11am-6pm; Farmyard and adventure playground open 10.30am-5.30pm; Carriage House restaurant and Stables grill and drinks open 10.15am-5pm. Hot food served at lunchtime; The Cavendish Rooms open 10am-4.30pm. Hot food served at lunchtime.
Last admission one hour before closing.
Ticket prices for 2010 were unavailable as we went to press. Check the website for prices and online discounts.
2009 prices: Discovery Pass valid for one visit to the House and two visits to the garden and/or farmyard, all within seven days: Adult £17.60, Child £11, Family Ticket £52.80.
Farmyard and Adventure Playground: Adult £5.50, Child £5.80, Family Ticket £21.45.
Chatsworth House, Bakewell, Derbyshire DE45 1PP
Tel: 01246 565300 www.chatsworth.org

Getting close to the deer at Dunham Massey is really special.

Clitheroe Castle, Grounds and Museum

Towering above the charming town of Clitheroe is the 800-year-old Norman keep of Clitheroe Castle, which following a restoration project and complete refurbishment of the associated museum was reopened in May 2009. We visited on a Sunday and found free road parking in the town centre, however on busier days it may be worth heading for a car park. Alternatively, arrive by train, as the station is only 0.2 miles away.

The keep itself is small, in fact the second smallest in Britain, but considering its age, it is pretty much intact. There are two ways up, either by climbing about 100 steep steps, or via a buggy-friendly path to the museum entrance and then approximately 10 steps. It is worth the trip as the views of the town and surrounding Ribble Valley are breathtaking. Just below the keep is a beautifully designed outdoor creative activity space that wouldn't look out of place at a French chateau. My children enjoyed listening to the panpipes, communicating through a pair of funnels and looking through a periscope. There are several benches in this area, where we sat and ate a picnic whilst admiring the view.

After lunch we headed into the Steward's House (dating from the 1700s) and modern atrium, which together house the two-story museum, café, shop and temporary gallery. At the entrance to the museum the boys were delighted to be provided with activity backpacks which contained a full explorer's kit of pith helmet, magnifying glass, pencil case, clip board and a sheet of items to spot. The museum's key exhibits included fossils telling of elephants and hippos in the area; a brilliant audio-visual presenting the castle's history; costumes ranging from lords to serfs to try on; and an Edwardian kitchen and collector's study to explore. There are plenty of hands-on exhibits for little ones throughout the museum. There was a lift to the first floor and a buggy park for those with pushchairs. As we'd packed a picnic we didn't experience the café, which was a shame as it looked very inviting. Cakes were priced in the region of £2.75 with main meals approximately £5.99.

There are 18 acres of formal gardens surrounding the castle and we finished our visit by taking a stroll through the rose garden and down to the children's play area. If you have time it is well worth having a nosy round Clitheroe as there is a great selection of independent shops there.

Unisex baby-change is in the museum.
Apr to Oct 11am-5pm, Nov-Mar 12-4pm.
Adults £3.50, children free.
Clitheroe Castle Museum, Castle Hill, Clitheroe BB7 1BA
Tel: 01200 424 568 www.lancashire.gov.uk/clitheroecastlemuseum

The views from the 800-year-old Norman keep of Clitheroe Castle are breathtaking. It is certainly worth the climb.

Dunham Massey

Dunham Massey is a personal favourite for easy, enjoyable walks. The grounds of this country estate are beautiful – a stunning mix of parkland and maintained gardens (you have to pay extra to get into these unless you're a NT member). There are plenty of deer roaming free and you can get close for the children to have a good look. A moat surrounding the early Georgian house is full of ducks and swans to feed, whilst nearby rabbits hop around. I spent a lot of time here when my son was a baby as there are no steep hills and the wide paths make it ideal pushchair terrain. Now he is older there are loads of broken tree trunks lining the walk which are perfect for climbing over. The other aspect that is a big hit is the sawmill, where the giant waterwheel has been restored to full working order.

There's a designated picnic area outside but if you haven't packed your own the restaurant in the converted stables does great home-cooked food, including an irresistible cake selection. 'Trustyboxes' containing a ham or cheese roll, a piece of fresh fruit, a jaffa cake bar and an orange juice are available for children for £2.95, as well as small portions of the hot meals on offer (£3.50-£4.50). They also serve baby deli food for 0-10 months, pure fruit ice cream lollies and Innocent smoothies. There's a large separate room just off the main dining area specifically aimed at families. It has highchairs and toys, so it doesn't matter as much if

the kids run riot there. Also in this room you'll find a baby unit with a microwave and bottle warmer. There's lift access throughout and baby-changing is in the main toilet block adjacent to the restaurant.

The house is worth a look if you've got older children or easy-going babies. But it's perhaps less interesting for toddlers and you can't really take prams inside. However, front-carrying baby slings and hip-carrying infant seats are available for loan.

Whilst in the Dunham area you may want to think about paying a visit to Ash Farm, which produces ice cream that must rate as some of the best in the world! The mother and daughter team create flavours as diverse as fruit cake, lavender and ginger, in varying quantities ranging from a simple cone or tub to two-litre containers ideal for the freezer. The ice cream shop is open daily 12-5pm (12-6pm in summer and on fine days) and there is a pleasant enclosed garden with tables and chairs in which to sit and gorge!

Ash Farm, Station Road, Dunham Massey WA14 5SG
Tel: 0161 928 1230
Dunham Massey Park: Summer Daily 9am-7.30pm; Winter Daily 9am-4pm (or dusk if earlier).
Stables Restaurant: Summer Daily 10.30am-5pm (hot food 12-2.30pm); Winter Daily 10.30am-4pm.
House: Summer Sat-Wed 11am-5pm.
Garden: Daily 11am-5.30pm.
House and Garden: Adult £9.40, Child £4.70, under 5s free, Family ticket £23.50. Garden only: Adult £6.60, Child £3.30, under 5s free. Family Ticket £16.50. Car Park £5.
Dunham Massey, Altrincham, Cheshire WA14 4SJ
Tel: 0161 941 1025 www.nationaltrust.org.uk

Quarry Bank Mill and Styal Estate

Quarry Bank Mill is a great place to go on a rainy day and if it does turn out nice, the gardens are beautiful and the walk down by the River Bollin is easy for pushchairs and toddlers. There is a good play area at the start of the walk plus, as an added incentive, a small café selling ice lollies, cakes and cups of tea.

Inside the mill, it is pretty impressive. You can't take a pram as you start at the top and wind your way down, but shoulder seats for babies and hip carriers for toddlers are available for a deposit of £5. These can be collected at the Mill entrance. There are interactive exhibits and as you walk around, guides in traditional costume will give you demonstrations and potted histories of certain pieces of equipment. Be warned, if you have a child who doesn't tolerate a lot of noise, this is not the place for you. When the machines are running, the volume is incredible. At the bottom of the mill, there is a spectacular water wheel, the most powerful in Europe.

The Apprentice House is a guided tour that is booked in time slots and has limited availability. It is aimed at older children as the tour involves how the Victorian children used to live, where they slept, and even a vegetable garden. The Secret Garden is a bit tricky with pushchairs as it's built on a slope, plus there is a river at the bottom. Children's garden tracker packs are free to borrow from the garden steward in the hut.

The restaurant is child-friendly, offering lunchboxes at £2.95 or a child's meal at £3.50-£3.95. No baby food is provided but they are happy to microwave food and bottles. There is a small play area and highchairs available.
Mill and Apprentice House: 1st Mar-31st Oct Daily 11am-5pm, 1st Nov-12 Dec Wed-Sun 11am-4pm, 13 Dec-23rd Dec Weekends 11am-4pm, 26th Dec-31st Dec Daily 11am-4pm. Estate: Daily 8am-6pm.
Mill only: Adult £7.35, Child £3.90, under 5s free, Family £18.60. Mill and Garden or Apprentice House: Adult £10.50, Child £5.25, under 5s free, Family £25.20. Mill, Garden and Apprentice House: Adult £14.20, Child £7.05, under 5s free, Family £35.40. Car Park: £4.
Quarry Bank Mill and Styal Estate, Styal, Wilmslow, Cheshire SK9 4LA. Tel: 01625 445896 www.nationaltrust.org.uk

Haigh Hall and Country Park

During the summer holiday heat wave, we zipped up to Wigan and spent a glorious day here. I know we're a family that's become increasingly obsessed with trains, but the fact that Haigh Hall has got a rather good one made the day for us.

The winding country road brings you in at the top of the estate – you arrive at the pay and display car park, adjacent to Haigh Hall Golf Club and right next to the café, shop, outbuildings (including toilets) and children's playgrounds. A short walk down a hill brings you to the Hall itself. Georgian Grade II listed, this is generally closed to the public, however you can book in for Sunday lunch and afternoon teas – we peeked in and there were quite a few families having a rather nice looking cream tea!

Beyond the Hall, you then have 250 acres of park and woodland boasting magnificent panoramas as far as North Wales. We of course headed straight for the miniature train, which is about five minutes further on from the Hall. It runs at weekends and every day during the summer holidays from June to September from 1-3.45pm and costs £1 a ride. The steam engine takes you on a 15-minute or so trip around the woodland and is really good fun. As if that wasn't enough, there's also a super-mini railway track in the woody area just behind the platform run by enthusiasts. It's not well signposted, so ask the staff on the larger train for directions. When we went, there were about seven or so weaving in and out of the trees – Will and I jumped on board and zipped off (word of warning – it is quite hairy!).

Next we took an hour-long stroll through the beautiful woodland; there are plenty of nature trails on offer for all levels of walking ability and biking is clearly popular too. We were feeling a bit peckish by now, so headed back to the café – which unfortunately was heaving. The food on offer was a bit limited but Will was happy enough with a hot dog and chips. We just about managed to get a seat outdoors in the cobbled courtyard. I think I'd consider taking a packed lunch next time. Because it was the school holidays, there were tons of children's activities taking place in the courtyard area. I was very impressed because they were extremely well priced and nicely imaginative; everything from making up garden hanging baskets to painting ready-made bird boxes. Our final stop was the playground – plenty of swings and a climbing frame but frankly not much else. The crowds were thronging by this point and we decided to quit while ahead!
Winter Daily 9.30am-4pm, School Summer Holidays Daily 9.30am-5pm. Car Park £1.50.
Haigh Country Park, Haigh, Wigan WN2 1PE
Tel: 01942 832 895 www.wlct.org

With magnificent veiws towards the Welsh Hills, Haigh Hall is an enjoyable day out. Will looking cool in his shades!

Lyme Park

Lyme Park is a stunning mansion house that closely resembles an extravagant Italianate palace surrounded by gardens, moorland and ancient deer park. It was used as the setting for the 1995 TV version of Jane Austen's Pride and Prejudice starring Colin Firth. If you go hoping to see Mr Darcy appearing from the lake, prepare to be disappointed, but if you are looking for somewhere to take the children where they can run around in beautiful surroundings then Lyme Park fits the bill.

It's an ideal venue for meeting friends with children, and is perfect for picnics. After paying the parking entry fee, you proceed down a long driveway with the imposing view of the house ahead, to the car park which is positioned within easy access of everything. There are plenty of picnic areas and lots of open space for the children to explore. Heading towards the timber yard there is a lovely stream and pond, which makes an ideal paddling pool in the summer. On the opposite side of the pond, over a bridge, we found a steep bank to scramble up and plenty of fallen trees to climb on. The pretty timber yard housed a coffee shop, toilets and plant shop.

The highlight for the children was the extensive play area. Built from wood with a bark floor, it is nestled in amongst the trees, creating much-needed shade on a hot day. It is really well designed, with

three different areas catering for all age groups. A particular favourite with the under fives seems to be a piece of equipment that acts like a set of scales – children sit on a small seat suspended from a rope that is counter-balanced by another seat and rope, creating a unique see-saw effect.

We ended our visit with a short stroll in the deer park but by that stage the kids were getting weary and so we didn't last long, although we did catch a glimpse of one of the fallow deer that roam freely.

The most obvious structure in the park other than the house is a tower called the Cage, which stands on a hill to the east of the approach driveway. I think it looks like a cross between The Tower of London and a castle. It isn't open all the time and the route to it is not pram-friendly. It was originally a hunting lodge then later used as a park-keeper's cottage and as a lock-up for prisoners. There isn't much inside except a spiral staircase to climb, but the views towards Manchester are spectacular. There was also a large wooden 3D jigsaw of the Cage for children to play with, which fascinated my four-year-old.

The house itself is also worth a visit – it has a wonderful collection of tapestries, clocks and beautifully furnished rooms. The Victorian garden has roses, sunken parterre and a reflection lake. Baby-change facilities are available.

House and garden: 27th Feb-31st Oct Fri-Tues 11am-5pm.
House by guided tour only 11am-12. Numbers restricted.
Park open all year daily 8am-6pm.
Timber Yard Coffee Shop open daily 11am-4pm.
Car park £5. Pedestrians free.
House and Garden: Adult £9, Child £4.50, under 5s free.
House only: Adult £5.95, Child £3, under 5s free.
Garden only: Adult £5.60, Child £2.80, under 5s free.
Lyme Park, Disley, Stockport, Cheshire SK12 2NR
Tel: 01663 762023 www.nationaltrust.org.uk

Norton Priory

I ended up at Norton Priory quite by accident but I am very glad I did. The approach is through a dull business park that is off putting, but once inside the grounds you will find a little haven of rural England.

We were two families and a dog (who was allowed everywhere except the café and walled garden). We also had scooters in tow, which the staff were happy for us to take in. The children were initially drawn to the gift shop, which sold a selection of pocket money toys as well as more educational items. After persuading them there was more than a gift shop on offer we scooted through to the indoor museum, which houses some remains of the priory church and tells the story of priory life. This was the perfect size for little ones, offering a range of interactive areas where they could try brass rubbing and magnetic fishing, among other activities.

Once the children had explored the skeleton

Mulberry picking at Norton Priory was a delicious highlight. Sam and Ollie showing off their red-stained hands!

exhibit we headed outside into the undercroft, which the children walked straight through, much more interested in clambering on the excavated remains of the priory dormitory outside. After tiring of climbing they sped off on their scooters towards the sculpture trail but were stopped in their tracks by an excavated drainage channel, which proved great fun to jump across and pass over on a small footbridge. I took this opportunity to have a look in the medieval herb garden before settling down on a nearby bench. It was then that we spotted the highlight of our visit, a mulberry tree, overflowing with the sweetest mulberries, ready for picking. Twenty minutes later our whole party were licking their red-stained lips and trying to hide their red-stained fingers. The sculpture trail was another hit as it was a little like a maze. Everywhere seemed accessible with a pram except a viewing gallery, which was reached via a spiral staircase.

On returning to the indoor museum we headed to the Refectory café before tackling the St Christopher gallery, which houses a large sandstone St Christopher together with some high-tech screens, hands-on activities and the all important dressing up.

There is also a walled garden to visit, which is a five to 10-minute walk from the entrance. Storysacks are to be found in the museum gallery and are available at no cost. Baby-change facilities are also available.
Apr-Oct Mon-Fri 12-5pm, Weekends 12-6pm. Walled garden 12-4pm.
Adults £5.50, Children £3.95, Family £13.50, under 5s free.
Norton Priory Museum and Gardens, Tudor Road, Manor Park, Runcorn, Cheshire WA7 1SX
Tel: 01928 569 895 www.nortonpriory.org

Tatton Park

Tatton Park is one of Britain's great country house estates and it's on our doorstep. It's a fine neo-classical mansion set in 50 acres of beautiful gardens but admittedly not a major attraction for toddlers. Where Tatton comes into its own for the under fives is in what surrounds the house and garden. Its 1,000-acre parkland is home to deer, cattle and sheep and boasts a rare breeds farm, an adventure playground and even a land train. Tatton also hosts a heap of special events throughout the year. The day we went there was a selection of small fairground rides.

We left the car in one of the huge fields dedicated to parking and decided to stroll to the farm as it didn't look too daunting for our three-year-old. This is a beautiful traditional farm with all you'd expect (see Home Farm on page 45).

We took the land train back to the main estate, stopping at the Stables Restaurant for lunch (the toilet block in the courtyard has baby-changing facilities). From there, it was fairground rides all the way to the adventure playground. We found this exceptional. Containing over 30 rides, it's a massive space set in beautiful surroundings and has been very well thought out.

Tatton Park's a really big deal. It's dominated this part of Cheshire for over two centuries and is, quite literally, a national treasure. If you don't fancy any of the above, just explore the park by foot, bike or even horse. With its woodland, ponds and lakes, this is a stunningly beautiful estate.
Up to March 26th 2010
Park: Tues-Sun 11am-5pm; Gardens, Shops and Restaurant: Tues-Sun 11am-4pm; Farm: Weekends 11am-4pm.
27th March-3rd Oct
Park: Mon-Sun 10am-7pm; Gardens: Tues-Sun 10am-6pm; Mansion: Tues-Sun 1-5pm; Farm: Tues-Sun 12-5pm; Shops: Tues-Sun 10.30am-5pm; Restaurant: Mon-Sun 10am-6pm.
Last admission one hour before closing.
Car Park £5, free to walkers and cyclists.
Adult £4.50, Child £2.50, under 4s free, Family £11.50.
Totally Tatton ticket (entry to 3 attractions) Adult £7, Child £3.50, under 4s free, Family £11.50.
Tatton Park, Knutsford, Cheshire WA16 6QN
Tel: 01625 374400 www.tattonpark.org.uk

Tatton Park is a 1,000-acre wonderland for the under fives.

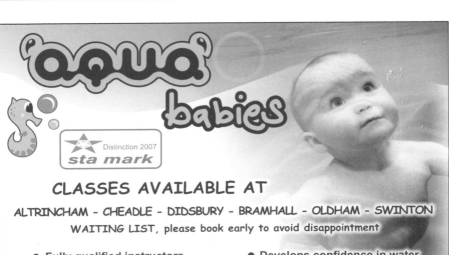

Greater Manchester may well be land-locked but fortunately it is within a stone's throw of the west coast of England, which has a great selection of beaches – perfect for day trips.

"Manchester's got everything except a beach"

Ian Brown, Stone Roses

Ainsdale Sands

On a glorious summer's day, we set the sat-nav for Ainsdale, one of the largest areas of wild duneland left in Britain. You can enter the reserve from the beach or one of the numerous access points. We actually drove onto the sands, which was great fun for the little ones, though at one point we were concerned we'd get stuck (don't worry, there's a jeep going up and down pulling out any stranded vehicles!). Thankfully we didn't, and plonked ourselves down at the furthest point along the beach. In hindsight, this perhaps wasn't the best location as the refreshment van and toilets were located where you drive in, so miles away. We were woefully unprepared, without breakers or a picnic, but thankfully we had remembered buckets and spades so the kids got digging.

The dunes are as you'd expect – magnificent – and the children loved rolling down them. I don't think you'd bother with a pram round here, although nearby is the Sand Lakes Nature Trail which has access for prams and wheelchairs and takes you round a small pool. The award-winning beach at Ainsdale is stunning and we even went for a paddle. A cliché yes, but it felt like being abroad. After a couple of hours, our next mission was to find food, and quickly. The van on the beach was more fast-food style, which we didn't fancy so we drove back into Ainsdale itself. By this point the kids were in hunger meltdown so we flung ourselves into the nearest place available, a bar

called Bar Mio. They were very welcoming and did us a couple of paninis. A better choice for the children would probably have been The Pantry a couple of doors down, which had a kids' menu.

Beach parking £3.50 per day. Beach entrance toilets open daily throughout summer and ad hoc in the winter.

Ainsdale Discovery Centre, The Promenade off Shore Road, Ainsdale-on-Sea, Near Southport PR8 2QU
Tel: 0151 934 2967 www.sefton.gov.uk

Formby Point Red Squirrel Reserve

This reserve is National Trust owned and includes a pine forest squirrel reserve and Formby Sands. This is uncommercialised stunning natural coast without a pier or prom in sight. If you're heading to the squirrel reserve first then park under the trees, but if you are intending to take a Crackerjack-worthy collection of items onto the beach it is better to park a little closer and walk back to the squirrels unladen.

A short hike over grass-covered sand dunes from the car park takes you to the wild open beach of Formby Sands. The dunes are great for 'sand sliding' and the firm sand is equally as good for football as it is for making sandcastles. With its exposed position, kite flying is popular, but the wind eats its way into everything, so be prepared for sand sandwiches!

Even with a three-wheeler it is difficult to push a pram over the sand dunes but the squirrel reserve is very pram-friendly. The reserve borders the dunes and is home to one of the UK's last remaining colonies of red squirrels. You can purchase bags of nuts at the entrance lodge to encourage the squirrels down from the trees. In recent years numbers have declined due to squirrel pox, however from a very low base, breeding in 2009 has doubled their numbers and hopefully this will continue.

There are toilets next to the reserve, which is some distance from the beach. On a warm day there is an ice cream van but nowhere else to purchase refreshments, so pack a picnic.

Toilets and car park: Summer 9am-5.30pm, Winter 9am-4pm. Car Park £4.20.

Formby Point Red Squirrel Reserve, Victoria Road, Freshfield, Formby, Liverpool L37 1LJ Tel: 01704 878591 www.nationaltrust.org.uk

St Annes

St Annes is a much smaller, quieter beach resort than neighbouring Blackpool but still has the pier and promenade, with all the attractions that young children love at the seaside. A day trip here is a regular occurrence in our household.

We usually park in the pay and display car park by the Beach Terrace, a lovely stand-alone café with great views about 500m south of the pier – ideal for a quick cup of tea before you start. Baby-changing and highchairs are available. Then we head north along the prom towards the pier – often the boys take their bikes, as it is an ideal surface to cycle on and they can get to the attractions a bit quicker. Spoilt for choice they begin on their favourite, the little train, which takes a circular route round the crazy golf taking in a tunnel along the way. From there it's on to the netted trampolines. There are a number of other attractions including boats and a bouncy play area, all suitable for children under five.

The pier is a little bit tired but full of the type of rides that small children adore. Most of them are open from Easter until the October half-term. Costs vary, but are in the region of £1.50 and generally cash only.

The beach itself is beautiful, and on the north side of the pier it is bordered by sand dunes which can either be explored or used as shelter from the wind. During the summer months, the tide is low during the main part of the day, so it is a long walk to the sea. If the walk seems a bit too far, there is a purpose-built paddling pool for toddlers on the promenade, close to the pier, for a splash.

There is also a café on the pier, and adjacent to that a fish and chip shop. For lunch however we either return to the Beach Terrace Café or more commonly pack a picnic. After lunch we make sandcastles on the beach before the boys are lured to the donkeys and the inflatable bouncy slide. Exhausted from all the fun they always fall asleep within five minutes of leaving St Annes.

Beach Terrace Café: Mon-Sun 9am-dusk.

Beach Terrace Café, South Promenade at jct with Fairhaven Road, St Annes FY8 1NN Tel: 01253 711167

Pier Café: Easter-31st Oct Mon-Sun 10am-6pm, 1st Nov-Easter Weekends 10am-4pm.

The Pier Café, St Annes Pier, South Promenade, St Annes FY8 2NG Tel: 01253 788510 www.piercafe.co.uk

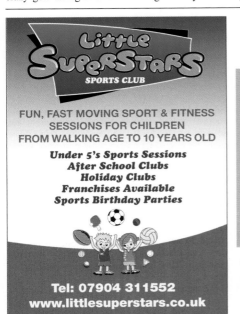

Attractions and theme parks

The diversity of attractions outside the city are amazing – and you don't have far to travel to reach them. Whatever you are looking for – from indoor waterparks and adventure theme parks to the more traditional farm and funfair entertainment – there is definitely something for everyone.

Attractions and theme parks

Apple Jacks Farm

Looking for a cheaper alternative to the zoo, we headed for Apple Jacks Farm. But cheap it isn't, and at first my heart sank when we went through the entrance as it is clearly designed for large crowds. Once in, however, it was pleasantly quiet.

Although doubtful we would find enough to keep five-year-old Lucas amused, there was no need to worry. Apple Jacks has plenty on offer, not least of which are a giant hay mountain and archery range, both of which were big hits. Another favourite was the sandpit diggers but these were definitely over-shadowed by the Pillow, an inflated yellow rubber rectangle roughly 40 foot long that is basically a different take on the bouncy castle theme. Kids run up the sloping sides and jump around on the top while the adults sit and watch, although obviously small children would need parental assistance.

Apple Jack's speciality is mazes and it features a vast, five-acre maize version that is so enormous it is possible to get lost for hours! There are at least three others of varying levels of difficulty and style so if your children are maze-mad, this is the place to go.

Other key attractions include a wild west show, open land play area, pedal carts, giant games and Spooky World. There is also the beautiful lake to walk around. Strangely enough, one of the biggest hits was the tractor ride, which takes you straight through the middle of a pond. The simple pleasures!

17th July–12th Sept Daily 10am–6pm, 16th Oct–14th Nov Daily 12–10pm. £10 per person.
Apple Jacks Farm, Stretton Road, Stretton, Warrington WA4 4NW
Tel: 01925 268495 www.applejacksfarm.co.uk

Apple Jacks has plenty to keep youngsters busy, not least of which is a giant inflatable pillow, a different take on the bouncy castle theme.

Blackpool Sandcastle

An indoor waterpark with something for everyone. As soon as you leave the changing rooms you feel like you are on holiday, with the temperature at a tropical 84 degrees! You pay to enter whether you go on the slides or not so you may as well join in. You can even hire swimsuits and a towel for £4 so there are no excuses.

There are 18 slides in all. Definitely worth a try is the world's longest indoor roller coaster waterslide at 250 metres called the Masterblaster – if you are brave enough and over eight years old! For younger kids there is everything from a wave pool to a pirate ship play area, lazy river, bumpy slides and several tunnels. As long as younger children sit on your knee they can also go on some of the more adult rides.

The waterpark opens at 10am and the car park next door was full by 9.30am. We parked behind the Pleasure Beach (£6 per day) and walked round. There are lots of tables to eat lunch at and various fast-food outlets, but prepare to queue. Thankfully there was no problem heating bottles or baby food. There are separate male and female changing rooms, plus a family changing room, which along with the female toilets has baby-changing. Lockers, some of which are located by the pool, require a refundable 50p. We were there for over six hours and had a blast.

Summer Daily 9.30am–6pm, Winter Weekends 10am–4.30pm. Times vary throughout the year so it's worth checking the website. Adult £10.85 (£14.20 including Hyperzone), Junior (8–13 years) £8.85 (£11.85 including Hyperzone), Junior (6–7 years) £8.85 (£10.85 including Hyperzone), Child (2–5 years) £6.85, under 2s free.
Sandcastle Waterpark, South Beach, Blackpool, Lancashire FY4 1BB
Tel: 01253 343 602 www.sandcastle-waterpark.co.uk

Blackpool Tower

The day before we went, we heard dreadful reports about Blackpool Tower, but as we'd pre-booked we decided to go anyway – thank goodness! It turned out to be a lovely sunny day and there was not a queue in sight. Result! The entrance leads straight into the aquarium, which although small is more than enough to satisfy the kids. Towards the back, along with fruit machines, is a cloakroom for storing a pushchair. This level also has baby-changing, as does Level 5.

We thought it best to head to the Tower Top first – a lift takes you most of the way – where you'll find the 'Walk of Faith', a two-inch thick glass

Blackpool Tower's 'Walk of Faith' is not for the faint-hearted… 380 feet up and nothing but a piece of glass between Nuala, Matthew, Christopher, Daniel… and the ground!

panel capable of withstanding the weight of five baby elephants. Five-year-old Christopher was in the middle of it before he realised and when he looked down his face was a picture. Some 380 feet up, looking down on the building below, he thought it was hilarious! We then climbed the stairs to the top three levels up. The views were amazing! On a clear day you can see from North Wales to the Lake District. Note that the climb is not suitable for pushchairs and it is closed when winds reach 40mph (they often get up to 100mph!)

Next we visited the Tower Ballroom where, complete with an organist in bow tie, several couples were ballroom dancing. Stuck in a bit of a time warp yes, but the boys loved it and they particularly enjoyed the Cha Cha! Then it was on to Jungle Jims, an indoor soft play area with a separate toddler section, lots of seating for adults and a bar offering tea, coffee and beer. The kids would have stayed there all day if we had let them.

We went to Bickerstaffe's for lunch, a pasta and pizza restaurant. There is also the self-service Restaurant 1894.

After that we set off to Jurassic Walk, a dinosaur exhibition that included a 3D film. Although I found it disappointing, the kids loved it and also enjoyed walking through the land of the dinosaurs afterwards. Then it was time for the circus. The performance went on for two hours, including the interval, which might be a little too much for a toddler, but it was fantastic! Fast paced, with lots for grown-ups and kids, amazing acrobats and lots of comedy bits, it kept us all laughing.

A couple of tips: we parked in the shopping centre next door, and pre-booked tickets on the internet and saved about £3 per head. We were there from 10.30am-6pm and managed to be busy all the time, but felt we had missed out on the seaside. Maybe we should have booked the earlier circus showing of 1-3pm and spent less time at Jungle Jims! Due to the fact the Tower was built in 1894, there are several times when you have to lift pushchairs up and down steps. It is tatty and worn in places but is slowly being modernised (it takes seven years to paint) and is definitely worth a visit!

Mon-Sun Summer (Mar-Sep) 10am-11pm, Winter (Oct-Feb) 11am-5pm. Adult: £16.95, Child:£13.95, under 90cm free. Discounts available online. Tesco vouchers are valid against the full admission price. Blackpool Tower, Promenade, Blackpool, Lancashire FY1 1BJ Tel: 01253 622 242 www.theblackpooltower.co.uk

Diggerland

When you're faced with five children ranging in age from two to nine, it can be tricky finding somewhere with something for everyone, but Diggerland is a strong contender. The entrance fee is fairly steep at £15 per person. Children under three go free but unfortunately there's no family ticket available. However, you can book online and save £2 a person, or take advantage of the two for one voucher enclosed in this book!

From the minute you arrive, Diggerland is pretty impressive – there are JCBs lined up on either side just waiting for someone to have a go. They are all static but you can move the arm and bucket around and there are loads of levers to play with. A good place to start is the Mini Diggers. There are 12 of them, all of which do different activities with their buckets. Five-year-olds can have a go on their own but younger children need to ride with an adult. Opposite are their giant counterparts – three enormous diggers on big piles of mud, which can be used to dig holes or just move earth from one pile to another.

In the centre of the park are three areas: the first contains dumper trucks; the second, skid steers that go really slowly but are difficult to manoeuvre; and finally the tractors, which are extremely quick. Again you have to be five years old to drive but only three to go on all of the rides.

The café is still being built so in the meantime, take a picnic. There are plenty of picnic tables outside and some inside. Baby-changing is by the main building.

Other attractions are go-karts for older children; the Sky Shuttle – where you sit in the bucket of a digger and are transported 50 feet into the air, and Spin Dizzy – an enormous digger with seats in its bucket that spins you round until you literally plead to get off! Both these rides are for three years and over but I would think twice about letting a three-year-old on Spin Dizzy. Also a Mitsubishi Pajero has been done up to look like a police car which, from nine years old, you can have a go at driving around a track. For a more sedate time, try the tractor that pulls a long line of trailers slowly around the park, or Dig-a-round – a carousel with buckets instead of seats. There are also coin-operated dodgems and an indoor soft play area.

We went in the winter and it was very quiet, but other mums who have been in the summer say the longest wait they had was 10 minutes, so a thumbs up on that front. For children mad about diggers it is an absolute must.

13th Feb-31st Oct Weekends and daily during school holidays.
Feb and Oct 10am-4pm, Mar-Sep 10am-5pm.
3-65 yrs £15, under 3s free.
Pre-booked online tickets £2 discount.
Diggerland, Willowbridge Lane, Whitwood, Castleford, West Yorkshire WF10 5NW
Tel: 0871 22 77 007 www.diggerland.com

Gulliver's World

Gulliver's is an amusement park designed for families with children between the ages of two and 13. It is made up of themed areas within which you will find a ride to suit your child's age. Our under fives were well catered for.

Gulliver's has improved its facilities over the past year and has a new indoor play section for smaller children. In here you'll find a mini-supervised pirate ship ride as well as an area with shop, garage and post box for the children to get into some

You can ride on the diggers from three years old and drive one from only five years old!

role-play. Add the café into the mix and you can enjoy a pretty relaxing time.

Back outside, we particularly liked the train ride, which takes you around the Lost World; the pedal tractor driving school; and the mechanical diggers. There is also a mini canyon rapid ride (you get wet on this one!) and a swinging pirate ship. I had to drop out of this and leave Ollie and Felix in the hands of a mother with a stronger constitution. Fortunately we found the staff at Gulliver's fabulous and if you have a little one or mum who has bitten off more than she can chew they were happy to stop a ride mid flow where possible. The food on sale tends to be fast-food style, but there are pack lunches available and also plenty of play areas with picnic tables.

After lunch the kids headed for the wooden child-sized village in Western World, complete with chapel, jail and pirate ship climbing frame. The rides in Circus World are also perfect for under fives. This area does look a little tired and could do with a lick of paint but this is something most five-year-olds would not notice!

One thing to note is that on several rides children under 90cm are not allowed on and those between 90cm and 120cm (who have paid the full entrance price) have to be accompanied by an adult.

Whilst small compared to some theme parks, there is still plenty of walking to be done so I would recommend taking a pushchair or hiring one from guest services for £3 per day. Also available are nappies, dummies and lost identity stickers.

Open usually March-October weekends except for school holidays when open daily 10.30am-5pm.
Adults and children £13.50, children under 90cm free.
Gulliver's Theme Park Warrington, Old Hall, Warrington WA5 9YZ
Tel: 01925 444888 www.gulliversfun.co.uk

Jodrell Bank Radio Telescope

In truth there's not much at Jodrell Bank for toddlers but it's such an extraordinary place, you should go anyway. It's only 10 minutes from Alderley Edge so after a walk in the woods why not pop in for a cup of tea and a quick scoot around the visitor centre (the gift shop is pretty good for children) before heading outside to marvel at the sheer spectacle that is Jodrell Bank. Your children will be agog each time the massive dish of the telescope makes one of its rotations. There is a children's playground suited to older children next to the car park and a 35-acre arboretum with various trails to explore.

Normal opening hours are 10.30am-5pm. However, during the winter the visitor centre is closed on Mondays, open 10.30am-3pm Tues- Fri, and 11am- 4pm on weekends. There are occasional days when the centre is closed so check the website for more details.
Adults £2, Children £1, under 4s free.
Jodrell Bank, Macclesfield, Cheshire SK11 9DL
Tel: 01477 571 339 www.jb.man.ac.uk

Red House Farm

Red House Farm has got a bit of everything – a farm shop serving up fresh produce and regional specialities; an award-winning tea room dishing out doorstopper sandwiches and tempting cakes and an outdoor area with sandpit and motorised mini vehicles.

The tea room has a good children's menu with things like a picnic platter or scrambled eggs. The staff are helpful and will happily heat up baby bottles. The little play area is in view of the tea room, which makes lunchtime relatively relaxing. Just remember to bring some change as the motorised mini-diggers and tractors need £1 coins to operate.

In the summer there is a Maize maze with a barbecue, bouncy castle, pedal quad bikes, play area, and a quad barrel train. Granny and Will squeezed themselves into blue plastic oil-drum type things (Will was too young to ride on his own) and off they disappeared. They returned five minutes later a bit muddy and definitely windswept – Will seemed to enjoy himself though not sure about Granny!

Animals wise, there aren't loads – usually a few pigs, ducks and rabbits. There is also a giant sandpit with various toys which kept Will entertained for the longest amount of time along with a straw mountain and Little Tikes play area.

Baby-changing facilities are in the unisex toilets next to the tea room. Car parking is free.
Tea room: Mon-Sat 9am-4.30pm, Sun 10am-4.30pm;
Farm shop: Mon-Sat 9am-5.30pm, Sun 10am-4.30pm;
Maze: July-Sept. Adult £5.95, Child £4.95, under 5s free.
Party of four (regardless of adult:child ratio) £19.50.
Red House Farm, Redhouse Lane, Dunham Massey, Altrincham
WA14 5RL Tel: 0161 941 3480 www.redhousefarm.co.uk

Southport Funfair Pleasureland

Pleasureland is somewhere I used to go as a child so it was great to head back and see how it had changed (early risers do note that the park doesn't open until around midday).

There are three car parks surrounding the funfair (prices range from £2-£5 depending on the time of year) so that is nice and easy. Entrance is free, then once inside you buy tokens for the rides which for the little ones cost between £1 and £2 each. There is quite an old-fashioned feel about the place, which I like. There are a good few rides for toddlers, from the Toyset Carousel (lots of vehicles) to the Thunderbirds Jetride (little planes going up and down) – but whilst the kids enjoyed it, it was surprising how fast the cost mounted up.

New for 2010 is an indoor play centre, which is aimed at 0-10 year olds, a useful fall back in case of rain. We played a bit of hook-a-duck, won a goldfish and an hour passed quickly. There are cafés on site but we'd brought a packed lunch so strolled down to the beach just a few minutes away. Alternatively, there is a retail park next door on the seafront with restaurants such as Frankie & Benny's and Nandos.

After lunch we walked down to the pier and enjoyed a ride up and down on the bright yellow road train. We were tempted by the Southport Belle, a Mississippi-style paddle steamer that cruises up and down the large Marine Lake, but as the weather was getting worse, we decided we'd have to save that one for next time.

Open Weekends in March, Easter Holidays, Bank Holidays, Daily mid-June to mid-September, all approximately 12-7pm.
If bad weather, phone ahead to check if open.
Southport Funfair Pleasureland, Marine Drive, Southport, Merseyside PR8 1RX
Tel: 01704 532 717 www.southportfunfair.co.uk

For those with a strong constitution Gulliver's World has lots of thrills up its sleeve.

OUT AND ABOUT

A trip to Thomas Land is a brilliant day out – totally exhausting but the children love every minute of it.

SplashZone

Housed at the entrance to Gulliver's World, from the outside SplashZone looks like nothing more than a grey industrial unit with a colourful tube slide snaking through it. But once inside it's a totally different story, best described as soft play meets water park, with loud disco music thrown in for good measure.

The idea of the centre is that adults sit dry at tables or on sofas at the side and watch the children play on the equipment or on soft matting in a fenced wet zone. As there is no standing water, there is no requirement to swim.

Our older children who are a little more independent disappeared into a haze of water jets and slides quite happily. But if you need to play alongside your children, be prepared to get wet! Adults are allowed to don their cossies if they want to.

There is a dedicated area for younger children at the far end of the wet zone, which features more gentle jets of water, a couple of small slides and two little receptacles of water to play in but it could do with some watering cans or buckets – it may even be worth taking your own along.

Staff are in attendance throughout and helpfully tried to warn me that a suspended giant water bucket was about to tip. Unfortunately I then walked straight into it's path and a nervous Felix got drenched!

Children can go between the wet and dry areas without having to dry off and change so it may be worth keeping towels with you to keep them warm during lunch. Pushchairs can be taken to the dry seating area, which is quite useful as there is no area for crawling babies, as even the floor in the dry area is cold and wet. Highchairs are available and jars of baby food for sale at the café. Courtesy shampoo and conditioner in the showers.

Booking is essential and is a two hour time slot.

School holidays Mon-Fri 10am-6pm, term time Tues-Fri 11am-6pm, Weekends 10am-6pm. Booking required.
Adults £2.50, children under 90cm £3.50, children over 90cm £5.50. For children aged two and over.
SplashZone, Gulliver's World, Old Hall, Warrington, Cheshire WA5 9YZ
Tel: 01925 230 088 www.gulliversfun.co.uk

Stapeley Water Gardens and Palms Tropical Oasis

Stapeley Water Gardens is essentially a large garden centre adjoined by The Palms Tropical Oasis – an aquatic and reptile centre. This is a huge glasshouse containing exotic plant life, trees, a rather good selection of lizards, snakes, spiders and meerkats as well as the Italian Gardens, complete with water features and a Japanese Koi Carp pool. Will had a good time running around but he did shy away from the opportunity to stroke a snake proffered by a friendly keeper. You do have to pay to get into Palms and it's not cheap, however there is a strong conservation ethos at the centre. We ended our visit with a coffee and snack in the café. This wasn't an enjoyable experience unfortunately – many of the empty tables were laden with used crockery (though someone started to clean them up eventually) and the floor was horribly dirty with food debris. The toilets were also very below par.

Daily 10am-5pm. Palms: Adult: £4.95, Child £2.95, under 3s free.
Stapeley Water Gardens, Nantwich CW5 7LH
Tel: 01270 623 868 www.stapeleywg.com

Thomas Land

A trip to Thomas Land at Drayton Manor Theme Park had to be worked out with almost military precision. We'd been warned by other parents who'd gone on a Bank Holiday weekend that the queues had been horrific, so we definitely wanted to go on a term time weekday. A good tip is that reduced price adult-toddler tickets are available mid-week during Staffordshire term times (these may differ from Manchester). There is lots of parking as you'd expect and we were able to park pretty close to the entrance.

Once in, we headed straight to Thomas Land, an attraction within Drayton Manor immediately on your left-hand side after walking through the gates. There are 12 themed rides. These include 'Harold's Heli Tours' (which you can see from outside – so no turning back without a major tantrum!) the 220m Troublesome Trucks roller coaster, Rockin' Bulstrode and Sodor Docks – a bumpy ride that rotates you 360 degrees – and Sodor's classic cars, where you steer a car through tunnels and a barn. Our children were aged two and three and in my opinion a little young for some of the rides. Bear in mind that generally you need one adult to accompany each child on a ride.

We packed a picnic but trying to find somewhere to eat it in the Thomas Land section was tricky. We later discovered that there are plenty more outdoor picnic areas in the zoo section, which isn't far away. There is a café in the Thomas area, one of several throughout the park. They stock Ella's organic range of food pouches for babies and toddlers.

After lunch we took a ride on Percy the train to Farmer McColls Farm, where there's a café, an exotic animal reserve and Spencer's Activity Park, a brilliant adventure playground. Then it was off to the zoo. We didn't get round all of it but we saw monkeys, penguins and tigers, among others.

We finished off with Emily's Adventure Play – a large indoor soft play area controlled on a time basis so it is never over-crowded. It's worth noting that no adults are allowed in the play zone. There is a good area for under twos as well as baby-changing on site.

There are toilets and baby-changing in Thomas Land and the zoo section but some could do with a facelift and could have been cleaner.

Overall it was a great day out – totally exhausting but the children loved every minute of it.

20th March 2009-31st October 2009. Daily 9.30am-5.30pm.
2009 prices Adult £25, Child £21, under 4s free,
Adult and Toddler (under 4 years) available only during
Staffordshire term time £15. Discounts available by booking online.
Thomas Land at Drayton Manor Theme Park, Tamworth, Staffordshire B78 3TW Tel: 0844 472 1960 www.draytonmanor.co.uk

After a lot of 'oooooohh, that's disgusting!!' hysterical screams and 'ouchs' from Sam we eventually made it round the Barefoot Walk.

Trentham Gardens and Adventure Play – Barfuss Park (Barefoot Walk)

We were recommended Trentham Gardens and the Barefoot Walk by a friend who loved it. We arrived to be greeted by a row of shops and a large restaurant, not overly impressed so far! After locating the entrance, right in the centre of the actually very nice independent shopping village, we headed into the gardens, which are absolutely beautiful.

Here there is an adventure zone with three different play areas, two large sandpits full of toys, diggers and wheelbarrows and the JCB track – a tarmac pathway with at least 10 pedal diggers in various sizes. The play areas are aimed at different ages and abilities. What I loved about it most though were the numerous deckchairs and picnic tables scattered around. Although not the sunniest day, it was great to just plonk down, admire the view and watch the children amuse themselves.

If you can rouse yourself, the one-kilometre Barefoot Walk (Barfuss Park in German) is well worth a try. After storing shoes and bags in the lockers provided, we set off across water, mud, rocks, stones and soggy hay. Strangely enough, the boys took a bit of persuading to wade through the mud but we eventually made it round. Double foot showers are provided at the end of the walk, although the mud does take a bit of washing off.

We'd brought a picnic, but a brand new café opened in 2009 with toilet and baby-changing facilities.

The lake and woodlands are immediately on your right as you come out of the gardens. Here there is a narrow gauge train that runs along the shore of the lake at £2 per person. There is also a 42-seat catamaran that cruises the lake for £2 per person or you can hire your own rowing boats for £7 per family. There are various walks around the estate, two of which are pushchair-friendly.

Summer Daily 9am-6pm, Winter Daily 10am-3pm.
Winter: Adult £5, Child 5-15 £3.50, under 5s free.
Summer: Adult £7.25, Child 3-15 £5.70, under 5s free.
Joint tickets available for the Monkey Forest.
Trentham Woodlands and Lake: 8am-8pm. Admission free.
For operating times of the train and the boat please see website.
The Trentham Estate, Stone Road, Trentham, Stoke-on-Trent, Staffordshire ST4 8AX
Tel: 01782 646646 www.trenthamleisure.co.uk

Cafés

Child-friendly cafés are a must if you're looking for a relaxing lunch with children. We've checked out some of the favourites – and even found one with an on-site crèche.

Café culture

Battery Park Juice Bar

A well-known institution amongst Chorlton-ites, we decided to give Battery Park a go with the kids in tow. Four of us went on a weekday for lunch – weekends do get very busy apparently. There is no children's menu so we decided on a cream cheese bagel and a couple of hot halloumi sandwiches to share. We split a milkshake between the children (they're enormous, very thick and did I mention delicious?!) and we settled for juices – the bill came to £18.35.

It's got a lovely atmosphere, a real community vibe – the café's split-level with wooden chairs and tables downstairs and a couple of comfy sofas in the back room upstairs. We took along a bag of toy cars and our two kept themselves entertained enough for lunch not to be too stressful. They have a highchair but there are no baby-changing facilities.

Quite frankly it's not brilliantly child-friendly and you'd struggle to get pushchairs in when it's busy but if you're passing, fancy a brilliant smoothie or a chunky sandwich, it's definitely worth a look.
Mon-Fri 8am-5.30pm, Sat 10am-6pm, Sun 11am-5pm.
Battery Park Juice Bar, 615a Wilbraham Road, Chorlton M21 9AN
Tel: 0161 860 0754 www.batteryparkjuicebar.co.uk

Café Seven

We've just discovered this café set in the leafy residential streets of Bowdon. There is plenty of parking on the road plus a little car park across the way. Don't be put off by its small appearance – when you get inside you'll discover there's another floor upstairs packed with leather sofas. On each floor there's a little child's table with stools, a few crayons and a couple of toys.

On our visit a group of NCT mums were getting their coffee fix. Caffé Latte is unique with an on-site crèche facility.

This is an extremely child-friendly environment and the staff seemed immune to the terrific amount of noise emitted by my eight-month-old. They're happy for you to park your buggies in the café's main thoroughfare and when we visited, the upstairs was very quiet so you could breastfeed in peace too!

Finally the food – it was a really nice simple menu offering very reasonably priced paninis, all-day breakfasts and salads as well as 'Kidditoasties' and 'Kiddisandwiches' for £2.30. All the food is prepared on the premises, with ingredients sourced locally. The handmade cake selection is irresistible – try the lemon drizzle cake or the jam centred shortbread – just delicious. All this makes Café Seven the perfect place to go and meet fellow mums with babies.
Mon-Fri 8.30am-3pm, Sat 9am-2pm. (Later openings planned for 2010).
Café Seven, 7 Vale View, Vicarage Lane, Bowdon, Altrincham WA14 3BD Tel: 0161 941 4663

Caffé Latte

Caffé Latte is unique on our list in that it is the only café we've come across that has an on-site crèche facility. Aimed at children aged from two to 12 years old, the crèche is open every day and you can just drop in without advance booking. You can leave your child for up to two hours while you either go shopping or relax with a coffee. This children's area is in a sound-proofed room off the café and is kitted out with a large table and chairs

Café Seven is incredibly child-friendly – the perfect place to go.

EATING OUT

LOVE Babies in the City

LOVE Babies in the City

EATING OUT

When we visited mid-week there were lots of mums and buggies – there is a buggy park within the shop that would fit about four pushchairs. The café is pleasantly decorated, although I found it a little sparse. However, I was soon distracted from the décor when my hot chocolate arrived.

The children's menu offers such items as a small glass of fruit juice or milk for £1, toast and crumpets with jam or nutella for £1.50 and soup and a sandwich for £3.50. Simple fare maybe, but it appealed to my toddler. For the grown-ups there are light bites such as pain au chocolat, or something a bit more substantial such as jacket potatoes, chilli with a hint of cocoa and toasties served with crisps, salad and coleslaw. As you would expect, chocolate features strongly on the dessert menu. Choose from the chocolate fondue, truffles that you make at the table or take a look at the display of chocolate cakes and muffins. If you are choc'd out, then try the scones and jam or tea breads.

The service was a little slow but accommodating and with a smile. Baby-change is on the ground floor. There is no nappy bin but nappy sacks are available, although you are asked to take them with you. The café is only a five-minute walk from Ramsbottom station on the East Lancs Railway (see page 37).

Tues-Sun 10.30am-5pm. Also at Deansgate, Manchester (Tues-Sat).
The Chocolate Café, 2 Bolton Street, Ramsbottom, Bury BL0 9HX
Tel: 01706 822 828 www.chocolate-cafe.co.uk

for activities such as painting and making hama beads. There is a television with movie choices and also toys and books for the younger ones.

As we'd arrived with small babies, we didn't get a chance to test the crèche but we did get to try one of their tasty paninis and homemade cakes. For little ones they are happy to make any choice of sandwich or toastie with prices starting from £1.80.

The café is light and airy with a modern feel and there's a microwave so you can heat up your own baby food (which I always prefer). The staff were very friendly, not batting an eyelid at the terrible mess my baby was making – hopefully they'll lower the age of the crèche so next time I can enjoy my latte in peace!

Crèche: Mon-Thurs £3.50 per hour,
Fri-Sun £4.50 per hour.
Café: Mon-Fri 8am-5pm, Sat 10am-5pm,
Sun 11am-4.30pm.
Caffé Latte, The Paddock, Handforth, Wilmslow,
Cheshire SK9 3HQ Tel: 01625 538949 www.caffelatte.org.uk

The Chocolate Café

Here you'll discover a ground-floor chocolate shop selling a gorgeous selection of handmade chocolates, and an upstairs café offering, amongst other things, 14 different flavours of hot chocolate that you make yourself by immersing a chocolate bar in hot milk! If you don't want your child to eat chocolate, it is probably best to avoid this place!

The Courtyard Coffee House and Penny-farthing Museum

Stuck for somewhere to go for lunch one day whilst visiting Knutsford, a local suggested The Courtyard Coffee House. I don't think we'd have found it otherwise, as it's tucked away in an inconspicuous spot off the main street. We were delighted to find a very cute, old-fashioned looking tearooms, which actually doubles up as a museum – it holds the world's largest collection of penny-farthings. These are all suspended from the ceiling so it's quite a spectacle!

Not surprisingly on a Saturday afternoon, there was a large queue, but once we made it clear that we were happy to sit in the outside cobbled area (the weather was chilly so no one else wanted to), we got seated quite quickly. The service was warm and friendly but the menu was divided into time zones, restricting what you can order at certain times, which was a bit frustrating. That said, the food was good and the scones amazing. And the outside area had a little wall fountain that kept the kids reasonably entertained.

Mon-Sat 9.30am-4.30pm.
The Courtyard Coffee House, 92 King Street, Knutsford,
Cheshire WA16 6ED Tel: 01565 653 974

Cafés

The Design Museum Café

If you're heading over to the pool at Hathersage, or even just on a day trip to the Peak District, then call in at David Mellor's Cutlery Factory and Visitor Centre. The country shop is a delight for all you foodie parents and the factory itself (set in the architecturally award-winning Round Building) is fascinating. However, the main attraction for children lies within the Design Museum Café.

The café serves up wonderful wholesome food and I can vouch for the sandwiches; I had the bacon and brie with onion marmalade, which was gorgeous. For children there are smaller but still pretty exotic sandwiches, including ham and piccalilli or cheddar with apple chutney from £3.60. The café is within a small museum showcasing some of Mellor's achievements – everything from cutlery and cathedral candelabra through to post-boxes, litter bins and benches, but the star of the show is the set of full-sized traffic lights flashing away alongside the tables. These keep children mesmerised whilst you tuck in – our son spent his entire lunch pushing the button waiting for the green man.

Country Shop, Design Museum and Café: Mon-Sat 10am-5pm, Sun 11am-4pm.
Cutlery Factory: Mon-Fri 10am to 4pm.
The Design Museum Café, Hathersage, Sheffield S32 1BA
Tel: 01433 650 220 www.davidmellordesign.co.uk

The star of the show at the Design Museum Café is definitely the set of full-sized traffic lights flashing alongside the tables.

Fruitcake

I was intrigued when Fruitcake was recommended to me as a café designed absolutely with parents and children in mind. Situated next to Alderley Edge's main high street, Fruitcake is enormous, which on a Saturday lunchtime meant for us there was no problem getting a table, plenty of room for the children to spread out and no issue with getting our pram in. Great start. In one area of the café there's a plasma screen (showing Sky Sports when we were there, but apparently it's often kids telly!) and in front of this is a really generous area given over to the children. There were loads of toys to play with: books, activity tables, cars, dolls, a kitchen – the lot. I don't think we've been to a better kitted out café that isn't situated in a soft play centre!

The menu is pretty varied with a special kids section. We chose Welsh rarebit, houmus and halloumi and a hot dog. With five girlfriends and 11 children aged between six months and five years (most of them noisy boys), I can think of no better place to go for lunch.

Mon-Fri 7.30am-5.30pm, Sat and Sun 9am-5pm.
Fruitcake, 6 The Parade, Alderley Edge, Cheshire SK9 7JX
Tel: 01625 590667

Get your girlfriends and kids together and head to Fruitcake!

Hullabaloo

We chanced upon this cute café on a shopping trip to Altrincham with our 18-month-old boys. It's fully organic serving great tasting food including sandwiches, salads, soups and platters. There's also a tempting range of homemade cakes and puddings – hard to resist.

What made it stand out most was its child-friendly policy. The staff were brilliant with the boys and the children's menu was excellent, with things like

houmus and pitta dippers for £3 and beans and cheese toasties for £2.85. There was room for pushchairs and a box of goodies for the children to dip into with colouring books, crayons and reading books. A great venue for lunch with little ones.
Mon-Sat 10am-4pm.
Hullabaloo, 5 Kings Court, Railway Street, Altrincham, Cheshire WA14 2RD Tel: 0161 941 4288

The Lavender Barn

Set in the village of Dunham, these cute little tearooms are a great find. Inside is a wonderful hotchpotch of tables, all painted in shades of lavender. Outside is a lovely courtyard surrounded by grass and lavender beds. A word to the wise though – cars can park directly in front on the grass, and a little way off, slightly hidden, is an unfenced pond.

The food is pretty basic: soup, sandwiches, salads and jackets, but everything is freshly made. The real appeal is the selection of cakes. The staff are friendly and the atmosphere relaxed, perfect for afternoon tea.

Anything lavender is for sale, whether it's in a pot, been turned into marmalade or a calming tea. Also based in the converted barn is Gingham & Roses, a great shop selling shabby chic, hand-painted furniture. As well as painting all the furniture on-site, Janet Quick runs courses to show you how to turn all your car boot pieces into something more desirable!
Tues-Sun 10am-4pm.
The Lavender Barn, Dog Farm, School Lane, Dunham, Altrincham, Cheshire WA14 4TR Tel: 0161 928 5377
Gingham & Roses, Janet Quick, Tel: 07932 229882

Oddest

Chorlton has always led the way in great independent eateries – and Oddest is a new kid on the south Manchester block. The third in the portfolio of 'Odd' establishments (the other two are city centre based), we gave the child-friendly service at this ostensibly grown-up bar 10 out of 10.

The Lavender Barn is not only painted lavender, it sells everything lavender too, even the ice cream!

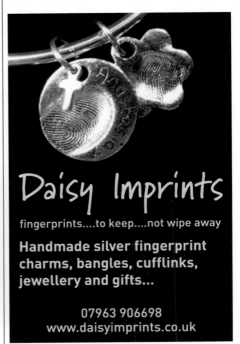
EATING OUT

Cafés

The décor is quirky and eccentric, with a mix of sofas, tables and chairs, plus a screen showing programmes on a loop (with the mute button on) – 'Lilo & Stitch' was playing when we were there.

The staff couldn't have done more – they use portable Totseats, which they helped us fasten to the chairs, and brought over crayons and paper for the kids. The children's menu has quite a lot of choice from soup at £1.95, egg and beans or fish fingers and fries at £3.75. There is even a selection of purees for babies at £2 each. The food was delicious and clearly homemade and the service was speedy. Do note though, it's a daytime-only haunt for families; come the evening it's DJs and beers – might leave the kids at home next time!

Open for food Mon-Thurs 11am-9pm, Fri 11am-7pm,
Sat 10am-7pm, Sun 10am-9pm.
Oddest, 414-416 Wilbraham Road, Chorlton, Manchester M21 0SD
Tel: 0161 860 7515

The Quays

Found on the banks of the Bridgewater Canal in the heart of Worsley village, The Quays is a perfect stop-off if you've been walking in the area. It's a very cute coffee house run by extremely friendly owners.

Though quite small, and a bit of a tussle with prams, you'll manage if it's not too busy. There's also a little outside area at the back for a fine day. Menu wise, there was a lovely range of homemade food on offer, all extremely well priced. For a two-course lunch of quiche and salad followed by lemon meringue pie for two adults, with drinks it came to under £10. Can't complain about that can you!

Mon-Sat 10am-4pm, Sun 11am-4pm.
The Quays, 11 Barton Road, Worsley M28 2PD
Tel: 0161 793 4615

Queenie Mumbles

Probably one of my favourite cafés to go to with children. The fact that it's never been nominated for a family-friendly restaurant award is definitely an oversight. Managed by a mum of four, a lot of thought has gone into making this small but

Quirky by name and quirky by nature – but Oddest definitely gets 10 out of 10 for child-friendly service.

perfectly-formed café an enjoyable place to eat with children. The food is mostly locally sourced and seasonal with everything being cooked to order. There is a very comprehensive menu but what's brilliant is that although there's an excellent platter and sandwich selection for the children, Queenie Mumbles will cook whatever they want: "if we have the ingredients we'll cook it".

There's a toy cart in one area of the café with lots of small activities designed for children to select something and take it back to their table to play with. Another excellent feature is the 'decorate your own cupcake' option on the menu – for £1.95 the children are given a plain bun and icing, sugar strands, dolly mixtures and the like to decorate it with.

Needless to say there are plenty of highchairs, and baby-change facilities are in the unisex toilet with wipes and nappy bags provided. In summer months, outside tables are also available.

Tues-Sun 10am-6pm. Closed Mondays.
Queenie Mumbles, 9 Goose Green, Altrincham WA14 1DW
Tel: 0161 941 2215 www.queeniemumbles.co.uk

Razma Reads

A wonderful children's bookshop (with an adult selection too) complete with a café; I love the opportunity to head down here to meet friends or buy a book. Razma Reads is located in the heart of Didsbury Village. It is housed in quite large premises, all on

Razma Reads is the only children's book shop in Greater Manchester, plus it has a cafe – what could be better!

I visited on a Tuesday lunchtime with my two-year-old and a couple of friends. The staff were very friendly and immediately interacted with my son. The café and deli appeared very 'glossy' with marble floors, large windows, spotlights and shiny display fridges filled with goodies, but despite the new surroundings it retained a family-run feel. There was also plenty of space, which made it great for prams or pushchairs.

There was no dedicated children's menu but when you primarily offer rustic pizzas, is there any need? We shared an anchovy and olive pizza, and my friends ordered a salad from the specials board and a toasted sandwich. Everything was delicious. Whilst the grown-ups concluded with a proper Italian espresso, Felix got stuck into Roma's award-winning homemade ice-cream. I couldn't help buying a tub for the freezer from the deli on the way out.

If this café was nearer to home I'd be popping in regularly for early tea with my children. Unisex baby-change and highchairs available.

Mon-Wed and Sat 9am-6pm, Thurs-Fri 9am-8pm, closed Sun.
Roma, 268 Bury New Road, Whitefield, Manchester M45 8QS
Tel: 0161 766 2941 www.roma.ltd.uk

Simply Books

Simply Books is a lovely bookshop in the centre of Bramhall village, with a great child-friendly café. Downstairs is a small children's table with a selection of books, but upstairs is a big communal table that can seat about 10 children plus lots of comfy chairs with more books and activities.

There is a Charlie and Lola themed menu for kids, and everything is freshly made and can be altered depending on your child's likes and dislikes. In general the choice includes a soup or sandwich, mini hot chocolate or juice, some fruit and a homemade cookie, all for £3.50. They are also more than happy to do mini-portions of anything on the menu. For adults the café offers a sandwich or soup, hot drink and a slice of homemade cake for £6.50 – well worth it.

Nothing has been forgotten here. As well as a lovely relaxed atmosphere, there are highchairs, space to park your buggy and a changing area for babies. Parking is limited on the high street although there are a number of

one level. This means there's room for a couple of sofas, about five tables and chairs and, every child's favourite, a wooden pirate ship large enough to clamber all over and sit inside. Although no meals are served here, there are hot and cold drinks and a range of cakes, together with child-friendly snacks such as raisins and smoothie pouches. In my opinion, a perfect place for a coffee.

Mon-Sat 9.30am-5.30pm, Sun 12-4.30pm.
Razma Reads, 794 Wilmslow Road, Didsbury M20 6UH Tel: 0161 438 6811
www.razmareads.com

Roma

This family-run deli, café and bakery has been in Whitefield for as long as I can remember. It was recently re-housed in a swanky new building, adjoined externally to a new Morrisons supermarket. Conveniently Roma now shares Morrisons' car park so there is bags of parking. It is also within spitting distance of the metro station and bus stops.

TOP FIVE CAFÉS

Fruitcake
More toys than you can shake a stick at – you'll never get the kids out!

Zest
A great café in a lovely setting serving some of the best mouth-wateringly indulgent hot chocolate ever.

Caffé Latte
Unique on our list because it's the only eaterie with an onsite crèche facility.

Roma
Award-winning ice cream and rustic pizzas what child could resist.

Café Seven
A mummy haven in leafy Bowdon. Just perfect

car parks. But the best bit about Simply Books is the valet parking! Yes, valet parking! Just park outside, run in and Andrew the owner will take your keys and park your car in their area round the back (apparently it's a bit tight!) Definitely a deserving winner of the Independent Bookseller of the Year 2009!

Mon-Sat 9.30am-5.30pm, or if the lights are on just go in!
Simply Books, 228 Moss Lane, Bramhall, Cheshire SK7 1BD
Tel: 0161 439 1436 www.simplybooks.info

Slattery's Pâtissier and Chocolatier

The real appeal of a trip to Slattery's is not the dining room on the first floor of the three-storey Victorian building that houses the Slattery empire but walking through the 'Willie Wonka'-style shop on the ground floor. Children cannot fail to be impressed by the rows and rows of superbly decorated cakes, gateaux, chocolates of every shape and size, sweets, and bottles of sarsaparilla. Unfortunately there are no oompah-loompahs but the 'chocolate factory' itself can be viewed through large picture windows at the rear of the shop.

The elegant dining room on the first floor, which can be accessed by lift, does not offer a children's menu although there are plenty of items that would appeal to a child and could be shared, such as jacket potatoes with a host of fillings (£6.75 with beans and cheese), toasted sandwiches (£5.55), an extensive breakfast menu or an afternoon tea (from £12.25). Plus, of course, there are plenty of delicious desserts and chocolate concoctions to try.

Although a bit on the pricey side, Slattery's is worth a visit for a special treat. Luckily for Ollie and Felix, their grandparents live only a block away, so they get to be indulged without me footing the bill – although I may end up paying the dentist in the end.

Mon-Fri 9am-4.30pm, Sat 9am-3.30pm.
Slattery, 197 Bury New Road, Whitefield, Manchester M45 6GE
Tel: 0161 767 7761 www.slattery.co.uk

A trip to Slattery's is a little like visiting Willy Wonka's chocolate factory – the only thing missing are the oompah-loompahs.

Time for Tea

Time for Tea owner Julie believes that tea can only be enjoyed out of a china cup, so on entry to these tearooms you'll soon notice the shelves heaving with old-fashioned and novelty china teapots; in fact there are over 50 of them and you can ask to choose one specifically to have your tea from too!

The café is quite small, with around 10 tables, but we got our prams in fine and were warmly welcomed. The menu is simple, serving home-cooked food at unbeatable prices; Welsh rarebit at £2.85, bagels with cream cheese for £2 and poached eggs on toast at £2.85, to name but a few. We very much enjoyed tea the old-fashioned way and tucked into some fine cakes. For those with toddlers, there is a small children's corner with a few toys, but due to the amount of china around you'd probably be advised to accompany them in here!

Tues-Sat 9.30am-5pm, Sun 12-4pm.
Time for Tea, 416 Bury New Road, Prestwich Village M25 1BD
Tel: 0161 773 3612 www.timefortearoom.co.uk

Thyme Out Deli

This is a great little spot to go with children on a summer's day as at the side of the building is a lovely fenced herb garden complete with pebbled paths, parasols and plants for sale. It can also be accessed via a side gate, which is useful if you have a pram. We have visited several times with a large group of friends and their children. Taking along a few toy cars and a bucket, the children have enjoyed messing around in the pebbles whilst waiting for their lunch.

The best thing about Thyme Out is its gorgeous fenced herb garden – perfect for a summer's day.

A good drinks menu offers fresh smoothies (£2.95 each), with interesting names such as the 'Neneh Cherry', together with a selection of herbal teas, coffees and milkshakes. The staff are also more than happy to make a large jug of cordial for children to share.

The deli offers some terrific choices from the ubiquitous olives, rocket and Parmesan with cold meats to tasty salads, such as the grilled goats cheese and pear (£6.50). There are some good options for children too, including pizza (£6.75), pasta, croque monsieur (£4.95) and paninis. The kitchen is also willing to adapt dishes for children where possible. There is no baby-change facilities.
Daily 9am-5pm.
Thyme Out Deli, 147 Nell Lane, Manchester M20 2LG
Tel: 0161 434 8686 www.thymeoutdeli.co.uk

Trifles Bakery
Situated on a pedestrian street in the centre of town, this award-winning family bakery and café tempts you in with its display of beautifully-decorated cakes. It is a little pokey with a pram but you could leave it on view outside or fold it away and tuck it behind the entrance door.

We visited on a Saturday and it was packed so we had to wait a few minutes for a table. The children kept themselves occupied drooling over the cakes and once we were sat down the service was pretty quick. The boys enjoyed a hot homemade pie between them with side salad, which at £2.90

was great value for money. I tried the Trifles' Panini (£4.90) and it was delicious. There is plenty on the drinks menu including flavoured coffees, milkshakes and orange juice or blackcurrant cartons. For dessert you can try something from the menu such as ice cream or scones but it is very hard to bypass the cake display.

This is a casual café with a bustling atmosphere which is worth going to if you are in town. Toilets are on the first floor but there is no baby-change.
Mon-Sat, 9am-5pm.
Trifles Bakery, 25-29 Market Avenue, Town Centre,
Ashton-under-Lyne OL6 6AL
Tel: 0161 330 2005 www.triflesbakery.co.uk

Zest
I was recommended Zest by my mother-in-law, a local to the area with very discerning tastes. While my husband walked the dog round the adjacent Doffcocker Lodge (a small  local nature reserve) on a rainy afternoon, I took the children in for a snack. The food is sourced locally and absolutely delicious, with a range of sandwiches and light meals, including Blackpudding Tower, Lancashire rarebit and both a meat and vegetarian tasting plate. We opted for a homemade scone and a hot chocolate. The hot chocolate is made with real chocolate and although expensive at £2.95, was quite honestly the best I've ever had. It was wonderfully indulgent, and a great alternative to pudding. A children's menu is available which offers smaller portions of the main dishes.

There are plenty of highchairs and baby-changing facilities are currently being installed in the new bathrooms. During 2010 a new decking area is planned overlooking the nature reserve; it will have a retractable roof so on those nice sunny days you can sit outside. So my mother-in-law was right (aren't they always!) A great recommendation.
Mon-Fri 10am-6pm, Sat 9am-6pm, Sun 10am-4pm.
Zest Fine Food, Doffcocker Roundabout, 877-879 Moss Bank Way,
Bolton BL1 5SN Tel: 01204 492 300 www.zestfinefood.co.uk

If you fancy a mouth-wateringly indulgent hot chocolate, Zest is the place to go.

Cafés

If you're in need of a reviving cuppa, a bite to eat or maybe something stronger, here's our top 10 favourite cafés to wheel your buggy in to.

Cafés in town

Café at the Rylands

A real treat in the heart of the city, the library is one of Manchester's treasures and whilst you'd never consider it a place for the kids, the café in the modern extension is terrific. It manages to maintain some of the library's serenity whilst still feeling relaxed. We were there for a midday lunch and had no trouble bagging a large coffee table with two sofas. The children's menu was well priced (mains, a cookie and a drink cost £3.25) and offered a decent selection of paninis, sandwiches and Manchester sausage on toast. Food is wholesome and mainly locally-sourced. Don't visit without trying the hot beef sandwich with Lancashire Blue cheese – it's delicious.
Mon and Sun 12-5pm, Tues-Sat 10am-5pm.
The John Rylands Library, 150 Deansgate, Manchester M3 3EH

Café Revive at Marks and Spencer

When I'd just had my first baby and I was out shopping in the city centre, Café Revive became a regular haunt. I made sure I timed it early enough to get a seat before the lunchtime rush and I enjoyed sitting there with a coffee and sandwich looking out of the floor-to-ceiling glass windows towards St Ann's Square. The staff were unerringly helpful – always offering to carry my tray to the table as I negotiated my pram. They'll provide bottle warmers and there's baby-changing in the toilets within the café.
Store open Mon-Fri 9am-8pm, Sat 8.30am-8pm, Sun 11am-5pm.
Café Revive at Marks and Spencer, 7 Market Street, Manchester M1 1WT
Tel: 0161 831 7341 www.marksandspencer.com

House of Fraser (Kendals) – Restaurant on the 6th Floor

I'm fond of shopping at Manchester's landmark department store, so being able to combine it with a coffee or snack with my little boy is an added pleasure. The restaurant is extremely child-friendly with the staff giving me tap water

Café at the Rylands is a real treat in the heart of the city.

with a straw for Will and offering to carry my tray to the table. It's all one level with a fair amount of space for prams and there is now a small children's play area too. They have children's lunch boxes or a hot meal for £3.50 including an activity pack. You can also buy the items separately, which is useful. There are highchairs and they will heat up bottles etc. For really little ones, they stock the Baby Deli range of meals. Baby-changing (together with a toyshop, shoes and childrenswear) is on the same floor. There are a few steps up to the toilets, but if that's going to be tricky, try the additional baby-changing on the third floor which doesn't have this problem.
Mon-Fri 9.30am-7pm, Sat 9am-7pm, Sun 11am-5pm.
House of Fraser, Deansgate, Manchester M60 3AU
Tel: 0161 833 0025 www.houseoffraser.co.uk

Manchester Cathedral Visitor Centre

Hidden in the basement of the visitor centre is a pleasant self-service café restaurant, which is very handy for The Arndale, Selfridges and The Triangle. There is a friendly atmosphere and the staff are more than happy to help you if you have children in tow. If you want a hearty lunch at a good price, there is plenty on offer such as braised lamb shanks, three cheese and red onion tartlet, or if you prefer, simpler options like jacket potatoes, sandwiches and pastries. Because it is self-serve there isn't a long wait at the table for your food. This always seems to be of utmost importance to my hungry boys. The café shares the same space as the Hanging Bridge, a 15th Century medieval bridge that originally connected the church with the medieval town. It is one of Manchester's oldest structures, and a scheduled monument. There is a lift to the basement. Baby-change and highchairs available.
Open from 10.30am daily, serves food from 12.15-3.30pm.
Manchester Cathedral Visitor Centre, 10 Cateaton Street, Manchester M3 1SQ Tel: 0161 835 4030 www.mcvc.info

The Midland Hotel

For a special treat, dress your little cherubs in their Sunday best and head for afternoon tea at the grand old Midland Hotel. Served daily, from 2.30-5pm, children will love the dainty finger sandwiches and delightful cakes served on pretty cake tiers. We shared an adult's tea between us and it was plenty for an adult and two children. It is advisable to book ahead. Baby-change facilities and highchairs.
Daily 2.30-5pm. Costs a minimum of £16.95 for afternoon tea.
The Midland Hotel, 16 Peter Street, Manchester M60 2DS
Tel: 0161 236 3333

Oklahoma

A café with a difference, Oklahoma is a bit bonkers and all the better for it! On one side there is a shop with shelves crammed full of quirky retro stuff, jokey and wacky gifts, imported goods and a great selection of cards, and on the other there's a mainly veggie café with an eclectic mix of comfy chairs and tables. It's bustling at weekends and yes you'd struggle a little with a pram when it's very busy but Oklahoma is something different. Staff absolutely welcome children and it's really worth a trip if you're after an alternative present combined with a good coffee or

TO FIND OUT ABOUT BUS, TRAIN AND TRAM SERVICES TO EACH VENUE PHONE TRAVELINE ON 0871 200 22 33

EATING OUT

Oklahoma is a bit bonkers – and all the better for it.

yummy milkshake. Foodwise options include a sweet potato and cheese for £5.20, scrambled egg on toast or cheese toastie for £3.50. There are two entrances, both involving small steps. There are also two highchairs and one unisex toilet with a baby-changing surface.
Mon-Fri 9am-7pm, Sat 8am-7pm, Sun 10am-6pm.
Oklahoma, 74-76 High Street, Manchester M4 1ES
Tel: 0161 834 1136 www.oklahomacafe.co.uk

Podium Restaurant Bar and Lounge
Situated on the ground floor of the imposing Hilton Hotel, Podium is open in the mornings for a full English or simply pastries with a smoothie and coffee. It is great if you are with a pram because it is so spacious and there are conveniently positioned baby-change facilities. You can either eat in the lounge area or the more formal restaurant. We opted for a pastry in the lounge, where the children enjoyed looking out of the floor-to-ceiling windows at the hustle and bustle of Deansgate. It is very handy for the Museum of Science and Industry (see page 12), which is only a five-minute walk away.
Open for breakfast: Mon-Fri 6.30-10.30am, Weekends 7-11am. Also open for lunch and dinner.
Hilton Manchester Deansgate, 303 Deansgate, Manchester M3 4LQ
Tel: 0161 870 1600 www.hilton.co.uk/manchesterdeansgate

Selfridges Exchange Moet Bar and Restaurant
This is the restaurant located on the second floor – rather temptingly, the same level as the women's clothing. We've been a few times for lunch as we love the views out of the big glass windows towards the Manchester Wheel. We always have a very pleasant time here as the staff are extremely good with babies and children. The system changed slightly on my last visit as there's no longer a dedicated children's menu – you can now choose off the main menu and they'll make it a kid's size and halve the price (approximately) or they can rustle up what they call a 'plain menu' where basically they'll endeavour to cook whatever simple food you'd like to request for the children such as sausage and mash or chicken and chips. Toilets with baby-change are close by on the second floor.
Mon-Sat 10am-11.30pm, 12-5.30pm, Sun 12-5.30pm.
Selfridges Manchester, Exchange Square, 1 Exchange Square, Manchester M3 1BD Tel: 0161 838 0540 www.selfridges.com

St Ann's Saturday Café
At the geographic centre of Manchester, the café of St Ann's Church is a peaceful retreat from frenetic shoppers – great if your kids are getting tetchy. If you go into the main church entrance, the small café, staffed by volunteers, is at the back of the church. It sells homemade sandwiches and slices of cake, all served with a smile and at a nice price. The tea and coffee is all accredited by Fair Trade. If you find the café's full, the Reverend is happy for you to sit in the pews! There is a book stall selling some children's books. There is a highchair but currently no baby-changing facilities.
Saturday 10am-3.30pm.
St Ann's Church, St Ann Street, Manchester
www.stannsmanchester.com

Teacup on Thomas Street
Formerly known as Cup, this is an appealing, independent café – no global branding here. It's all good home cooking and great smoothies. In its revamp, the beautiful display of porcelain cups have now been moved from the centre of the café towards the back in a little gallery.
Teacup's a pretty sizeable space so there's plenty of room for prams and staff are very welcoming. When we went at the weekend it did start getting very busy after 1pm, so bear that in mind. Foodwise you can grab a halloumi kebab for £4.25, scrambled eggs on a bagel for £3.25 and a selection of wonderful pastries, among others. There is only one unisex toilet but it does have a baby-change table.
Mon-Fri 9am-6pm, Weekends 9am-7pm.
Teacup, 53-55 Thomas Street, Northern Quarter, Manchester M4 1NA Tel: 0161 832 3233

EATING OUT

Restaurants

Manchester has a fantastic child-friendly restaurant scene. Whether you are looking for proven favourites such as pizza and pasta houses, or have a taste for something a little more exotic such as Indonesian or Greek, here is an insight into the whole gamut of venues on offer, all of which have baby-changing, highchair and bottle-warming facilities unless stated otherwise.

Dining with the kids

Barburrito

Previously listed in The Guardian's Top 50 healthy fast-food places and garnering various accolades such as 'best newcomer' and 'award-winning and cool', Barburrito continues to be one of Babies in the City's favourites, too. New for 2010 is the Bambino menu for kids of 12 years and under. They can choose from Bambino bowls (rice, beans, meat and salsa) or burritos (chicken, beans, pork), both priced at just £2.50. You order your dish at the counter, the staff prepare it freshly in front of you (which the children enjoy watching), you pay, the kids get given a balloon, you sit yourselves down and enjoy. For me it was the perfect lunch – tasty, healthy food and ready quickly.

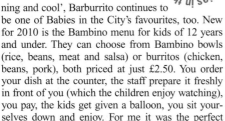

The restaurant we visited, at the Trafford Centre, was spacious so taking in buggies was no problem whatsoever. There is another Barburrito in Piccadilly Gardens in Manchester city centre, but this is aimed more at the business lunch brigade with bar stools and high tables.

Check out the website before you go as there are regular offers.

Mon-Fri 11.30am-10pm, Sat 11am-10pm, Sun 12noon-10pm.
Barburrito, 134 The Orient, The Trafford Centre, Manchester M17 8EH
Tel: 0161 747 6165 www.barburrito.co.uk
Also at Manchester city centre.

Brasserie Chez Gerard

We really put Chez Gerard to the test! It was Saturday teatime in mid-December with the Christmas Market across the road and absolutely heaving with people. I don't think I've ever seen Manchester city centre busier. We fought our way to the door and asked if they had a table for three; we hadn't booked. The manager hesitated for just a moment before racking his brains and smiling 'yes, but only for an hour or so'.

Despite our son being in a terrible mood, the staff were terrific and couldn't do enough for him. The waitress was even on hands and knees, scrambling around locating lost crayons to colour in the children's menu. It was good value; a basket of baguette with butter, a main course, soft drink and dessert for £5.95. Main choices were chicken with new potatoes, fish and chips, hamburger and chips, penne pasta and a cheese or plain omelette. The choice of dessert was impressive too – ice creams and sorbets, fresh fruit, mixed grapes and a Belgian waffle with hot chocolate sauce.

This is a good choice for a family meal in the city centre. Adult food is tasty and the staff really couldn't have been better.

Sun-Thurs 9am-10pm, Fri and Sat 9am-10.30pm.
Brasserie Chez Gerard, 2-8 Commercial Union House, Albert Square, Manchester M2 6LW
Tel: 0161 834 7633 www.brasseriechezgerard.co.uk

Café Metro

If you fancy fish and chips then you will be hard pushed to find a better spot to dine than Café Metro, situated at Blackfriars between Bury and Whitefield. Offering fabulous adult and child-sized portions of meat puddings, fish, scampi and a host of non-chippy items, such as Whitby Crab starter, you will be spoilt for choice. Although it is more expensive than a takeaway (£3.45 for children's cod and chips, £7.85 for adults), the restaurant is a charming place to eat. It has been tastefully decorated and tiled in black and white throughout. It is also the proud recipient of Britain's 2009 'Loo of the Year' award, which although doesn't have baby-change facilities, is spotlessly clean so you won't mind changing your little one on the floor while you enjoy the piped music and admire the bouquets of flowers.

To the rear of the café, accessed via patio doors, is a large wooden deck with tables overlooking a wooded dell. There is also a fenced area for under-threes to play in complete with a playhouse. Steps down from the deck and a path lead to a fenced wooden play area for older children, which has a barked floor. The café has its own car park and is on a main bus route.

Daily 11.30am-9.30pm.
Café Metro, 825 Manchester Road, Bury, Lancashire BL9 9TP
Tel: 0161 796 0134 www.metrofishbar.co.uk

Café Rouge

Café Rouge was a winning choice for me when I wanted to meet up with fellow mums and babies. We used to meet mid-morning, post one feed and pre-another, discussing the sleeping patterns of our newborns over a hot chocolate and a croissant.

The thing I liked most about Café Rouge was at

EATING OUT

"Arriba, arriba" down to Barburrito. Where you can get tasty, healthy Mexican food with a speedy service.

this time of day it was usually pleasantly quiet. So a collection of novice pram drivers with our precious cargo didn't feel so intimidated!

I've since returned with my toddler and found the staff just as amenable and the children's menu fairly priced with a good selection such as chicken, mash and gravy or cheesy omelette and fries, with dessert and drink for £4.95. Most branches have step-free access and outside seating.

Mon-Sat 9am-11pm, Sun 9am-10.30pm.
Café Rouge, 651-653 Wilmslow Road, Didsbury, Manchester M20 6QZ
Tel: 0161 438 0444 www.caferouge.co.uk
Also at The Trafford Centre and Manchester city centre.

Carluccio's

Going to Carluccio's for lunch is always a treat – a perfect, delicious escape. The waiting staff fall over themselves to coo at any babies and always seem to have time to engage visiting children.

Babies in the City LOVE Babies in the City

The kids menu at £6.25 is excellent value, with a good choice of dishes such as breadsticks and a soft drink to start, followed by pasta with different sauces, lasagne or ravioli. It also offers smaller portions of items off the main menu if nothing else appeals. And then to finish is the gorgeous ice cream, which I have to confess is simply divine. A great little activity pack keeps the children entertained between courses and nothing is a problem for the staff.

Mon-Fri 8am-11pm, Sat 9am-11pm, Sun 9am-10.30pm.
Carluccio's, 3 Hardman Square, Spinningfields, Manchester M3 3EB
Tel: 0161 839 0623 www.carluccios.com
Also at The Trafford Centre.

Coriander Restaurant

We didn't start our night aiming for a curry with the children, but that's where we ended up at an unusually late hour of 7.30pm. We quickly ordered poppadoms and even got the boys trying the dips while we glanced through the menu. It was only after a few minutes that we realised it was in fact the children's menu. It is a very extensive list, priced around £7.90 for a main course, rice and chips including a drink or ice cream. We ordered one curry for them to share, which was plenty.

There are no baby-changing facilities or crayons, but the staff are very friendly and accommodating.

Coriander uses all natural ingredients and has no added food colourings. I have to say that the meals were all delicious. So curry with the kids? No problem.

Mon-Thurs 5.30-11.30pm, Fri and Sat 5.30-12pm, Sun 3-10pm.
Coriander Restaurant, 279 Barlow Moor Road, Chorlton-cum-Hardy, Manchester M21 7GH Tel: 0161 881 7750
www.corianderchorlton.co.uk *See website for special offers.*

Restaurants

Croma

With friends up for the weekend and us all wanting a good lunch before they headed back down south, we opted for the ever-reliable Croma in Chorlton. The more I go to this locally-based chain, the more I enjoy it. The pizzas are consistently good, the waiters always calm and it is excellent value for money. The children's menu includes a drink, pizza or pasta dish, salad sticks, ice cream and a cromaccino (frothy milk), all for £4.95. The staff don't even bat an eyelid when most of the salad sticks and colouring pens provided end up on the floor. My sceptical southern friends were highly impressed and even offered to pay the bill!

Mon-Wed 12-10pm, Thurs-Sat 12-11pm,
Sun 12-10.30pm.
Croma, 500 Wilbraham Road, Chorlton,
Manchester M21 9AP
Tel: 0161 881 1117 www.croma.biz
Also at Manchester and Prestwich.

Dimitri's

For me, this great Greek restaurant brings back memories of long leisurely evenings spent with friends – so I was a little apprehensive about allowing my two-and-a-half year old to blow a hole in those rose-tinted glasses. But I need not have worried. Things got off to a great start, with the houmus and pitta bread having the same effect on my daughter as the San Miguel had on me – soothing.

A main of pasta bolognese for her (okay so it's not exactly Greek, but anything for an easy life) and fish kebabs for us got a serious thumbs up all around. The kids' bit of the menu has all the firm favourites – so even fussy eaters are well catered for. We had a lovely time – I'd say that this place is as close as you can get to a romantic evening when you've got a little chaperone in tow. The staff were really friendly too – they even told me I was a Pretty Princess – at least I think they were talking to me!

Daily 11am-midnight.
Dimitri's, Tonman Street, Deansgate, Manchester M3 4FN
Tel: 0161 839 3319 www.dimitris.co.uk

The Dinnerstone

Situated in the village of Uppermill and adjacent to Saddleworth Moor, it's a lovely drive out to The Dinnerstone. Parking is limited on the high street but the restaurant has a car park at the back.

On the waiter's recommendation, I opted for Ham Hock Tagliatelle, which was absolutely gorgeous though not the cheapest at £10 (it was the same price for most of the pasta dishes). Children's portions were generous so little ones could probably share, a main course costs £5.50 and pizza £6.75. The choice of children's meals was good and included breaded haddock fingers, free-range sausages, linguine and pizza. My five-year-old went for the 'make your own pizza' option. Elsewhere this usually means the child is supplied with the raw ingredients to build their pizza before it's cooked so you can understand the disappointment when it arrived fresh from the oven. I did pull the waiter up on this as the menu stated 'make your own' but it seems that this actually means children simply choose their own toppings – which definitely needs to be clearer on the menu.

The Dinnerstone is a nice place for a treat. As we were leaving we realised it does a cheaper menu from 3-6pm at the weekends and from 5-7pm during the week, with pizza and pasta dishes starting from £4.95.

Tues-Thurs 11am-2.30pm, 5-8.30pm,
Fri 11am-2.30pm, 5-9.30pm,
Sat 12-9.30pm, Sun 1-7.30pm.
The Dinnerstone, 99-101 High Street,
Uppermill, Saddleworth, Oldham OL3 6BD
Tel: 01457 872 566
www.dinnerstone.co.uk

Dukes 92

A favourite of ours pre-children, we decided to return to Dukes with our three-year-old in tow. For those who don't know it, Dukes 92 is located in a fabulous spot in the Castlefield area of central Manchester at the meeting point of the Bridgewater and Rochdale canals – in fact it takes its name from the adjacent Duke's Lock.

The pub-café interior is nice and spacious with a selection of booths or tables and chairs – it's all on the flat, so easy to get in with a buggy and park up next to your table. The canal-side patio has plenty of seating too but of course is very close to the water's edge.

Dukes specialises in pate and cheese (for the adults) as well as having sandwiches, salads and pizzas on offer. The kids' menu had four options – pizza, pasta, haddock goujons or chunky chicken, all priced at £4. Drinks and desserts are extra. The portions were very generous and the food tasty.

Babies in the City LOVE in the City

TOP FIVE RESTAURANTS

Croma
Manchester's pizzeria that never fails to deliver. Consistently good food and service with a smile.

Café Metro
A brilliant play area makes this the perfect place to enjoy fish and chips and Whitby crab.

Carluccio's
Going to Carluccio's for lunch is always a treat – it's a perfectly delicious escape.

Tampopo
Award-winning family restaurant, this noodle bar and its spicy crackers always hits the mark.

Barburitto
A consistent favourite – tasty, healthy food that is ready quickly. A winning combination.

EATING OUT

Croma appeals to children of all ages – from the games on the menu to the cromacinos.

All told we had a lovely time – it's not cheap, our bill came to £25 for three meals and soft drinks – but it's a perfect setting particularly on a sunny day.

There is free parking in Dukes' car park next door or on the street in front.

Lunchtime menu Mon-Thurs 12-3pm; Fri-Sun 12-4.30pm.
Dukes 92, 18 Castle Street, Manchester M3 4LZ
Tel: 0161 839 8642 www.dukes92.com

El Rincon De Rafa

This well-known Manchester institution was regularly frequented by the younger and more single me, so what would it be like to return with two children in tow? The 20 or so steep steps down to this hideaway basement restaurant are the first indicator that babies probably don't visit that often. Once I'd safely and extremely slowly navigated these (God bless the Bugaboo), I was asked by the waiting staff whether I'd booked – yep, despite it being 5pm on a Saturday, the restaurant was bustling. "Errr, no I haven't!" Things were not looking good at this point and all I could think was that I had to get all the way back up those steps without even a hint of chorizo getting near my lips.

Thankfully all was not lost – after a bit of pondering, the waitress found me a table right next to the entrance, which was handy for parking the pram, and then went on the hunt for a highchair. The atmosphere at El Rincon is great – it is a brilliant place to just hang out. The tapas menu means that even for the most fussy child (for which my three-year-old ticks the box) there's usually something they'll have a go at. We ordered a wonderful selection of Serrano ham, Spanish omelette, prawns, meatballs, garlic bread and Manchego

cheese. The all-Spanish staff were totally charming and absolutely delightful with the children. They heated up baby food in the microwave and did their very best for us. A most enjoyable time indeed.
Mon-Sun 12-11pm.
El Rincon, off St John's Street, 244 Deansgate,
Manchester M3 4BQ Tel: 0161 839 88199

The Fat Loaf

We worried a bit that we'd be too disruptive for this smart bistro in Didsbury, but the staff couldn't do enough for us. It's part of a local, independent chain and is advertised as a family-friendly restaurant – a billing it definitely lived up to.

We had a very cosy early supper by a wood-burning stove as a welcome respite against a snowy January evening. It's not the cheapest, but deals are usually available. I'd recommend the pre-6pm light bites menu as perfect for a young family. We ordered plain grilled fish with vegetables from the children's menu for our four-year-old. The quality was excellent; it was a really good, healthy meal and made a welcome change from the usual fare of chicken nuggets.

In summer, The Fat Loaf has a weekend hog roast out the front. It's a really good spot for lunch if you're heading to Fletcher Moss Botanical Gardens.
Mon-Sun 12-10pm.
The Fat Loaf, 846 Wilmslow Road, Didsbury, Manchester M20 2RN
Tel: 0161 438 0319 www.thefatloaf.co.uk
Also at Altrincham and Sale.

Felicini

Although pretty much an institution on Didsbury High Street, funnily enough I'd never actually tried Felicini until one lunchtime when friends and I

Restaurants

were passing and a board outside advertising a cut-price pizza deal enticed us in.

As it's quite a swish restaurant, we requested a table in a quieter bit so we wouldn't disrupt the other diners – the waitress sensibly suggested we sit towards the back in one of the large leather-seated booths. She was very accommodating, bringing crayons and paper out for the children and obliging with a large jug of tap water for everyone.

Felicini provides an impressive variety of Italian dishes for children on its Bambini menu – from spicy sausage penne to margherita pizza. A main meal and ice cream from this will cost you £5.95. However, due to the pizza deal on offer on the main menu, we opted for this, ordering three between three adults and five children. They were delicious, but what was even more delicious was the bill – in total just £15 to feed eight of us. Bellisimo!

Daily 11am-11pm (food service from 12 noon).
Felicini, 747-751 Wilmslow Road, Didsbury, Manchester M20 6RN
Tel: 0161 445 2055 www.felicini.co.uk

Lunch at Felicini was a huge success. Fantastic food at an even more fantastic price. It's definitely worth a visit.

Giraffe

Myself and the boys were in town early on a Saturday evening in the run up to Christmas. Having been turned away from another restaurant in Spinningfields despite not being full (we only wanted a quick snack for the boys), I expected the same treatment from Giraffe. Nothing could have been more different, the staff were extremely welcoming and quickly sorted the kids out with balloons and a Giraffe stirrer, which they loved.

From Chicken Schnitzels to a Sunshine Power-food Salad, Giraffe is all about exploring different foods from around the world.

The children's food portions were generous and tasty so plenty for me to try too! The smoothies at £2.10 are delicious but a bit pricey, however as part of the Kids Meal Deal they were a steal.

A new children's menu is coming out as we were

going to press which will offer a main course and a drink for £4.50. Thanks to the accommodating staff and our voucher, I will defintely be heading back!

■ **See the voucher at the back of the book for a 20% discount off all meals at Giraffe.**
Mon-Sat 9am-12pm, Sun 9am-11pm.
Giraffe, The Trafford Centre, 136 The Orient, Manchester M17 8EQ
Tel: 0161 747 2100 www.giraffe.net
Also at Spinningfields and Manchester Airport Terminal 1 Airside.

Gourmet Burger Kitchen

The menu has a whopping 28 burgers to choose from with some very tasty twists on the classic burger. Gourmet Burger Kitchen is certainly child-friendly, there's a dedicated children's menu where they can order a burger (vegetarian option available), fries and drink for £5.95. Or there's the option to have chicken pieces instead for the same price. Our little boy wasn't perhaps quite at the age where he could get stuck into the food so it was a bit wasted on him. The food was delicious but there are no activity packs for little ones so take your own entertainment.

Sun-Thurs 12-10pm, Fri 12-11pm, Sat 12-11pm.
Gourmet Burger Kitchen, Spinningfields, Bridge Street,
Manchester M3 3ER Tel: 0161 832 2719 www.gbk.co.uk
Also at Didsbury and Wilmslow.

Gusto

Gusto is a modern Italian restaurant offering more than just pasta and pizza. We arrived for an early lunch and although the waitress was very friendly and helpful, service was a bit slow and with three children it needed to be quicker. They were all easily distracted with pretty comprehensive activity packs and this kept them going until their pizza bases arrived ready for them to create their masterpieces. The cost was £5.95 for a pizza with a choice of various toppings. This also included dessert and a chef's hat. There is an alternative three-course menu which includes starters of calamari, garlic bread or ham and melon, a selection of pasta dishes for the main course, plus dessert. Gusto stocks the organic BabyDeli range which start at £2.35 for a four-month-old baby puree meal.

For myself I ordered the penne pasta with salmon, peas and baby spinach; I had about three mouthfuls and the boys stole the rest, so I can honestly say the pizzas were good as that's what I ended up eating! There was no problem getting them all wrapped up to take away as we had loads left over. Two pizzas between three children would have been plenty.

After 6pm the children's menu stops and though they were happy to have children in the restaurant they could only provide a small version of the adult meals at a reduced rate.

Phoebe's chuffed with her 'Giraffe' shaped stirrer.

Mon-Fri 11am-11pm, Weekends 10.30am-11pm.
The kitchen opens from 12 noon.
Gusto, 756 Wilmslow Road, Didsbury M20 2DW
Tel: 0161 445 8209 www.gustorestaurants.uk.com
Also at Knutsford and Alderley Edge.

Jam Street Café

I'd only been to Jam Street Café in the evening for drinks and a spot of dinner, so thought it was worth a try in the name of research to come back during the day with the kids.

In the traditional sense they are not child-friendly. There are no baby-changing facilities, little room for pushchairs and no obvious children's menu. But they do a great breakfast (available until 3pm) for £5.80, which is perfect to share with a little one, or they are happy to go off piste and cook some beans on toast or something similar.

A children's favourite is the ice cream sundae or a babychino (warm frothy milk with chocolate sprinkles). The staff are lovely and didn't seem to mind too much when four mums with a child each took over the small café. They were more than willing to warm up a bottle of milk and grab a highchair from the basement.

In the evening the café turns into a bar and food finishes around 9.30pm so kids have to leave by then.
Sun-Thurs 10am-midnight, Fri-Sat 10am-1am.
Jam Street Café, 209 Upper Chorlton Road, Whalley Range, Manchester M16 0BH Tel: 0161 881 9944

The Lead Station

An informal and popular café bar where you can have a leisurely breakfast, pop in for coffee and cake or dine on three courses. Housed in a former police station, it always seems to be teeming with children of all ages (particularly around the early dinner slot of 6-8pm). This really helps to provide its informal and friendly atmosphere.

We are regulars, in fact my four-year-old is so accustomed to the menu that he usually places his order as we are being shown to a table. The boys love it because the children's menu is good and the

Restaurants

staff always take time to have a giggle with them. I love it because it is a night out in a trendy café bar. Some favourites on the menu are bangers and mash, steak, dips and pittas, and usually several delicious vegetarian options.

In summer there is a pleasant outdoor seating area to the rear. If you come armed with a pram, don't be put off by the three steep steps at the entrance and the swinging double doors – once you get past this it's plain sailing. The Lead Station had a makeover in 2009 – there is now new seating to the front exterior and the baby-change has been rehoused in the refurbished ladies' toilet.

Sun-Weds 11am-9.30pm, Thurs-Sat 10am-10pm.
The Lead Station, 99 Beech Road, Chorlton, Manchester M21 9EQ
Tel: 0161 881 5559

Loch Fyne

My first trip to Loch Fyne was with friends in the evening and I had a great time so I was looking forward to returning with the children so that they could check out the fish tanks and the colourful array of lobsters, crabs, langoustines and oysters on display.

The staff were great with Harry and Sam and took them over to the fish tanks for a short lesson in crustaceans, and at one point a waiter brought a live lobster to the table, which went down really well.

Loch Fyne has a children's menu and for £6 you have a choice that includes haddock goujons,

pan-fried salmon or moules mariniere with chips plus an ice cream. Drinks aren't included in the price. If your child doesn't like fish, there are alternatives such as sausages or pasta. The menus double as colouring sheets and there are plenty of crayons.

Although Loch Fyne is one of the more expensive places on our list, it has regular offers on so it's worth checking the website before you visit.

Mon-Thur 9am-10pm, Fri-Sat 9am-10.30pm, Sun 10am-10pm.
Loch Fyne, 848 Wilmslow Road, Didsbury, Manchester M20 2RN
Tel: 0161 446 4190 www.lochfyne.com
Also at Alderley Edge, Knutsford and Warrington.

The Olive Press

Part of chef Paul Heathcote's restaurant collection, the Olive Press chain is brilliantly child-friendly. The Little Olives menu selection is impressive and at £4.95 very good value. The 'make your own pizza' option is hugely popular in our household – a small pizza base is brought to your table with various toppings – the children then make their own concoction and it's whisked off to the oven. But if that doesn't take their fancy you've got plenty of pasta or grill dishes to choose from. They also get a drink (fruit juice, coke, milkshake) and dessert (knickerbocker glory, strawberries, chocolate cake) included. The standard of food is high both for adults and children and service has always been great.

Note: for pram pushers, there are a few steps up to the main door in the Manchester branch and then down again at the other end.

Mon-Thurs 11.45am-10pm, Fri-Sat 11.45am-11pm, Sun 12-9pm.
The Olive Press, 4 Lloyd Street, Off Deansgate, Manchester M2 5AB
Tel: 0161 832 9090 www.heathcotes.co.uk
Also at Bolton, Cheadle Hulme, Clitheroe, Leeds, Liverpool, Preston and Warrington.

Will putting the finishing touches to his pizza at The Olive Press.

mums already ensconced in a very cosy area in the middle of the café with a couple of sofas and some low-level tables, plus a TV that staff had kindly turned over to CBeebies!

The Orangery has an extensive menu and although we didn't try them, the children's meals included chicken nuggets with chips, grilled cheese ciabatta and macaroni cheese for £4.50 each, all with a complementary soft drink. This is a friendly place to hang out for a coffee and bite to eat with babies and little ones – and if you were on your own I'm sure it wouldn't be long before you got chatting to other mums.

Daily 9am-11pm (children's meals served 10am-7pm).
The Orangery, 54 Heaton Moor Road, Heaton Moor, Stockport SK4 4NZ
Tel: 0161 442 7771 www.theorangerywinebar.co.uk

Pizza Express

Pizza Express is a pleasant dining experience and delivers consistently good pizzas. They are very family-friendly and are more than used to the odd tantrum. You can watch pizzas being made in the open kitchen, but unfortunately you can't make your own (although some branches now cater for children's parties where you can do just that).

The Piccolo children's meal is three courses for £6.10. This includes dough balls, pizza or pasta, salad and dessert, plus a Bambinoccino – frothy milk with

Harry is excited by the prospect of dinner! The fish tanks at Loch Fyne are full of lobsters, crabs, oysters and lan-

The Orangery

We'd been recommended The Orangery in Heaton Moor by a mum who regularly meets there with her NCT group. So when we took our babies for a light lunch we weren't surprised to find a group of

Restaurants

chocolate sprinkles, that give parents an extra 10 minutes for a latte. With the usual supply of crayons and colouring paper, this is a good place to start if you're not used to going out for dinner with a toddler.

Mon-Thurs 11.30am-11pm, Fri and Sat 11.30am-11.30pm, Sun 11.30am-10.30pm.
Pizza Express, South King Street, Manchester M2 6DQ
Tel: 0161 834 0145 www.pizzaexpress.com
Pizza Express restaurants are located all over Greater Manchester.

Shimla Pinks

It was a cold wet Sunday approaching tea time and we could only think of one thing that would warm the cockles of our heart – curry! We hoped our two-year-old would feel the same!

We headed for Shimla Pinks. At an embarrassingly early 5.30pm we were first to arrive in the restaurant, but it filled up pretty quickly. They don't have a dedicated kids' menu, but will do half portions of anything on the main menu, and if your children aren't familiar with spicy food, they will fry up some plain chicken with boiled rice.

The staff were friendly, the food hit the spot, and we even got a balloon when we left. The only downside was that they don't have baby-changing facilities, but they are moving premises early in March 2010 to Spinningfields, and the new place will be well kitted out for kids – the chef is even hoping they'll have a proper children's menu, so I'd say it will be worth a visit.

Mon-Fri 12-11pm, Sat 3.30-11pm, Sun 7-11pm.
Shimla Pinks, Crown Square, off Bridge Street, Manchester M3 3HA
Tel: 0161 831 7099 www.shimlapinksmanchester.com

Kids love the dough balls at family favourite Pizza Express.

Strada

I think the pizzas at Strada are pretty much the best you can get. We tried out the city centre branch in the Spinningfields area with the children one Saturday lunchtime. I was surprised at how quiet the restaurant was, but this meant there was no problem getting a table. There was no children's menu (though according to the manager one is being tried out in Wilmslow) or activities, but a smaller version of any adult meal can be supplied. We stuck to pizzas (average price for an adult size £8.95) and when they arrived, our three-year-old's wasn't much smaller than ours! The food was as tasty as ever and despite gorging ourselves, there was plenty to take home afterwards and the staff happily provided us with a doggy-box. Not the cheapest Italian on the block but still one of my favourites.

Mon-Sat 11.30am-11pm, Sun 11.30am-10.30pm.
Strada, 4A Leftbank, Irwell Square, Spinningfields, Manchester M3 3AN Tel: 0161 819 5691 www.strada.co.uk
Also at Wilmslow.

Tai Pan Restaurant

If you're looking to introduce the kids to Chinese food, then the Tai Pan may well fit the bill. Located in purpose-built premises on Upper Brook Street, free on-site parking makes it very easy and the children will find the supermarket downstairs an interesting contrast to Sainsbury's.

Upstairs (there is a lift for your pushchair) the restaurant is popular with Chinese families, bearing testament to the excellent food. The waiters aren't the friendliest in the world, but the food is pretty quick and fairly reasonably priced. There are plenty of highchairs and baby-changing is available. There is no children's menu but my five-year-old got stuck into my won ton soup, absolutely loved the roast duck and prefers chinese vegetables to broccoli. A good jumping off point is crispy duck pancakes; not many children can resist getting messy with their food.

We took loads of toys and pens, but if the young ones do get bored there's a large fish tank to amuse them while you quickly pay the bill!

Mon-Sat 12-11.30pm, Sun 11.30am-9.30pm, Bank Holidays 12-9.30pm.
Tai Pan Restaurant, Brunswick House, 81-97 Upper Brook Street, Rusholme, Manchester M13 9TX Tel: 0161 273 2798

Tai Wu

The Tai Wu on Oxford Road opposite the Palace Theatre has always been a favourite in our family. It's a brilliantly popular restaurant, full of Chinese families. We either arrive a few minutes before it opens at 12, (though we are still never first in line!) or leave it until later when things have quietened

There is no dedicated children's menu at Strada but it is a really child-friendly restaurant.

down. You will probably still have to take a ticket and wait in the bar area for 15 minutes.

Tai Wu serves traditional dim sum from trolleys pushed around the restaurant. The benefit is food available immediately, but you can still order from the menu.. With all the various dishes arriving in different bamboo baskets, children are interested and might try stuff they probably wouldn't at home. The service is quick, they have plenty of highchairs and really seem to like children. They don't provide colouring pens or activity packs. The toilets are downstairs but there is a baby-changing table in the disabled toilet at the end of the bar.

Also downstairs is an all you can eat buffet, which is available pretty much all the time, good if you're in a hurry or want to try a variety of different dishes but remember, it does have a one-and-a-half hour time limit so you can't stay all day!
Mon-Sun 12noon-2.45am, Dim Sum Mon-Sun 12-4pm.
Tai Wu, 44 Oxford Road, Manchester M1 5EJ
Tel: 0161 236 6557 www.tai-wu.co.uk

Tampopo
After reading the rave review in last year's Babies in the City, I couldn't wait to try out Manchester's very own noodle chain – Tampopo. It didn't disappoint. We went on a Saturday for lunch and though busy, we got a lovely welcome and thankfully a table too! Crayons, menus and children's chopsticks were quickly doled out and our drinks order promptly taken.

The food options for the children were chicken satay or noodles, plus an ice cream or sorbet for £3.95 or a choice of a small version of anything off the main menu for £4.50. We chose chicken noodles, which to our delight our son Will was willing to try and in fact did a pretty good job of polishing off. Meanwhile, for the record, the adults' Pad Thai and vegetable tempura were simply delicious. I wholeheartedly recommend Tampopo as a great place to introduce your kids to extremely tasty yet reasonably priced pan-Asian food.

Mon-Fri 12noon-11pm, Sat 11.30am-11pm, Sun 12noon-10pm.
Tampopo, Triangle Shopping Centre, 38 Exchange Square, Manchester M4 3TR
Tel: 0161 839 6484 www.tampopo.co.uk
Also at Albert Square and The Trafford Centre.

TGI Friday's

TGI's is a great place to take the kids and it is very child-friendly. There are highchairs aplenty and it's always nice to be greeted with colouring sheets and crayons. There is a children's menu that not only offers staples such as pasta and burgers, but for the more adventurous, fajitas and quesadillas, although a word to the wise – the portions are enormous.

Mains for children start at £2.99 with desserts from 99p and drinks from £1.29. For the babies TGI's offers free Hipp Organic food for 4-10 month olds if an adult is dining. As the atmosphere is loud and noisy it did not seem to matter that my little one was screaming lustily when we got there, but fortunately he was soon pacified by the balloons and general vibrancy of this fun eatery.

Mon-Fri 11.30am-11pm, Sat and Sun 12-11pm.
TGI Friday's, Valley Park Road, off Bury New Road, Prestwich M25 3AJ Tel: 0161 798 7125 www.tgifridays.co.uk
Also at Cheadle, Sale and The Trafford Centre.

Wagamama

With a name that translates as wilful or naughty child, surely Wagamama must be the place to go with children for dinner?

We visited the Spinning-fields branch of this rapidly-expanding noodle bar chain. It is set on ground level in a state-of-the-art building, with floor to ceiling windows overlooking trees festooned with fairy lights and it always seems to have a buzz and energy about it.

The staff are friendly and the food is consistently good. Highchairs clip straight on to the tables so there's no problem sitting wherever you like and a noodle doodle colouring sheet and crayons are brought to your table.

A child's main course starts from £4.05 for a mini chicken ramen – chicken breast served on a noodle soup. Priced separately, desserts include vanilla ice cream at £1.10 or natural flavoured

If you want to introduce your children to chinese food then head to Tai Pan.

lollies at £1.55. Drinks are either freshly squeezed orange or apple juice at £1.50.

With a speedy service and informal approach (your order is written on your paper placemat by the waitress), Wagamama is definitely a great choice.

Mon-Sat 12-11pm, Sun 12-10pm.
Wagamama, 1 The Printworks, Corporation Street, Manchester M4 2BS Tel: 0161 839 5916 www.wagamama.com
Also at Spinningfields, Manchester.

Zizzi

When this Italian restaurant chain moved into Didsbury village, giving a previously miserable and derelict corner building a welcome makeover, us locals were clamouring to give it a try. We found a large, bright restaurant with a warm welcome. I was most taken with the new interior. Taking its inspiration from Didsbury's history as the founding place for the RSPB (Royal Society for the Protection of Birds), I think this informs the design to great success. Anyway, less of the wallpaper.

Our waitress was lovely, putting me, my friend and our five monkeys in a large corner booth so we could spread out and not bother anyone else. We'd packed our own toys so the kids really just got on with it. The food was enjoyable enough – the little ones can choose from the Bambini menu priced at £5.95 for a snack (dough sticks), main meal (pizza or pasta) and sweet (ice-cream). Nothing unusual but good quality and a lovely environment.

Mon-Sat 12-11pm, Sun 12noon-10pm.
Zizzi, 700 Wilmslow Road, Didsbury, Manchester M20 2DN
Tel: 0161 434 5923 www.zizzi.co.uk
Also at Spinningfields, Manchester.

EARLY YEARS NURSERY SCHOOL

For children aged 2-5 years

We see each child as an individual

"A truly inspirational nursery…"
Lynsay Marsh

"From the moment I walked in I knew it was a special place"
Rebecca Sandiford

- Principal is an educational author
- Mature, experienced staff including four qualified teachers and six qualified nursery nurses
- No staff turnover - allowing children and parents to form long-term relationships
- Open 8am-6pm throughout the year

Telephone: 0161 448 1114

30 Palatine Road, Withington, Manchester. M20 3JJ

Pubs and inns

If you like nothing better than a gorgeous pub lunch after a hike in the country with the kids, then these are the places to head for.

Pubs and inns

The Axe and Cleaver

Amidst some beautiful Cheshire countryside you'll find this attractive pub, part of the Chef & Brewer chain, within the winding roads of Dunham Massey. One glorious summer's day, after finishing Tuesday morning toddler group, we set out en masse to give it a whirl for lunch. With five mums and eight children, we were really going to put it to the test. First impressions were certainly good – we sat in the pretty beer garden at the back, which is full of wooden tables and chairs and overlooks fields and the car park. There's no play equipment, but the children kept themselves amused as there is space to run about and hide under trees. The pub also has a recently renovated interior, which is fresh and modern but retains a cosy atmosphere with open fires being lit on colder days.

The menu had a good array of dishes on offer, including a quite substantial kids' menu. We ordered quickly as everyone was starving! Unfortunately, as it was lunchtime on a sunny day, the pub was inevitably busy which led to a 30-minute delay in our meals arriving. The staff were apologetic when they finally did bring it out, although the food wasn't all quite ready at the same time either which caused some bickering (amongst the adults!) It was nice though and I would certainly go again, but it may be a good idea to check on the waiting time if you are in a rush.
Food served: Daily 12-10pm.
The Axe and Cleaver, School Lane, Dunham Massey, Altrincham WA14 4SE Tel: 0161 928 3391

The Clog and Billycock

We had such a fantastic meal here, I cannot recommend it enough. Part of the award-winning Ribble Valley Inns chain, The Clog and Billycock serves up wonderful food all with contemporary twists on local favourites and as much as possible sourced from local suppliers. The fish pie and beetroot and curd crumpet that we had were sensational. Unfortunately you can't book unless you're a party of six or more and be warned, this place is popular; although when

we arrived at 12.15pm on a bank holiday weekend, we were able to get a table no problem. It's a large, spacious pub beautifully designed with flag floors and open fireplaces. The atmosphere is warm and friendly – the service was perfect and quick (but not too quick!)

On the day we visited, there were plenty of children of all ages eating so I didn't feel awkward about arriving with three-year-old Will and 13-week-old Ellie. You choose your own table, so I made sure I picked one next to another family with young children rather than those enjoying a peaceful meal without! We were given a fun sheet with crayons and a sticker and the children's menu (with kiddie-sized cutlery). This offered tempting dishes such as deep fried cauliflower fritters with curried mayonnaise or haddock and real chips. The main meals for the kids were between £4.50 and £6.50. The quality of the food was top notch and in my opinion worth the money. There's no play area but The Clog and Billycock is located in picturesque countryside and we concluded our day with a walk round Witton Country Park, minutes drive away. All told, a perfect pub.
Lunch: Mon-Sat 12-2pm, Sun 12-8.30pm.
Afternoon bites: Mon-Sat 2.30-5.30pm.
Dinner: Mon-Fri 6-9pm, Sat 5.30-9pm, Sun 12-8.30pm.
The Clog and Billycock, Billinge End Road, Pleasington, Blackburn, Lancashire BB2 6QB
Tel: 01254 201 163 www.theclogandbillycock.com

The Little Mill Inn

Down narrow and winding country roads, on the westerly edge of Derbyshire's rolling hills and next to a babbling river complete with restored working waterwheel, you'll discover The Little Mill Inn. Dating back to the 18th Century when it was a candlewick mill, this is a lovely country pub. Armed with two babies and two energetic four-year-olds, we descended on a quietish sunny weekday in the school holidays.

First impression is what a fantastic location, second is what an amazing slide – it really is enormous. The children's play area, built into the steep grassy banks surrounding The Little Mill Inn, is terrific – Will and Toby loved running amok exploring and it's all within your eyeline if you're sat in the outside eating area. Inside we received an extremely warm welcome; laid out as you'd hope all traditional pubs should be, with large fireplaces and low ceilings. I'd imagine this place is equally pleasant to visit on a less fine day. There was plenty to choose from off the menu serving traditional pub fare both for adults and children.
Food served: Mon-Fri 12-8pm, Sat 12-9pm, Sun 12-7pm (carvery until 4.30pm).
The Little Mill Inn, Rowarth, via Marple Bridge, High Peak, Derbyshire SK22 1EB
Tel: 01663 743178 www.thelittlemill.co.uk

The Inn at Whitewell

If you've made the effort to get to the Wild Boar Park (see page 41) why not drive round to the beautiful Inn at Whitewell. Dating back to the 1300s, with roaring fires and spectacular views over the Forest of Bowland, the romantic feel of the place takes you back to times before the nippers.

The Little Mill Inn has a fab children's play area including the longest, steepest slide I've ever seen in my life!

The Inn at Whitewell is good with the kids but even better if it's just the two of you!

Although ostensibly not the most child-friendly of places – there are hazards (water, log fire, steps…!) everywhere – children and dogs are very welcome. The kids loved the stuffed animals on the wall.

The bar area is enormous and there is a superb menu. Lunchtimes are busy and you can only book a table in the dining room in the evenings, but if you're unlucky enough not to find a table you shouldn't have to wait long. They will do a smaller version of many dishes and, quite simply, offered excellent quality food. A main course is around £10 with a child's portion at £5.50.

Whilst there's no dedicated outside play area as the inn is right next to the water's edge, there's a large patio for summer lunch. You can also, without the pushchair, enjoy a walk along the River Hodder from the bottom of the car park.

As soon as you arrive, you realise you would like to stay longer and settle in for the afternoon. So my advice is find someone… anyone! to babysit; call in some favours and go for the night. I bet the breakfast takes some beating!
Food served: Daily 12-2pm, 7.30-9.30pm.
The Inn at Whitewell, Near Clitheroe, Lancashire BB7 3AT
Tel: 01200 448 222   www.innatwhitewell.com

Joshua Bradley and The Bluebell Centre, Gee Cross

The Joshua Bradley does a roaring trade in family meals, mainly due to its large and well-equipped beer garden. There are loads of outdoor tables, a duck pond, rope swings in trees, a playground and a field. Inside there's a formal restaurant, 'The Orangery' with waiter service, but really you can eat anywhere if you order at the bar. Food is plain, traditional pub grub; this certainly isn't a gastro-pub but the décor is pleasant, the staff are attentive and the ambience is very friendly. This area is known locally as the Bluebell Centre as it also comprises a café (10am-4pm, though we found it a bit erratic) and a Paint-a-Pot studio called 'Wild Orchids' where we happily whiled away half-an-hour after lunch.
Food served: Daily 12-10pm.
Joshua Bradley, Stockport Road, Gee Cross SK14 5EZ (you'll find it at the Bredbury end of Stockport Road)
Tel: 0161 406 6776   www.hydesbrewery.com

Plough and Flail

With pretty much an unbeatable setting and serving terrific food, the Plough and Flail is a lovely place to visit. Myself and two girlfriends plus children arrived on a scorching hot summer's day. We were delighted to find a wonderful grassy outside seating area across the car park from the pub with a large wooden climbing frame on a bark-chipped surface. The boys got stuck in straightaway. Unfortunately, due to health and safety regulations, we were informed that the pub isn't allowed to serve food or drinks in this area. This created a bit of a palaver, as we had to move back to the pub's patio area once our food had arrived and because this was some distance from the aforementioned climbing frame, it did cause the children to become a bit grumpy.

The children's menu was quite comprehensive, serving choices such as kid's steak with chips and vegetables or sausages, mash and onion gravy, all priced at £6.50 – so not cheap, but in fairness the food was very good and the children wolfed it down. Options for adults ranged from sandwiches at £6.50 to main meals, such as my delicious fish and chips for £12.75. On the weekday during term-time that we visited, the Plough and Flail became very busy – so I suspect on weekends it will be heaving. As with most popular places, booking would be advisable.
Food served: Mon-Thurs 12-2.30pm, 6-9pm; Fri and Sat 12-2.30pm, 6-10pm; Sun 12-8pm.
Plough and Flail, Paddock Hill, Mobberley, Cheshire WA16 7DB
Tel: 01565 873 537   www.thedeckersgroup.com

A rare opportunity to sunbathe. Soaking up the rays at the Plough and Flail.

The Roebuck

This Grade II listed country inn in Mobberley came highly recommended and following my visit, justly so. Having booked in advance, which we did easily enough on the day, we turned up with two rather irate and hungry children. Our waitress was wonderful; on seeing that our original table wasn't in a brilliant place for the pram and highchair, she swiftly moved us to a better position. She also took our order quickly, brought bread out to pacify the children and the meal was delivered as promptly as possible.

The food was excellent, with a kids' selection and most of the adult meals able to come as children's portions as well. Whilst it's not terribly cheap – our meal without puddings or starters came to £34.80 without a tip – this is a beautiful pub and probably somewhere you'd prefer to come just the two of you so you could savour the atmosphere

Pubs and inns

The Axe and Cleaver is great for a lime and soda (ha ha we all know it's a G&T) after a toddler group.

more than children allow! Although we came in winter and were confined to the roaring fires indoors, the beer garden at the rear of the pub was large and pretty so I'd imagine The Roebuck would be a perfect spot in summer, too.

For those that wish to work up an appetite before lunch or burn it off afterwards, there are some nice easy walks directly accessible from here.

Food served: Mon-Fri 12-2.30pm, 5.30-10pm, Sat 12-9.30pm, Sun 12-8pm (9pm in summer).
The Roebuck, Mill Lane, Mobberley Near Knutsford, Cheshire WA16 7HX Tel: 01565 873322 www.theroebuck.com

The Three Fishes

The Three Fishes is a bit off the beaten track but definitely worth the trip if you are looking for a top quality meal with a top quality kids' menu. We have been there for special occasions with all the family, which prompts a note of warning – you definitely have to book (although this option is available only for parties of six or more). If not, your names go on a blackboard waiting list and be aware that the lunch menu is served only until 2pm on Saturdays – it's snacks afterwards. Don't be put off by the thought of a crammed full restaurant though, it is well worth the wait and the food is served quickly.

The menu is exceptional quality pub grub, with a three-course menu for kids! Portion sizes are large for the children, but in my opinion, not over-facing; mine always have room for the pancakes for pudding and manage to squeeze in a natural milkshake. Although The Three Fishes is extremely welcoming to children and has colouring available, there is nothing else to entertain them so I take my own selection of hot wheels, trains and Polly Pockets to keep them amused.

We have been taking our children to The Three Fishes since they came out of highchairs and we think it is a fabulous, friendly place for a special meal. The bonus to this pub is that the surrounding countryside is so nice, providing plenty of trails to trek along, so you can all walk off your over-indulgence! Enjoy!

Lunch: Mon-Sat 12-2pm, Sun 12-8.30pm.
Afternoon bites: Mon-Sat 2.30-5.3pm.
Dinner: Mon-Fri 6-9pm, Sat 5.30-9pm, Sun 12-8.30pm.
The Three Fishes, Mitton Road, Mitton, Near Whalley, Lancashire BB7 9PQ Tel: 01254 826888 www.thethreefishes.com

The White Hart

Set on a hillside in the countryside, with impressive views over Oldham and Manchester, this is a traditional pub serving wholesome and some locally sourced food and ales. Its website states humorously, "children are welcome... and help to control sometimes badly behaved adults whom are obviously not tolerated!"

We found the atmosphere a little stiff and starched but the staff were very polite and we had an enjoyable lunch. The pub has tables set for dining and a snug area where you can just enjoy a drink. The children's meals are excellent quality but some may find them expensive at £7 for a main. The children's White Hart sausage and chipped potato meal is large enough to feed two toddlers so it can be shared or taken home in a doggy bag. The adult's menu offers oysters, Goosnargh duck, Saddleworth sausages and mash, together with a great cheese menu, which you can wash down with traditionally brewed ale or a Highland Malt (starters average £5 and mains £15).

To the rear and side of the pub is a pleasant garden with pub tables where you can soak in the view whilst children let off a bit of steam. The White Hart also has a restaurant and hotel. Dovestones reservoir is 2.5 miles away if you fancy a walk beforehand. Baby-change and highchairs available.

Breakfast: Mon-Fri 7am-9.30am, Weekends 8am-10.30am.
Lunch: Mon-Sat 12-2.30pm, Sun 1pm-7.30pm.
Eves: Mon-Sat 6pm-9.30pm, Sun from lunch until 7.30pm.
The White Hart, 51 Stockport Road, Lydgate, Oldham OL4 4JJ Tel: 01457 872566 www.thewhitehart.co.uk

Worsley Old Hall

As we all know, little ones can't sit still for long, so on a warm day Worsley Old Hall is a good choice if you want a leisurely lunch. The elegant 16th Century hall (formerly the home of the Duke of Bridgewater) is set in its own grounds overlooking Marriot Worsley Park Golf Club. You can sit and relax on the terrace and savour your dessert and coffee whilst your children run around on the lawn or clamber and climb on fallen branches in full view. The food is from the Brewers Fayre chain, of which the hall is now part. There is a children's menu that tries to promote healthy eating, with main meals costing £3.99, or £4.50 for a main and dessert.

Food served: Mon-Sat 11am-10pm, Sun 12-10pm.
Worsley Old Hall, Worsley Park, Walkden Road, Worsley, Manchester M28 2QT Tel: 0161 799 2960 www.brewersfayre.co.uk

Granny and Ellie on the swings at The Joshua Bradley.

Gardening is lots of fun with little ones, so combine this activity so with a visit to an extra special garden centre.

Green-fingered mums

Bents

Bents is rather like the Harrods of garden centres. It's truly a destination garden centre – when I visited there were literally coach loads of people spilling in! If you'd not already gathered, Bents is huge. It's got an enormous shopping section with concessions selling everything gift-wise from children's clothes and toys to books and candles. Of course there's also a huge array of plants and gardening associated merchandise to look at as well.

The café is equally huge and the same can be said for the portions of food. Personally I found them too big and thus a tad on the expensive side. It was a friendly restaurant though and the staff are very helpful. Highchairs are available along with baby-changing facilities.

Mon-Sat 8.30am-5.30pm, Sun 8.30am-5pm.
Bents, Warrington Road, Glazebury, Warrington, Cheshire WA3 5NT
Tel: 01942 266300 www.bents.co.uk

Ned Yates is a perfect meeting place for mums and tots.

Ned Yates

A lovely place to visit, especially on a sunny day, as the café has loads of outdoor seating right next to an enclosed children's play area. This contains a couple of slides, swings and a wooden rocking horse, all on a bark-chipped surface. There is even a small croquet section on a patch of Astroturf!

The café itself is large and airy with a sofa area and toys for the children to play with. There were plenty of mums and babies on the day I went, so I think it must be an unofficial local meeting place! The café serves really delicious adult food ranging from ciabattas to freshly-made salads. For the children, breakfast choices (served till 11.30am) include eggs and soldiers, for lunch, mezze or kids' fun boxes for £3.95, amongst other things.

Mon-Fri 9.30am-5pm, Sat 9.30am-4.30pm, Sun 10am-4.30pm.
Ned Yates, Cottage Grove, Wilmslow, Cheshire SK9 6ND
Tel: 01625 522 128

Vicarage Garden Centre really feels like you have stepped into a secret garden.

Vicarage Garden Centre, Carrington

Step through the garden centre to the vicarage garden and you feel like you have walked into a chapter of Frances Burnett's 'The Secret Garden'. From benches surrounded by honeysuckle, overflowing herbaceous borders, woodland walks and ducks in the peace garden, to Billy and Wilf the goats – there is something here to capture your imagination. If that all fails, why not sit in the shade of a gigantic Gunnera ('giant rhubarb') whilst your children play in the adventure playground. Poo's pantry is at the heart of the garden and serves a small range of drinks and snacks such as muffins and crisps. Highchairs and baby-change available.

Mon-Sat 9am-5pm, Sun 10am-4.30pm. Oct-Mar closed on Thurs.
Poo's Pantry: 10.30am-12.30pm and 2pm-4pm daily, closed Thurs.
Vicarage Gardens, Manchester Road, Carrington M31 4AG
Tel: 0161 775 2570 www.vicaragebotanicalgardens.co.uk

Willow Pool Garden Centre and Baron Antiques

To describe Willow Pool as eccentric is a bit of an understatement. The place is teeming with colour, plants, fountains and architectural reclamation, together with the odd Blackpool illumination, duck pond and pirate statue, which will delight little ones. A visit here is not complete without taking in the Tea Rooms. Be prepared to be spoilt for choice as to where to sit. Choose from one of the two indoor rooms, with roaring fires and stained glass windows, or on a warmer day sit al fresco under a wrought iron gazebo. Or better still, sit outside in your own thatched and heated gazebo as we did and let your children make as much mess and noise as they like without any disapproving looks.

The menu is plentiful and the Tea Rooms are licensed if you fancy a tipple. Beware of the desserts though – they are fabulous but monstrously sized! Highchairs are available but may be difficult to use in the thatched gazebos.

Daily 9am-6pm. Tea Rooms 10am-5pm.
Willow Pool Garden Centre and Nursery, Burford Lane, Lymm, Cheshire WA13 0SH
Tel: 01925 757 827/01925 754 543 www.willowpool.co.uk

Classes and activities

The following classes offer a variety of activities, essentially they have similar benefits for children, from learning to share and taking turns, building confidence and self-esteem, or simply for you to spend time with your child. It's also a good way to get out of the house and meet other parents!

Singing, sticking and sports

ART AND CRAFT

Mucky Pups If you have a child that likes to help decorate your home unasked, then you will enjoy Mucky Pups. Each week there is a different topic like Creepy Crawlies and all the activities follow that theme. Seven stations are set up with an activity on each table, plus playdough. There is enough gluing, sticking and painting to keep active hands occupied for hours, plus you don't have to clear up afterwards. At the end of the class there is an opportunity to show off your best piece.

Classes are £6 for an hour and include a drink and a biscuit.
Bramhall, Brooklands, Wilmslow, Timperley and Knutsford
Tel: 07511 622445 www.mucky-pups.com

COOKING

Kiddy Cook This is a cooking class designed for children aged 2-11 years to encourage them to learn about food and explore new flavours in an educational and fun way. I tried the 'Cookie Tots' sessions for the 2-4 year old range and it was incredible how much teacher Nikki fitted into 45 minutes.

Sessions start with a warm-up to music using actions that mirror culinary activities such as rolling out pastry or kneading bread. Then a puppet called Katie Custard is brought out to tell the children what they'll be cooking and hand out recipe cards – the children have to identify the ingredients they will need from Nikki's bag. The day I went we made 'Mice in Jackets' – cheese-filled jacket potatoes. Afterwards there's a short story, then a bit of hands-on craft work. Next the children take part in a 'show and taste' session, when Nikki brings out a piece of exotic fruit for them to examine and try. A song then rounds it all off.

Cookie Tots costs £5.95 a session (ingredients and utensils provided) and you sign up per half-term. There is a £10 joining fee, for which you get an apron, recipe cards and a personalised recipe card holder.
Bowdon, Bramhall and Wilmslow
Tel: 07976 619648 www.kiddycook.co.uk

MUSIC AND ENTERTAINMENT

Baby Sensory I thought this was such a sweet class, with many different elements loved by all the babies. Each session is divided into three parts and there is something new every week. First is the sensory element. In our class, the teacher handed out small balloons with rice inside to handle and listen to,

bowls of fruit and vegetables to touch and feel, and laminated cards with pictures to look at. All these activities were accompanied by music ranging from classical to pop. One aspect I particularly liked was that we sat on wonderfully soft rugs placed on crash mats so there were no uncomfortable knees for mums!

The second part was exploratory. This took place in another part of the room, with lots of toys and activities set out. The class I went to had a small ball-pit, little tents, a large inflatable mattress for babies to lie on – with puppets to entertain them with – a bouncy horse and a couple of activity gyms. The little ones loved it and it was also the time for mums to have a chat, which was nice. Finally it was back to the sensory area, where my class ended with lights out and illuminated wands for babies to hold, fibre optic lights for them to look at and bubbles. The thing I liked most about Baby Sensory was its gentle pace, enabling you to really focus on the time spent with your baby.

£6 per class, suitable from birth-13 months.
Bramhall, Cheadle, Heaton Moor, High Lane, Knutsford, Lymm, Macclesfield, Nether Alderley and Warrington.
Tel: 0161 486 6102 www.babysensory.co.uk

Baby Sensory – relaxing time out from busy lives.

Baby Sign Time Run by the infectiously smiley mum of two Liz, Baby Sign Time has an extremely friendly and welcoming vibe. The one-hour session is divided into two parts. The first half includes signing and music fun with the babies, whilst the second half features playtime on the mat with toys for the little ones whilst mums enjoy social time with tea and cake.

The idea is that you learn to use hand signs and gestures with your baby when you talk to them, who then will be able to use these gestures to

Learning to communicate early at Baby Sign Time.

communicate before their spoken language develops. Using plenty of different props, which are dished out to everyone, Liz leads the babies and mums through lots of different signs with the aid of singing well-known songs. On the day I went the theme was animals, so amongst other things we used very simple signs like Tiger, Elephant and Giraffe and sang 'Row Row Row Your Boat' with a sheet and cuddly toys, 'Peter Rabbit' with the aid of colourful feather dusters (which my baby wouldn't stop eating!) and 'Old McDonald' using puppets. The time raced by and all the babies and toddlers seemed to love every minute.
£45 for 10 weeks.
Knutsford, Macclesfield and Wilmslow
Tel: 01565 872010 www.babysigntime.net

Babywinks A fun, fast-paced and jam-packed 30-minute class that incorporates movement, dance, singing and instruments for those aged 4-18 months. First there's a warm-up to music, with familiar songs such as 'Twinkle Twinkle' being belted out. Then, my favourite part of the class – Nuala hands out cute, furry monkeys dangling on elastic for you to bounce around whilst singing the 'Five Little Monkeys Jumping On The Bed' song. Other elements of Babywinks involve baby signing, instruments such as shakers and bells to play with and the ever popular bubbles. We finished off with more singing and a huge inflatable ball bouncing across a large parachute pulled tight by the adults. Everyone clearly enjoyed themselves!
£3 per session paid termly; £10 registration fee for insurance.
Bowdon, Chorlton, Didsbury and Sale
Tel: 0161 432 3624 www.kiddiewinksonline.com

Jabberjacks Jabberjacks is a music-based activity class for babies to pre-school children. Each session starts with a welcome song and shaking hands with the leader. The focus then shifts to the mystery box, singing 'What is in the box today?' Goodies vary from puppets and wands to bubbles and instruments. The box is opened two or three times each session

with a new discovery every time. There is a sharing toy which is passed round then each child gets to explore a bag full of things like a teddy bear's picnic, pet grooming kit or musical instruments.
Fees range from £4.75-£5.20 and are paid termly in advance with a one-off £10 registration fee which includes a Jabberjacks T-shirt.
Bramhall, Bowdon, Cheadle, Didsbury, Marple, Poynton, Prestbury, Prestwich, Sale, Timperley and Wilmslow
Tel: 0161 442 9911 www.jabberjacks.co.uk

Kiddiewinks This is a class that does not stop from the moment you arrive until you sing the final song. Every five minutes a new activity begins so there is no time to stop and think, let alone get bored! Each week has a different theme that also incorporates the pre-school curriculum.

The class I went to was titled 'Growing'. First we started with animal puppets and what their young were called; then we talked about healthy eating and exercise which then moved into a 'growing up dance' with pom-poms! A bit of quiet time was next as out came little bags containing babies with baths, bottles and clothes. Sticking with the growing theme, the children also had a go at planting pansies in a pot and decorating it with lots of stickers, plus they got to take them home.
Classes are one-hour long (from walking to pre-school age) during term time and are £4.50 per session payable per term. This includes juice and biscuits at the end.
Bowdon, Didsbury, Chorlton, Cheadle and Sale
Tel: 0161 432 3624 www.kiddiewinksonline.com

Rhythm and Rhyme This was the first class that I enrolled in with my baby and we loved it. Children and parents sit in a circle for the 45-minute sessions which involve singing, instruments, banging on the big drum, playing with a large 'parachute' sheet, dancing to jazz, classical or pop music and at the end, everyone's favourite – blowing bubbles. Our teacher was lovely and really enthusiastic.
The sessions are designed for babies from five months to pre-school and cost £48 per 12-week term.
Bramhall, Cheadle, Chorlton, Didsbury, Heaton Moor, Sale, Timperley, Urmston
Tel: 0161 860 0911 www.rhythmandrhyme.co.uk

A fun, fast-paced class sums up Kiddiewinks.

Classes and activities

Rhythm Time This is a great musical interaction class, well thought out and designed to help a child's development – it's also fast-paced and really enjoyable for parents and babies alike! First of all there's a bit of an introduction where everyone in the group says their baby's name and how old they are. Then it was straight into the first song and shaking the maracas!

The next musical interlude involved sliding the babies up and down mum's knees whilst singing – they all adored it. As well as musical instruments, there are lots of props used throughout the class which makes it interesting for everybody – Ellie's favourite was the glittery pom poms which we're told help stimulate eye-tracking as well as being great fun. Rhythm Time ended with more singing and bubbles and the class went home very happy indeed.

Sessions cost £3.75 per child paid termly.
Greater Manchester and Cheshire
Tel: 0161 476 2136 or Head Office on 0121 711 4244
www.rhythmtime.net

Sally Jolley Music Group This is a fantastic little group although I am totally biased as I have been going to it for over two years. Friends from a toddler class introduced me and the arrangement is that Sally comes to your house and takes an interactive music session lasting 45 minutes for a small group aged from two-and-a-half years to school age.

The group runs every other week, so it's not a huge commitment on your time. The variety of instruments and puppets Sally has built up over the years is amazing and the children love it when it's their turn to 'host' the group.

Classes are geared towards eight to ten children in a group.
The cost is £45 per session divided by the number of children.
Tel: 01663 765877

Tiny Talk The concept behind Tiny Talk is that the classes teach baby sign language. To the uninitiated, like myself, the class appeared to be fundamentally made up of singing with the usual actions attached. So when I went we had 'Incy Wincy Spider', 'Head Shoulders Knees and Toes' and 'Old MacDonald' amongst others. We learnt a couple of specific signs in the class but not as much as I was expecting, which was absolutely fine – it was a fun group, led by a great teacher and the babies enjoyed the songs.

Tiny Talk classes last for one hour with the final half-hour being given over to 'social and support' time – basically a friendly natter with everyone over tea and biscuits with toys out for the babies.

Tiny Talk is aimed at birth to two-year-olds, classes approximately
£4.50 each and you can drop in or book a term of six for £24.
Altrincham, Bramhall, Stretford, Warrington, Wigan, and Wilmslow
Tel: 07889 626553 www.tinytalk.co.uk

Bubbles at Rhythm Time a favourite with babies and children.

NATURE AND WILDLIFE

Forest School Set in a small woodland hidden in the heart of suburban Manchester, the Forest School provides a structured woodland playgroup. Run by a qualified Forest Teacher, each weekly session introduces the children to a different aspect of woodland life through stories and exploration. The sessions run all year, allowing children to experience nature through the seasons.

Whilst there are naturally no formal toilet facilities, there is a 'wee-tree' and plenty of space to change nappies! There are healthy drinks and snacks provided. Classes are weekly, Wednesday from 1-2.30pm (during term time) and held in Paupers Wood, Nell Lane, Didsbury.

It costs £4 per session on a drop-in basis. Numbers are limited for
safety reasons. Suitable from 18 months to pre-school.
Tel: Mary Maclachlan 0161 445 3520/07790 368117
www.foresteducation.org

SPORTS

Baby Yoga This is a great low impact workout for you and your baby. Sessions start with some light stretches and a dry massage for the babies followed by gentle movement to songs and an easy workout for the adults. I loved the lie down at the end, which if you can get your child to lie still will have you asleep in less than five minutes.

For the babies the advantages are clear – it is good for digestion, coordination and movement. For the adults, it is an hour out of the house doing something a bit different and really bonding with your baby.

Classes start from eight weeks old after babies have had their hip check and go on until about a year.

Classes are an hour, with a maximum of 10 adults, courses
are booked in four week slots based in Didsbury.
Tel: 07956 216218

Kindergym When children arrive at the South Manchester Gymnastics Centre, they can't wait to get started. Set in a huge industrial unit, there are two large rooms full of equipment. In the first, an obstacle course is set up that children can get straight on and work their way round. When the class gets started it's with a warm-up involving hoops and music which then leads back onto the obstacle course before finishing with roly-polys.

You can then move into the second room, where there's a huge trampoline, swing ropes, bars and rings, all over giant pits of soft foam. You're free to jump in too, although you do look a bit foolish trying to get back out again.

You take turns on the trampoline and it's free play until the class ends with the hokey-cokey. All the children love it and woe betide if you try and leave early!

Sessions last for one hour and parent participation is necessary. Kindergym is aimed at children from 18 months to four years old and costs £30 for an eight-week course. There is also an annual insurance payment of £10.
South Manchester Gymnastics Centre, Fenside Road, Wythenshawe, Manchester M22 4PD
Tel: 0161 491 0415 www.southmanchestergymnastics.org

The Lesley Taylor School of Dance Bolero it isn't, but I defy anyone not to be equally enchanted by the sight of a bunch of three-year-old girls flitting around in pink tutus. The teacher, Lesley Taylor, has a magical way with her charges and is much more interested in having fun than discovering the next Jayne Torvill.

The first session (in the Cheadle class) is free – which is a good job because most little ones are too shy to join in on their first visit. There's also no pressure to buy all the gear until you want to – or until you get bullied into it by your three-year-old. So there's nothing to stop you giving these classes a try.

Little Superstars is perfect for energetic children – and parents.

Once my little girl got the bug it became the highlight of her week. I think it's excellent value and is great for coordination and confidence, not to mention shoring up those future Olympic chances!
Prices for the dance classes start from £2.75 per session.
Cheadle, Timperley, Bollington and Sale
The Lesley Taylor School of Dance
0161 483 1331/07702 808467 www.lesleytaylor.net

Little Kickers This is all about one thing – football! Two pop-up nets are set up and loads of balls are kicked around, and that's before the class even starts. I'm not sure who enjoys it more, the children or the parents. Two coaches are on hand so parent involvement can be as much or as little as you prefer.

The class starts with all the children on the mats doing a gentle warm-up. Then there are a series of games such as 'traffic lights', which shows who has been listening when the red marker is held up. Lastly, and clearly the favourite bit – penalties – a chance to score a goal with loads of cheering from the parents.

Sessions at the School of Dance are great for coordination and confidence.

There are two different 45-minute classes available: Junior Kickers for two to three-and-a-half year olds, and Mighty Kickers for three-and-a-half to five.
Both cost £6.50 per session and are paid every half-term. There is also a £16 one-off membership fee which includes a football strip.
Didsbury, Altrincham, Sale, Bowdon, Lymm, Prestwich and Whitefield
Tel: 0161 442 5713 www.littlekickers.co.uk

Little Superstars is an activity class covering general sports including rugby, golf, cricket and football. After a good warm-up, various games are played that change every 10 minutes, with an emphasis on colours and counting.

Each session then focuses on one main sport and involves parents in one-to-one with their children after a demo from one of the brilliant coaches. For example, the basketball session involves bouncing and catching the ball, then scoring baskets in smaller, specially adapted nets.

This is not the sort of thing you go to and put your feet up while your children run around – parental participation is essential. So get your gym shoes on and show your kids what you're made of in this excellent class.
Little Superstars holds 30-minute sessions for walking to two-year-olds and 50-minute sessions for two to five-year-olds. The cost is £4.75 per class payable per term and includes a free T-shirt.
Bowdon, Altrincham, Knutsford, Hale Barns, Appleton, Wilmslow, Marple, Middleton, Prestwich, Oldham, Hyde and Prestbury
Tel: 07904 311552 www.littlesuperstars.co.uk

CLASSES AND ACTIVITIES

Classes and activities

Enjoy low-impact workouts for you and your baby at Yoga Manchester.

Mini Movers These open play sessions are run by Stockport Council's Play Development team. The hour-long classes involve parent and child interaction with either soft play, bat and ball or various climbing frames. They end in circle time with group singing and activities. There is a progressive badge scheme and each term badges are awarded by Max the Rabbit for skills demonstrated each week.
Mini Movers is for children aged 18 months to starting school. It's £3.50 per session and you sign up for a term.
Bramhall, Cale Green, Cheadle, Edgeley, Marple and Reddish
Tel: 0161 474 4471 www.play.dev@stockport.gov.uk

Mums on Mats After baby number two, my body was definitely in need of a MOT but having had a Caesarean, I was concerned not to push it too quickly; friends recommended Mums on Mats. This is a post-natal class which works on toning and strengthening your whole body, with particular attention given to regaining your pelvic floor and stomach muscles. What is extra special about this class is that you get to take your baby along too so you don't need to worry about childcare either.

So I rocked up for my first session. Instructor Maria (herself a mum of three) is absolutely terrific. She makes sure everyone gets individual attention and it's a wonderfully rewarding way to spend an hour.

All the babies are in car seats asleep or gurgling on yoga mats watching and if any of them do get a bit tetchy and you're in the middle of a position, Maria comes over and gives them a hold whilst you finish off. The information imparted about the best way to get back in shape post-baby was up-to-date and first-rate. I'd been suffering from a great deal of back pain and Maria concentrated on this specifically, alleviating the problem greatly. I cannot recommend Mums on Mats highly enough!
£30 for a course of six or £6.50 pay as you go. Suitable from your six-week check.
Didsbury and Alderley Edge
Tel: 0844 730 800 www.glofamily.com

Tumble Tots This group is split into three age brackets – Gymbabes is for the youngest set, and is ideal if your six-month-old is desperate to get moving. The group starts with some warm-up songs and actions, then it is free style around the equipment before more songs and stickers at the end.

As your child grows and starts to walk, the classes adapt accordingly. First to Tumble Tots, which encourages balance, climbing, coordination and independence. Then on to Gymbobs for school age children.

There is a member of staff per six children so there is a lot of encouragement and the group is friendly and welcoming.
Classes last approximately 40 minutes and cost £5.70 each, paid in half-term blocks. There is also a £20 annual membership fee to cover insurance.
Bowdon, Chorlton, Knutsford, Hale and Didsbury
Tel: 0161 499 3699 07812 144450 www.tumbletots.com

Yoga Manchester Located in a beautiful studio with smooth wooden floors and perfect lighting, this post-natal mum and baby yoga class is an oasis of calm.

The hour-long session is roughly divided into three sections. The first concentrates on mum. So with baby lying on the yoga mat in front of you, you do a series of gentle exercises that include lots of pelvic floor work and concentration on breathing – an essential part of yoga of course. My personal favourite was 'Yogic Peekaboo' where you inhale whilst gazing upwards, then exhale coming down to kiss your baby.

Next is the Baby Yoga section, which includes things like singing 'Horsey, Horsey' whilst baby is sat on your right-angled leg and having baby lying on your legs whilst you circle them doing gentle bounces singing 'Round And Round We Go'. The third section is for mums and babies and involves some more lovely interaction between you both. The class finishes with relaxation techniques. Afterwards everyone hangs around for a chat and a cup of tea. A brilliant class.
Classes cost £6 per session or £10 for two. All classes are drop in, no need to book. Suitable from birth onwards. Pre-natal yoga and pilates classes also available.
Didsbury and Heaton Moor
Tel: 07821 607 505 www.yoga-manchester.co.uk

SWIMMING LESSONS

Aqua Babies This is a well-thought out, enjoyable class that not only gets babies used to the water and on their way to learning to swim, it also, very importantly, helps parents' confidence. Classes are small and take place in lovely heated pools with experienced, friendly teachers.

Aqua Babies starts by warming up the little ones in the water, for example by swishing them from side to side and then round and round on the spot. Next, toys are brought out and babies are encouraged to 'kick kick' (with you holding of course!) towards them, as well as across the pool, learning to hold on to the side when they get there. The class also includes singing; one song in particular, 'Twinkle Twinkle', during which parents float babies on their backs, moving them gently round the pool, which makes them very mellowed out!

Getting babies ready for going under water is another element. In this, Aqua Babies uses the 'Ready, Go, Lift…' cue so that when parents go through this motion, the babies know they're going to be taken under water momentarily and thus learn to be prepared. All told, this is an excellent swimming class for babies – I've just signed up my nine-month-old!

Costs are £10.50 per lesson paid in a block of nine or 10 weeks. Classes held in Bowdon, Bramhall, Cheadle, Didsbury, Oldham, Swinton and Timperley Tel: 0161 973 1931 www.aquababies.co.uk

The Elite Swim School I was struggling to find a class for both my three and five year old boys. We were no longer members of a gym and Sam was getting bored watching Harry have his lesson at the local pool. Thankfully we were recommended Richard's lessons, which are based at the pool at Manchester High School for Girls.

With 21 years' teaching experience and a recent gold medal at the National Swimming Championships, you know you are in good hands. Both boys were assessed on their abilities and put into classes accordingly. This is a step up from parent toddler swimming groups and the children are in the pool on their own. Thankfully Richard is in with them and by the end of the lesson there are usually two other instructors in the water too!

Mums on Mats is a post-natal class that works on toning and strengthening your whole body.

Learning to swim with Aqua Babies is an ideal starting point.

Five-year-old Harry loves every minute of it. His younger brother Sam started off absolutely terrified and wouldn't get in at all, but slowly we are turning the corner and I am confident that he will love it too in the long-term.

Classes cost £5.25 per session and are payable in blocks of eight, with the first two sessions free. Exclusively for Babies in the City the first 50 people to book with Richard will pay half price. Withington Tel: 0161 748 8669 or 07977 235856 www.eliteswimschool.co.uk

Puddle Ducks When I went to a Puddle Ducks class in Warrington I'd forgotten how great it was to have lessons. The instructor is in the pool with you and you're taught tricks and techniques to encourage your child to be more confident in the water. The teachers are brilliant, and their confidence definitely rubs off! Lessons include lots of songs and games, and the only flotation used is a woggle (a long float tube).

There are different classes dependent on age (from under six months right up to five years) and they cost from £10 per session for a 12-week course. There are no more than nine children per class.

Alsager, Delamere Forest, Northwich, Sandbach and Warrington Tel: 01477 535527 www.puddleducks-swimming.co.uk

Water Babies While the main emphasis is on having fun, a Water Babies course is highly structured. About 95 per cent of the lesson takes place on the surface, the rest underwater, but the swims beneath the surface only last a few seconds and the babies I watched going under the water were absolutely at ease with it.

The lessons are run by very experienced teachers whose enthusiasm is contagious. Classes include lots of splashing and kicking, as well as singing, work with floats and toys, and for the older ones, jumping in off the sides. All told Water Babies was very impressive and I'll definitely be signing up for a course when my baby arrives.

Each lesson costs between £10.50 and £13 charged as complete terms of eight, nine or 10 weeks. Blackley, Bolton, Burnley, Bury, Manchester, Standish and Wigan Tel: 01204 846 003 Lymm, Standish, Warrington and Wigan Tel: 0161 357 0111 www.waterbabies.co.uk

Indoor play centres

Indoor play centres are a life-saver on a rainy day, and Greater Manchester has some brilliant venues. Here are some of the best available, where you can just turn up and play – no booking necessary.

Rainy day activities

BOLTON

Cheeky Chimps is based on the first floor of a converted mill in Atherton, with plenty of parking space available. Access is via an old goods lift. There are two toddler areas, one with a slide leading into a ball pit and the other also with a slide plus loads of soft shapes to play with. For older children there is a climbing wall and a football pitch. The main structure is only two storeys but with interactive elements dotted throughout. Because of the style of the building it's a little dark and you may need to encourage the children to play. There are plenty of tables and chairs and even on a busy day you should have no problem finding a spot to sit. The café is small but serves the usual range of snacks, with a children's meal deal costing £2.95.

A unique feature is the crèche facility, where you can leave your child in fully-qualified care for up to two hours so you can go shopping in peace. This does need to be booked a day in advance.
Mon-Fri 9.30am-6pm, Sun 9.30am-4pm.
Mon-Fri £4, Weekends £4.50, under 1s free.
Toddler Times Mon and Tues 10am-12,
Thurs and Fri 1-3pm. Crèche Mon-Fri
10am-4pm, for 0-10years, £4 per hour for up
to 2hrs, inc drinks and snacks.
Cheeky Chimps, Howe Bridge Mill, First Floor, Gloucester Street, Atherton M46 0JT
Tel: 01942 894 444 www.cheeky-chimps.co.uk

Rough'n'Tumble: one of many excellent play centres in the area.

Curly Whirleez is laid out on multiple levels with great facilities in its three sections. There's a toddler soft play area, tube slide, wavy astro slide, ball pool and car track plus a lovely (scaled down!) red double decker bus for the children to play in. There are also various activities on offer, including toddler yoga, pre-school gymnastics and parent and toddler meetings. A decent café serves sandwiches, soup, drinks, fruit etc.
Mon-Fri 9.30am-6pm, Weekends 9.30am-5.30pm.
Over 3s £4, under 3s £3.50, under 1s free.
Weekends over 3s £4.50, under 3s £4
Curly Whirleez, Boundary Industrial Estate, Millfield Road, Bolton BL2 6QY Tel: 01204 523620 www.curlywhirleez.co.uk

Party and Play Funhouse is huge and being housed in a massive warehouse, allows the parents' seating area to be in the middle of all the equipment so you can see your child playing almost anywhere in the room. The giant doors of the building are actually fully retractable, so in good weather they're opened up making this a great venue even on sunny days.

All the usual climbing structures can be found here – a four-lane wavy slide, a curly tree slide and perspex tunnels to crawl through. There's a good toddler area for under fours which has the bonus of Little Tikes Cars. There are also two enclosed trampolines and a climbing wall. The café menu is quite large and includes a tasty sounding breakfast. Lunchtime adult food ranges from a Greek platter to cheesy nachos whilst the children's menu has such meals as salmon fishcakes, sausage and chips and lunchboxes from £3.25.
Mon, Thurs and Fri 9.30am-7pm, Tues, Wed and Weekends 9.30am-6pm. Over 1s £4.99, under 1s £1.
Party and Play, South Westregen House, Off Great Bank Road, Wingates Industrial Park, Westhoughton, Bolton BL5 3XB
Tel: 01942 818195
www.partyandplayfunhouse.co.uk

Wobbly Bobs is smack bang in the centre of Farnworth town centre and is perfect if you're local to the area. It's a relatively small soft play centre but has enough to keep the little ones entertained, with a three-lane wavy slide, ball pit and ariel glide with buoy swing.
Daily 10am-6pm. Over 4s £4, under 4s £3, under 1s £1, non-walking babies free.
Free drink on entrance.
Wobbly Bobs, King street retail park, Farnworth, Bolton BL4 7AZ Tel: 01204 576 719 www.wobblybobs.net

CHESHIRE

Antz in your Pantz There are three zones here – a little area for the under ones where they can crawl and climb in a padded space with toys; a slightly larger section built on two levels with slides aimed at the 1-5year olds, and then the main area with all the usual equipment – astro slide, rope bridges, tunnels etc. A nice touch is the plentiful supply of ride-along cars and tractors as well as the small football area. A good selection of food and drink is available.
Mon, Weds and Thurs 9.30am-6pm, Tues 9.30am-4pm, Fri-Sun 9.30am-6.30pm. Over 3s £4.85, under 3s £3.85, active babies £1.
'Play and meal' deals on offer.
Antz in your Pantz, Unit 8 Crown Industrial Estate, Canal Road, Timperley, Cheshire WA14 1TD
Tel: 0161 962 2266 www.antzinyourpantz.co.uk

TO FIND OUT ABOUT BUS, TRAIN AND TRAM SERVICES TO EACH VENUE PHONE TRAVELINE ON 0871 200 22 33

The Sensory Suite at Mr Clown's is a real stand-out feature.

Mon-Sun 10am-6pm. Over 3s £4.95, under 3s £3.95, 6-12 months £1, under 6 months free. Tues-Fri 10am-3pm (term time) £3.25 including drink and a biscuit.
Fun4All, Queens Avenue, Hurdsfield Industrial Estate, Macclesfield, Cheshire SK10 2DG Tel: 01625 440 044 www.fun4all.co.uk

Geronimo is set out over two levels, with seating sections ideally placed near the play area. The equipment includes a football pitch and sports area, two-level adventure play frame, quad slide, slide swing, ball pools, toddler cars and a baby and toddler area. The food at Geronimo is lovely, whether you are after a homemade lunch (including menus for children) or simply a slice of cake.

Also worth looking out for are the 'mums and tots' sessions held daily on weekdays (during term time).

Mon-Wed 9.30am-5.30pm, Thurs-Sat 9.30am-6pm, Sun 10am-4pm. Over 1s £3.50, under 1s £1, under six months free.
Weekends, holidays and after 3pm Over 1s £4.
Kid for a quid on Wednesdays after school.
Geronimo, 348 Wilderspool Causeway, Warrington, Cheshire WA4 6QP Tel: 01925 244855 www.gogeronimo.co.uk

Fun4All is a bit tricky to find (turn down Queens Avenue when reaching the industrial estate), but persevere because once you make it, there is plenty of parking and an overflow next door in the Booker Cash & Carry. The centre is big and well lit, with a large separate area on two levels for toddlers. The main play is on three levels, with a 10-metre wave slide and although a little on the small side, the climbing wall and separate soft sports zone with football and basketball nets make up for this.

There are loads of tables and chairs, with a good selection of food available ranging from £2.95 for sandwiches, including my children's favourite – jam – to £3.95 for a larger meal including fish, pasta and chicken goujons.

The Jungle has got good equipment and is nice and clean. Highlights are probably the four-lane bumpy slide, which is long and fast, and the two enclosed trampolines. There are two small areas for under threes, a ball pit and an enclosed helter skelter slide. Sandwiches, toasties and soup are offered plus good coffee. Seating areas are on two levels. Friday from 4-6pm is Disco Night, where the lights are turned down and the music turned up. Every day

Indoor play centres

from 10am-3pm is a toddler session with arts and craft activities, music, book reading and 'funky fitness'. There is also an after school meal deal for £5.

Daily 10am-6pm. Members: £4 for the first child/£3.50 for additional children, Mon-Fri (term time) 10am-3.30pm – includes a free tea or coffee plus juice. After school, weekends and school holidays £4.50 for all children. Under 1s free at all times. Non-members 50p extra, you can sign up online.
The Jungle, 12 Chetham Court, Calver Road, Winwick Quay, Warrington WA2 8RF Tel: 01925 659995 www.thejungle.uk.net

DERBYSHIRE

Mr Clown's Fun Zone The main stand-out feature at Mr Clown's is undoubtedly the Sensory Suite. Two small rooms with their own entrance located to the side of the main area have been appropriately decorated with bean bags and padded areas. They utilise tools such as colour-change lighting, bubble tubes, UV light, fluorescent materials and fibre optics – all designed for visual and tactile stimulation. You do have to put your name down for the Sensory Suite in advance of your visit. You can either book a single space or can get a few friends together and reserve it entirely for yourselves for half-an-hour, plus you can use the soft play facilities afterwards.

The rest of Mr Clown's has all the usual soft play equipment and specific toddler areas – my favourite is the old-fashioned wooden carts that the boys loved pushing each other round in.

There is a simple and very reasonably priced menu, with paninis for adults starting at £3.50 and a children's menu from just £2. Baby jars are also on sale.

Tues-Sun, Bank Holiday Mondays 10am-5.30pm. 5-11 years £5.50, under 5s £3.50, under 1s £1, under 6 months free. Parent and toddler sessions in the Sensory Suite Tues, Thurs and Sat. Call ahead to book. Weekday £5, Sat £6. Can be booked for a private half-hour session for £20 or an hour for £35.
Mr Clown's Fun Zone, Unit 16C Etherow Industrial Estate, Woolley Bridge, Hadfield, Glossop SK13 2NS
Tel: 01457 865 650 www.mrclownsfunzone.com

CINEMA – BABY SCREENINGS

We've found two cinemas that offer special parent and baby screenings, Nappy Mondays at the Apollo in Altrincham and Newbies at the Odeon in both The Trafford Centre and Rochdale. Currently running once a week, there is no choice of film, but it is usually one of the most recent releases. Legally it has to be a 12A rating or below, as children are in the audience. You pay only for the adult, at normal cinema entrance price.

Altrincham Apollo is a fairly small cinema and was very quiet for our visit – there were only about 15-20 mums with offspring. Mostly they were babies on laps, but there were some toddlers. There is no official upper age limit for children, but older ones tend to get bored. The volume is a bit lower and lighting is kept slightly up throughout the film which allows for feeding etc. Bottle and baby food heating duty was taken on by the popcorn counter staff. Pushchairs are allowed right in to the cinema, which makes life a lot easier. During showings at The Trafford Centre Cinema, pushchairs have to be left outside in the office, which can be awkward if you have a sleeping baby.

Overall there is a very relaxed atmosphere. Whenever I have been, the babies present have all been remarkably well behaved, in fact I am always surprised at how little they disrupt the viewing. Baby-changing facilities are available.
Apollo Altrincham, Denmark Street, Altrincham WA14 2WG
Tel: 0871 220 6000 www.apollocinemas.co.uk
Nappy Monday 12-1pm, Adult £6.20, Babies free.
Odeon, The Trafford Centre, Manchester M17 8DF
Newbies Tues 11.30am, Adult £7.10, Toddlers up to four free.
Odeon, Sandbrook Way, Rochdale OL11 1RY
Tel: 0871 22 44 007 www.odeon.co.uk
Newbies Wed 1.40pm, Adult £7.70, Toddlers up to four free.

KIDS CINEMA

Every weekend most cinemas host screenings for children – ideal if you haven't been to the cinema with them before and aren't sure if they're going to like it. In most cases one adult is free per child or there is a nominal charge. They are not always the latest releases, but the majority of under fives don't seem to care what they're watching. This is a great rainy day activity and if you don't get too caught up buying popcorn and drinks, it doesn't cost the earth.

Apollo Kids Club *Sat 10am, Adult and Child £1.50,*
Apollo Altrincham, Denmark Street, WA14 2WG
Tel: 0871 220 6000 www.apollocinemas.co.uk

Movies for Juniors *Sat 10.10am, Adult £1, Child £1*
Cineworld, Ashton Leisure Park, Ashton-under-Lyne OL7 0PG
Cineworld, The Valley, Bolton BL1 8TS
Sat 10.20am, 10.30am, Adult £1, Child £1
Cineworld, Grand Central Square, Stockport SK1 3TA
Cineworld, Parrs Wood, Didsbury M20 5PG
Tel: 0871 200 2000 www.cineworld.co.uk

Kids Club *Weekends 11am, Child £2.45, Adults free.*
Odeon, The Printworks, Manchester M4 2BS
Odeon, The Trafford Centre, Manchester M17 8DF
Weekends 11.10am, Child £3.50, Adults free.
Odeon, Sandbrook Park, Rochdale OL11 1RY
Tel: 0871 22 44 007 www.odeon.co.uk

Kids AM *Weekends 10.30am, Child 95p, Adults 95p.*
Vue, Lowry Outlet Mall, Salford Quays M50 3AH
Vue, Middlebrook Leisure Park, Bolton BL6 6JA
Vue, Park 66, Pilsworth Road, Bury BL9 8RS
Tel: 08712 240 240 www.myvue.com

Indoor play centres

MANCHESTER

Anchor's Away Play A new addition to the world of soft play centres, I found Anchor's Away Play a perfect venue for the team of little ones we took along. It's not too big, and on the day we went, not too busy, so we were able to get a table next to the smaller soft play area aimed at toddlers. It meant we could pop our two early crawlers in there and whilst they were only a couple of feet away wobbling around in a padded section, we could sit back and enjoy a coffee and a chat. This area is also flooded with natural light so it feels nice and airy.

Meanwhile the older brothers had fun in the other half of the centre, which includes a little football area, slides, ball shooting machines and a zip wire, amongst other facilities. There are also two free games consoles for older children.

Although there is no baby food on sale, the staff are happy to heat up food and bottles. Our three-year-olds tucked into chicken and chips, which went down well.

Daily 9.30am-6pm. Over 4s £4, 1-3 years £3, 6 months-1 year £1, Under 6 months free. Weekends and holidays Over 4s £4.95, 1-3 years £3.95, 6 months-1 year £1, Under 6 months free.
Anchors Away Play, Simonsway, By Jn 4 M56, Manchester M23 2XQ Tel: 0161 437 0665 www.anchorsawayplay.com

Head Over Heels is one of the largest play centres in the UK and the proud owner of an award-winning restaurant (The Observer 2006/7).

There are leather sofas and comfy chairs next to the main play area which, at three storeys high with a three-lane astro slide, keeps the children suitably busy. There is also an exclusively under threes soft play section – quite sizeable and really well equipped, with things like a ball pool with air fountain, slide, perspex tunnel, soft play roundabout and animals, play house, ride-on cars and play panels, among other things. Worth a special mention is the disco room, new in 2009. Great for the mums and dads as a tv in the restaurant area shows the parents what their little ones are up to in there. Also funny for diners if an unsuspecting parent starts to 'get on down'!

The kids' menu serves favourites such as lasagne, chicken goujons and scrambled eggs on toast. The adults' menu has an excellent choice too. Staff are also happy to heat up baby food or bottles on request.

Daily 9.30am-6pm. Over 3s £4.95, under 3s £3.95, active babies £1.20, Non-playing babies free. Toddler activity mornings Mon-Fri 9.30-11.30am, £4.50, Playtime 11.30am-2pm £3.50, Non-playing babies free.
Head over Heels, Unit 1a, Albany Trading Estate, Albany Road, Chorlton, Manchester M21 0AZ
Tel: 0161 881 4433 www.headoverheelsplay.co.uk

Anchor's Away Play: a new addition to the world of soft play.

OLDHAM

Cheeky Chimps Activity Centre is surprisingly homely for a soft play venue. It isn't enormous but the space is excellently used with a three-tier main play area containing toddler and baby sections. There is a superb supply of toys for the children to play with, and a few fast and steep slides. The staff are friendly and keep everywhere immaculate – the baby-change facility with pretty pictures, a mobile above the changing mat and free nappy sacks was one of the best I've seen. The café's menu is simple, tasty and reasonably priced. The children opted for the lunchboxes, which include a sandwich, crisps, fruit juice, fruit or biscuit, balloon, crayons and colouring picture all for only £2.99.

Daily from 10am-5.45pm (check if you're intending to arrive after 3pm as it is sometimes booked for private parties). Weekdays term time, over 1s £3, under 1s £2; Weekends, school and bank holidays over 3s £4, under 3s £3, under 1s £2.
Cheeky Chimps Activity Centre, Acorn Street, Lees, Oldham OL4 3PD
Tel: 0161 626 2552 www.cheekychimpsplaycentre.co.uk

Kiddly Beanz Situated within a parade of shops in Failsworth, this centre is essentially half-café and half-soft play. The soft play section I'd say is more aimed at the younger end of the market. Set out over two levels, it's quite small in comparison to others, but our little ones found enough to do to keep them happy for half-an-hour or so. And the staff are extremely friendly – clearly a place for locals.

Open weekdays 9.30am-4pm (10am-4pm in school holidays). Weekends 12-4pm. Closed on Tuesday except in school holidays.
Kiddly Beanz, 28-30 Partington Street, Failsworth, Manchester M35 9RD Tel: 0161 682 3089 www.kiddlybeanz.com

Play! Although we went at lunchtime during half-term week, there was still plenty of parking and loads of tables available. Helpfully, tubs are provided to place your coats and shoes in and then carry to your table so you're not dropping everything

CLASSES AND ACTIVITIES

Indoor play centres

all over the floor. There's a three-tier soft play, with a three-lane slide and viewing tubes at the top and this kept our boys very busy for the allotted time.

There is a separate gated area for under-twos; this is mainly to discourage older children running in and out. We enjoyed reasonably priced, freshly made, generously filled toasties (there is a no deep fried food policy.) You can also choose from the usual range of sandwiches, paninis and hot food. Children's meals range in price from £1.30-£1.60 for a selection including beans on toast, jacket potatoes or fish fingers. A snack pack of sandwiches, drink, crisps and fruit is available for £3. On Thursday mornings during term time there is a free arts and craft session in the party area.

Mon closed (except Bank Holidays and school holidays 10am-5pm), Tues-Sat 10am-6pm, Sun 10am-3.30pm.
Weekdays Over 19 months £3.20, 6-18 months £1.80, under 6 months free. Weekends Over 4s £4, over 19 months £3.50, 6-18 months £1.80, under 6 months free.
Play! Unit 5 Laurel Trading Estate, Higginshaw Lane, Oldham OL2 6LH Tel: 0161 627 3000 www.playoldham.com

ROCHDALE

Mischief Makers is impressively clean with a small baby section; a toddler zone with a ball pit, giant wobbly skittles and a low slung circular swing; and an area for 5-11year olds which has a three-run astro slide, helter skelter and basketball court amongst other things, laid out over four levels. The menu's not as extensive as other places we visited but is adequate and low cost. Baby jars are available and cost 90p. Pizza and play sessions are run Mondays 4-6pm where you get playtime, pizza, juice and ice cream included in the price of £5.75.

Daily term time 10am-4pm, holiday time 10am-6pm.
Over 2s £4.25, under 2s £2.50, under 1s free (if with paying child).
No 1 The Pavilions, Bridgefold Road, Rochdale OL11 5BX
Tel: 01706 653 656 www.mischiefmakersltd.co.uk

Planet Play When you walk in to Planet Play you are faced with a large three-level play frame with a tunnel slide into an incredibly deep ball pit. This area is aimed at older children and also includes air-powered ball-guns, a scary spook room and zip wires. There are two other sections: one for under sixes, which includes a fast slide, ball pit and a big cooking pot style swing; and one for under threes, which although quite small does have a little house and small ball pit. There are also lots of ride-on vehicles. The café menu is very extensive.

Daily Mon-Sun 10am-6pm.
Over 18 months Mon-Fri before 2pm £3.50, after 2pm £3.75, weekends and holidays £4.25. 12-18 months Mon-Fri before 2pm £2, after 2pm £2.50, weekends and holidays £2.75, 6-12 months £1.
Planet Play, 2 Bradshaw Street, Heywood OL10 1PN
Tel: 01706 627627 www.planetplay.net

Clodagh racing to the top of the slide at Land of Play.

Snakes and Slides is a large soft play centre with a baby and toddler area. There is a wide variety of play equipment for older toddlers and children, including a traverse wall, a football zone and four-lane astro slide. The café seating area is directly between the play equipment and the entrance. A good selection of food is available.
Mon-Sat 9.30am-6pm, Sun 10am-5pm. Mon-Fri term time, parent and toddler sessions £3.50 before 2pm; after 2pm Mon-Fri, weekend and school holidays £4.50, 6-12 months £1, under six months free.
Snakes and Slides, Unit 3, Rule Business Park, Grimshaw Lane, Middleton M24 2AE Tel: 0161 653 1221 www.snakesandslides.co.uk

SALFORD

Little Monsters Mayhem is a very well thought out centre. Its three areas contain a baby part with soft shapes, mirrors and wall activities; an under threes section with slide and ball pit; and the main larger area for older children with a three-lane astro slide, zip wires, climbing walls and a perspex car you can pretend to drive. What does catch your eye is a mini-circuit with scooters that adjust to become ride-ons. There are comfy leather sofas and lots of tables and chairs. The café menu is simple but healthy with toasties, sandwiches and jackets. For £2.90 you can get a platter which includes a choice of sandwiches, fruit, crisps, yoghurt and drink.
Mon-Sat 9.30am-6pm, Sun 10am-5pm. Child £3.95, under 1s free.
Little Monsters Mayhem, Station Approach, 632 Liverpool Road, Irlam M44 5AD Tel: 0161 775 5515 www.littlemonstersmayhem.co.uk

STOCKPORT

Anchors Away Formerly known as 'Whale Around', this soft play centre has had a bit of a makeover, although the layout is pretty much the same as before. If you can't park on the road outside, there is parking available in the mill a few minutes' walk away. The centre itself is quite small and probably more suited to the younger end of the market. There are three different play zones for pre-walkers, toddlers and juniors with ball pits, slides and toys to play with. Term time toddler sessions, with £3 entry, include activities such as junk modelling and parachute play as well as a free drink and biscuit for each child. After-school meal deals are also available.
Mon-Sat 9.30am-6pm, Sun 10am-4pm.
Weekdays and term-time: Under 1s 50p, under 5s £3, over 5s £4.
Weekends and school holidays: Under 1s 50p, under 5s £3.50, over 5s £4.50.
Anchors Away, Houldsworth Mill, Houldsworth Street, Reddish, Stockport SK5 6DA
Tel: 0161 432 4020 www.anchorsaway.org.uk

Funizuz is split between two rooms. The first room has ball pits and a two-lane astro slide for older children as well as separate areas for under 18 months and under threes – seating is limited in this room. In the second room there is a small under fours area with a slide and perspex tunnel plus a café with lots of seating and a television. Children's meals include pasta, chicken nuggets, sausages or fish fingers, chips, yoghurt and squash for £4. There is also a good pottery workshop.
Mon-Sun 10am-6pm. Over 3s £4.50, 9 months-3 years £3.50.
Pre-school sessions 10am-2pm term time only £3, including juice and biscuits.
Funizuz, Brookfield Road Industrial Estate, Cheadle, Stockport SK8 2PN Tel: 0161 491 6611 www.funizuz.co.uk.

Rough'n'Tumble Meeting a friend over in Marple, we decided to convene at Rough'n'Tumble. Based in a large old mill on a bit of a hillside, the car park for the centre is on a different level so you will initially encounter outdoor steps down to the entrance. Once in, there are basically two sections; the first for little ones, where the majority of the café's tables and chairs are situated, together with sofas, laid out around the area so that you can keep a good eye on them. The second section, for the older children, is around the corner. I thought the toddler bit here was very good with two little wavy slides, ball pit, and padded objects to play with.

The adult and children's food we ordered was nice and tasty. I'd brought along my own baby food and was pleased to find a microwave for heating it up together with lots of utensils to use. All in all a well equipped facility.

Will paints a pot at the Bluebell Centre.

POTTERY STUDIOS

Pottery studios are a great place to visit. They're particularly good if you're stuck for present ideas for relatives or if perhaps the weather's off and you fancy letting your child's artistic temperament bloom. Prices usually range from around £5-£25 from simple mugs and plates to piggy banks, letter racks and teapots. In the list below, you'll find most of the studios have refreshments on site and some are linked with soft play areas.

The Art Café
Mon-Sat 10.30am-6pm, Sun 11am-5pm.
2 Century House, Ashley Road, Hale, Cheshire WA15 9SF
Tel: 0161 929 6886

Brookside Pottery
Next to miniature railway – see page 36.
Weekends 11am-4pm (can open any day so please call).
Brookside Garden Centre, Macclesfield Road, Poynton
Cheshire SK12 1BY Tel: Liz 07946 637 499

Crackpots Ceramics Café (also has soft play area)
Mon-Sat 10am-5pm, Sun 11am-4pm.
Unit 8, The Bridge Shopping Centre, Knutsford Road, Latchford, Warrington WA4 1JR Tel: 01925 638 313
www.crackpotscafe.co.uk

Funizuz Play Centre
Daily 10am-6pm (see soft play centre on this page).
Brookfield Road Industrial Estate, Cheadle SK8 2PN
Tel: 0161 491 6611 www.funizuz.co.uk

Pottery Corner
Tues-Sat 10am-6pm and Sun 11am-5pm (open until 8pm on Thursday).
34 Beech Road, Chorlton, Manchester M21 9EL
Tel: 0161 882 0010 www.potterycorner.co.uk

Paint a Pot
Thurs and Fri 11am-2.30pm. Sat and Sun 11am-4pm, Holidays open daily 11am-4pm (phone first to check).
The Bluebell, Stockport Road, Gee Cross, Hyde, Cheshire SK14 5EZ Tel: 0161 406 6993
www.paintapot.org.uk

Indoor play centres

BABY LOVES DISCO

If you fancy dancing to some club classics rather than the more traditional nursery rhymes, then this is the place for you. After a warm welcome from staff who'll safely store your pushchair, you head downstairs into Pure nightclub. It's like descending into a big children's party, except there's no birthday girl, the music isn't too loud – you can hear yourself speak – and the lights are not too dark to scare children. I was pleasantly surprised at the amount of dads there and though many had no doubt been coerced, they looked like they were enjoying themselves. For the children, there were balloons, shakers, scarves, face painting and an unlimited supply of healthy party snacks.

Upstairs, for babies and those not so keen on the music and lights, there is a chill-out room with comfy sofas, books, baby toys and mats.

The changing station is downstairs, with free nappies and baby wipes. The nightclub apparently gets a triple clean before any babies come through the door.
Monthly Sunday afternoon 2-5pm. Admission: £8 per walking person, crawlers free. Age: 6 months to 7 years.
Pure, The Printworks, 27 Withy Grove, Manchester M4 2BS
www.babylovesdisco.co.uk

CHILL FACTORE

If you're looking for something a little out of the ordinary, check out the Chill Factore. Real snow indoors all year round means a winter wonderland really is permanently on our doorstep here in Manchester.

Once inside you'll find all the trappings of an alpine village. Mums can get a fix of some delicious hot chocolate from the bars overlooking the piste, while the children will be looking wide-eyed at all that snow. Next to the main slope is the 'Snow Play Area', which is filled with mounds of real snow and pretend trees with a mini wooden chalet to play in. It's designed for 2-10 year olds and contains soft play toys like polar bears and penguins. This is great fun and entirely unique within the area, but the most obvious point to make is that it is of course extremely cold, so dress accordingly (gloves are essential). Suits are £5 to hire and gloves cost £3 to buy. Helmets, again compulsory, are supplied and are included in the entry fee. The smallest boot in snow play is size 8 for children. Under 2s can go in but parents have to provide their own wellies.

Private ski-lessons are available for those aged three years and up – £50 for half-an-hour. Saturday mornings also have group ski lessons – the Kindergarten Club is for those aged 4-6 years old. Tubing is available for children over four, and there's a luge for the over eights.
Snow Play is open daily 10am-9pm.
Adults £1, Children £6 (parental supervision at all times).
Chill Factore, Trafford Way, Trafford Quays Leisure Village, Manchester M41 7JA
Tel: 0161 749 2222 www.chillfactore.com

Mon-Sat 10am-6pm, Sun 10am-4pm.
Over 5s £5, under 5s £4, under 1s £1.
Parent and Toddler Time, term time only, Mon-Fri 10am-3pm, 1-3yrs £3.30 including child's drink and biscuit.
Rough'n'Tumble, Goyt Mill, Upper Hibbert Lane, Marple, Stockport SK6 7HX
Tel: 0161 427 0007 www.roughntumble.co.uk

Run of the Mill is really well thought out. We especially like this play centre because it seems particularly geared towards the younger set and isn't overwhelming like some of the others (despite the fact that it's big – over 10,000 square feet). There are up and over climbs, leapfrog trampettes, wavy slides, an enclosed sports pitch, sky gliders, a giant ball zone and a junior traverse wall, amongst many other things! For toddlers, there is a sweet little vehicle area with various ride-ons as well as a specially designed playframe for under fours, which also includes a baby playpen.

Another outstanding feature is the menu – freshly prepared, home-cooked food of a very high standard. We enjoyed a Lebanese influenced mezze, panini and kid's sole goujons.

On Mondays and Wednesdays around 11am there are stories, singing and crafts for toddlers.
Daily 10am-6pm. Over 3s £4.90, under 1s £1, under 3s £3.90.
Parent and Toddler sessions Mon-Fri 10am-3pm (term time), £3 including juice and a biscuit.
Good after-school meal deals (term time) on offer.
Run of the Mill, Pear Mill, Stockport Road West, Bredbury, Stockport, Cheshire SK6 2BP
Tel: 0161 494 7137 www.runofthemill.co.uk

TAMESIDE

Kiddie Chaos is set in a huge industrial unit with around 50 tables for parents. It does get busy at the weekends and when parties are on, but the size of the play area means there's room for everybody. There's a four-lane astro slide, enclosed football pitch, exercise balls, climbing rope, trampoline and excellent enclosed floor to ceiling slide. There is also a small area for babies by the under fives zone, which contains a two-lane slide.

Food includes fishfingers, chips, beans, pizzas and sausages for around £3.25.
Mon-Sun 10am-6pm.
Tot Time: Mon-Fri term time, 10am-2pm, £2.75 inc juice, biscuit and hot drink, or £5 for meal deal; 2-6pm £3.50 or £6 for meal deal; Weekends and School Holidays £3.95, Under 1s 50p at all times.
Kiddie Chaos, Unit 1, Gorton Crescent, Windmill Lane Industrial Estate, Denton M34 3RB
Tel: 0161 320 7774 www.kiddie-chaos.co.uk

Slide and Seek is set in a huge warehouse with a vast café area. The junior section is four levels high with a four-lane astro slide and also contains a basketball area with nets. Toddlers have their own two-lane slide and a ball pit; there are also Little

Soft play centres are a rainy day life-saver.

Tike cars in a circuit and a kitchen area. There is a baby zone with soft shapes and panel games. Children's meals start at £1.50 for pasta. There is also a pick and mix selection of chicken nuggets, fishfingers, chips, carrot sticks, beans and juice for £3.50 or lunchboxes for the same price.

Mon-Fri 9.30am-6pm, Weekends 10am-6pm. Toddler activity mornings term time Mon-Fri 9.30am-2pm £3.50, including juice and snack, Under 1s free. After 2pm, school holidays and weekends, Over 3s £4.50, under 3s £3.50, under 12 months free. Mon-Fri meal deal £6.50.

Slide and Seek, Unit A, SK14 Industrial Park, Broadway, Hyde SK14 4QF Tel: 0161 366 8080 www.slideandseek.co.uk

TRAFFORD

Land of Play Reputedly where footballer Ryan Giggs held his daughter's birthday party, the brand new Land of Play is in a bright and airy unit close to The Trafford Centre. The toddler/crawling baby section is excellent, with a good range of toys and soft play objects. The large indoor climbing frame has all the usual attachments, though isn't quite as big as others we've been to – frankly this made it quite nice if you're going with younger ones as you've not got lots of gallumping 10-year-olds running wild!

The motorised go-karts on a small custom-made racetrack caught my son's attention obviously. You have to pay £1 for these. They are fast so I decided it would be best if I rode on the back and helped him steer – utterly terrifying but he clearly enjoyed it.

There's an extensive menu serving home-made food and heating facilities for baby milk.

Daily 9.30am-6pm.
Weekends and school holidays: Over 3s £4.95. 1-2yrs £3.95, playing babies £1, non-playing babies free;
Weekdays and term-time: Over 3s £3.95, 1-2yrs £2.95, playing babies £1, non-playing babies free.
Land of Play, Units E&F, Astra Business Park, Guinness Road, Trafford Park, Manchester M17 1SU
Tel: 0161 872 9434 www.landofplay.co.uk

CLASSES AND ACTIVITIES

Swimming pools

Below is a list of toddler times and swimming lessons available in the Greater Manchester area. A number of councils offer free swimming for under 16s if you register.

Swimming pools

Under 16s swim for free if you register via your library or Town Hall for a Smart Card.
Farnworth Leisure Centre Six-lane main pool and a teaching pool. Parent and Tots sessions from 6 months to 5 years held Mon, Wed and Fri 12-1pm and cost £2.95 per session. There's no need to book; floats and toys are available. It's a life-guarded session, there is no instructor.
Swim Life lessons available from 3 years. A 10-week course costs £42.50, classes available Mon-Fri and Sat mornings.
Family swim main pool: Sat 9am-2pm, Sun 9am-4pm.
Family swim small pool: Sat 1-3.30pm, Sun 9am-3.30pm.
Adult £3.10
Brackley Street, Farnworth, Bolton BL4 9DZ
Tel: 01204 334477 www.boltonleisure.com
Horwich Leisure Centre Main pool, teaching pool and crèche. Parent and Tots sessions Tues and Thurs 12-12.30pm or 12.30-1pm for children aged 6 months to 5 years. It's instructor led with floats and toys and costs £3.75.
Swim Life lessons available from 3 years. A 10-week course costs £42.50, classes available Mon-Fri and Sat mornings.
Family swim main pool: Mon 3-7.30pm, Tues and Thurs 3-7pm, Weds 4-7pm, Fri 3-7.30pm, Sat 9am-2pm and Sun 9am-4pm.
Family swim small pool: Mon-Fri 3-4pm, Mon, Weds and Fri 6-7.30pm, Sat 12.30-3.30pm, Sun 9am-4pm. Café.
Adult £3.10
Victoria Road, Horwich, Bolton BL6 5PY
Tel: 01204 334488 www.boltonleisure.com
LadyBridge Leisure Centre One main pool with family swim Sun 9.30am-2pm. Swim Life lessons available from 3 years. A 10-week course costs £42.50, classes available Mon-Fri and Sat mornings.
Adult £3.10
New York Road, Deane, Bolton BL3 4NG
Tel: 01204 334432 www.boltonleisure.com
Westhoughton Leisure Centre Two pools with Parent and Tots swim lessons on Thurs 2.30-3.30pm suitable for children aged 6 months to 5 years. Floats and toys available and it costs £2.95 per session.
Swim Life lessons from 3 years. A 10-week course costs £42.50, classes available Mon-Fri and Sat mornings.
Family swim in small pool: Sat 1.30-4pm, Sun 9am-4pm.
Adult £3.10
Bolton Road, Westhoughton, Bolton BL5 3BZ
Tel: 01942 634810 www.boltonleisure.com

Sharples Leisure Centre One main pool. Swim Life lessons from 3 years (10-week course £42.50), Mon-Fri and Sat mornings. Aqua Natal Classes Thurs 6.30-7.30pm £3.60 per session.
Family swim Tues 5.30-7.30pm, Thurs 5.30-6.30pm, Fri 7-8pm, Sun 9.30am-1pm.
Adult £3.10
Hill Cot Road, Sharples, Bolton BL1 8SN
Tel: 01204 334224 www.boltonleisure.serco.com
Turton Leisure Centre One main pool. Swim Life lessons from 3 years. A 10-week course costs £42.50, classes Mon-Fri and Sat mornings.
Family swim Fri 5-7pm, Fri 5.30-7pm, Sun 9.30-10.45am.
Adult £3.10
Chapeltown Road, Bromley Cross, Bolton BL7 9LT Tel: 01204 334440
www.boltonleisure.serco.com

Under 16s free if you register via your sports centre or online for an Active Lifestyle Card £2.
Castle Leisure Centre Three pools and Parent and Toddler drop-in sessions with toys Mon & Weds 1-2pm, £3 for parent and toddler. Family session Sat 11.30am-5.30pm. Swimming lessons from three years, 10-week course £45.
Baby Pool open daily but times vary. Café.
Adult £3
Bolton Street, Bury BL9 0EZ
Tel: 0161 253 6513 www.bury.gov.uk
Radcliffe Pool & Fitness Centre No family swim, but advised to come with under fives in term-time when it's quieter and you can usually use the baby pool, which has floats and a small slide: Mon, Tues, Fri 10.30am-4pm; Weds 9am-1.30pm; Thurs 11.30am-1.30pm; Sat 11am-3.30pm and Sun 8am-1.30pm. Swimming lessons from 3yrs.
Free swimming session for parents whose children have a disability, Sunday 1.45-2.45pm. Family changing room. Crèche on site Mon-Fri 10am-1pm.
Adult £3
Green Street, Radcliffe M26 3ED
Tel: 0161 253 7814 www.bury.gov.uk
Ramsbottom Pool and Fitness Centre One pool. Mother and Baby sessions Weds 9.30-10.30am. Run with a teacher on a drop-in basis and costs £2.90.
Swimming lessons from three years (10-week course £45) Mon and Weds afternoons, Tues and Fri mornings, weekdays after school, Sat mornings and Sun afternoons.
Porritt Way, Ramsbottom, Bury BL0 0PT
Tel: 0161 253 7292 www.bury.gov.uk

New for 2010: two for one adult if you come with children.
Under 16s swim free if you register online or at your sports centre.
Manchester Aquatics Centre Manchester Aquatics has excellent pools! The large baby pool is open Mon and Weds 9am-5.30pm; Tues, Thurs, Fri 9am-8pm. There are specific Family Sessions held in the baby pool at weekends 9am-1pm, 1.30-3.30pm, 4-6pm. The other thing to bear in mind is that generally speaking the baby pool (which is open to all visitors, not just little ones) is quieter during school times.
The next pool is the 23m, which is quite a shallow pool allocated for 'social swimming' so children are happily allowed in this Mon and Weds 9am-5.30pm; Tues, Thurs and Fri 9am-8pm and weekends.
Adult £3.10
Swimming lessons from 6 months. A 10-week course costs £35, classes available weekend mornings. Up to the age of 3 adults must be in the water too.
There are four family changing rooms and you can lock your pram away at reception when you arrive. Café.
2 Booth Street East, Ardwick, Manchester M13 9SS Tel: 0161 275 9450
www.manchestersportandleisure.org
Abraham Moss Leisure Centre Baby Pool open 10.30-11.30am Sat and Sun (£2.40 for parents, free for babies but no toys). General swimming with children in the main pool is all the time except first thing in the mornings and 12-1pm when it's adults only. You can buy a family ticket for £6.
Swimming lessons from 4 years. A 10-week course costs £35, classes available Mon, Weds eve and Thurs.
Crescent Road, Crumpsall, Manchester M8 5UF
Tel: 0161 720 7622
www.manchestersportand leisure.org
Broadway Leisure Centre One main pool. Parent and Baby sessions Fri 1-2pm. Family swim for under fives weekends 12-1pm (no toys).
Adults £2.40
New Moston, Manchester M40 0LN
Tel: 0161 681 1060
www.manchestersportandleisure.org
Chorlton Leisure Centre Family swim (with toys) every Sun 10.15-11.30am (allowed two under fours with one adult).
Swimming lessons from 6 months to three and a half years old. Classes Mon-Sat mornings. Parents must be in the pool too. Swimming lessons also from four and a half years old on Mon, Weds, Thurs after school and Sat mornings (10-week course £35). Aqua Natal is a drop-in on Tuesday 12-1pm, mums can leave babies poolside whilst they swim. Midwives from St Marys Hospital are around. Changing cabins are poolside so baby-changing limited to changing mats.
Adults £2.40
Manchester Road, Chorlton, Manchester M21 9PQ Tel: 0161 861 0790
www.manchestersportandleisure.org

CLASSES AND ACTIVITIES

Forum Leisure Two pools. Parent and Toddler session for under 5s (no toys) in the small pool Mon, Wed-Fri 12-1pm (£2.40). Swimming lessons 0-18 months Tues 12-12.30pm, 18 months to 3 years Tues 12.30-1pm. A 10-week course costs £35. Family swims Wed 6-7.30pm, Thurs-Fri 6-7pm, weekends 3-4pm. Small pool open Sat 11-4pm, Sun 10-4pm. Café.
Adults £2.40
Forum Centre, Forum Square, Wythenshawe, Manchester M22 5RX Tel: 0161 935 4020
www.wythenshaweforum.co.uk

Levenshulme Swimming Pools Parent and toddler drop-in sessions with toys Weds 12-1pm and Sat 1-2pm (£2.30). Adults £2.40 (£1.90 with Manchester Leisure pass). Changing cubicles and baby-change poolside. Barlow Road, Levenshulme, Manchester M19 3HE Tel: 0161 224 4370
www.manchestersportandleisure.org

Miles Platting Swimming Pool Swimming lessons available from 6 months. A 10-week course costs £35.
Family swim every Saturday 10.30am-12pm. You can use the family pool Thurs and Fri 4.30-6.30pm (no toys).
Adult £2.40
Varley Street, Miles Platting, Manchester M40 8EE Tel: 0161 205 8939
www.manchestersportandleisure.org

Moss Side Leisure Centre Parent and toddler sessions for under 5s in the heated baby pool, Mon 12-1pm, 3.30-7pm; Tues 3.30-6.30pm; Weds 12-1pm, 3.30-4pm, 5.30-6.30pm; Thurs 5.30-7pm; Fri 12-1pm, 4-7pm; Sat 12-2pm; Sun 10-2pm.
Adult £2.40
Swimming lessons available up to 3 years. A 10-week course costs £35, classes available Tues and Thurs 12-12.30pm. Parents must be in the pool too.
Moss Lane East, Moss Side, Manchester M15 5NN Tel: 0161 226 5015
www.manchestersportandleisure.org

North City Family and Fitness Centre Parent, Babies and Toddlers sessions for up to six years (with toys) Tues 1-2pm. Cost £2.45. Public swim is generally every day from 3.30pm onwards.
Family swim weekends 9-11am.
Adult £2.40
Upper Conran Street, Harpurhey, Manchester M9 4DA Tel: 0161 277 1900
www.manchestersportandleisure.org

Withington Swimming Pool and Fitness Centre Family swim Sunday 10-11.30am (no toys provided). Aquanatal Fri 12-1pm.
Adult £2.40
Changing cabins are poolside with family changing area.
30 Burton Road, Withington M20 3EB
Tel: 0161 445 1973
www.manchestersportandleisure.org

OLDHAM

Crompton Pool Parent and Baby sessions with instructor in two one-hour slots Weds 9.30-11.30am £3.80.
Aquatots Daily swimming lesson for two and a half to four years £46 for 10 weeks.
Adult £3.30
Farrow Street, Shaw OL2 8NW
Tel: 0161 621 3260 www.ocll.co.uk

Failsworth Sport Centre Parent and Baby drop-in sessions on Tues 11.30am-12.30pm, Sat 11.30am-12.30pm. Costs £3.80 and is for under fives.
Brierley Avenue, Failsworth, Manchester M35 9HA Tel: 0161 621 3240

Glodwick Pool Parent and Baby drop-in sessions on Weds 10-11.30am with toys and music (actual class starts at 10.30am). Costs £3.80 and is for under fours.
Nugget Street, Glodwick OL4 1BN
Tel: 0161 621 3280 www.ocll.co.uk

Oldham Sports Centre Parent and Baby sessions with toys (drop-in for up to two and a half years) on Weds 10.30-11.30am and Fri 11.30am-12.30pm in the small pool: £3.80.

Aqua Tots swimming lessons available from two and a half years. A 10-week course costs £46, classes available Mon-Thurs after school, Fri 5.30-7.30pm and Sat 9am-1pm.
Adults £3.30, Under 18s £1.85, Under fours free. Family ticket £7.50. Pram-locks. Café.
Lord Street, Oldham, Manchester OL1 3HA
Tel: 0161 621 3220 www.ocll.co.uk

Royton Sports Centre Parent and Baby drop-in sessions on Thurs and Sat 12-12.45pm. Costs £3.60.
There is a crèche facility Tues, Weds and Thurs mornings.
Park Street, Royton OL2 6QW
Tel: 0161 621 3250 www.ocll.co.uk

Saddleworth Pool Parent and Baby drop-in sessions on Tues 12-1pm with toys. Costs £3.20 and is for under fours.
Station Road, Uppermill OL3 6HQ
Tel: 0161 621 3270 www.ocll.co.uk

Hathersage Open Air Swimming Pool

A sunny day in May and a teacher-training day in Didsbury, so school was out – a perfect opportunity to check out Hathersage open air pool without it being too busy. How wrong I was – little did I realise that everyone else had the same day off!

We arrived soon after lunch (there are two sessions a day if you're not a pass holder) and despite the long queue, we got in. Because of the limit on numbers it actually wasn't too crowded. Access to the pool is via about 20 steps and there is no lift so be aware of this if you're taking a pushchair.

It's a shame that old-fashioned lidos are a thing of the past as it was absolutely wonderful to be swimming outside and with stunning views of the surrounding Peak District to boot. The water is kept at a very warm 29 degrees and there is a grassed area to lay out your towels. If you need shade, there is a covered veranda and even an old-fashioned bandstand.

There are very good, separate changing rooms for men and women, together with a family changing room with baby-change facilities. You'll also find outside hot showers by the pool.

A nice touch is the Pool Café, where you can buy a take-away and eat directly by the pool or go downstairs and eat inside the café. Hot food, including a great portion of chips, drinks, ice creams and sweets are available all day. For a choice of sausage, burger, fish fingers or pizza with chips and beans, the cost is £3.25; sandwiches start at £1.75 and ice cream is £1 a scoop.

An aqua fun session is held a couple of times a week at no extra charge, with a variety of floats and pool toys.

Non season ticket holders: 3rd Apr-21st May, 3rd-25th Sep, Mon-Fri 7.30am-6pm, Weekends 7.30am-5pm; 22nd May-2nd Sep, Mon-Fri 7.30-9.30am, 10.30am-12.30pm, 1.30-3.30pm and 5-7pm, Weekends 7.30-9.30am, 10.30am-12.30pm, 1.30-3.30pm.
Aqua Fun Mon 5-6pm, Sat 3-4pm.
Adult £4.40, Child £2.30, Family £11.
Hathersage Swimming Pool, Oddfellows Road, Hathersage, Hope Valley S32 1DU Tel: 01433 650 843 www.highpeak.gov.uk/culture/Hathersage

Swimming pools

Under 16s swim free if you register for a pass.
Central Leisure Centre Parent and Baby drop-in sessions up to five years, with toys on Mon, Weds and Fri 12.30-1.30pm, £3.30. Swimming lessons for over threes, 11-week course £39.05. Daily from 4pm.
Adults £2.80
Entwisle Road, Rochdale OL16 2HZ
Tel: 01706 924213 www.link4life.org
Middleton Arena Leisure Centre Aquatots (a Parent and Baby drop-in session with toys for children up to five years) Mon 10-11am, Tues 12.15-1.15pm, Wed 11.45-12.45pm, Thurs 12.15-1.15pm, Sat 10.30-11.30am and 3-4pm. Most sessions with instructor (£3.10). Those without (Mon and Sat mornings) £2.80.
Adult £2.80
Suffield Street, Middleton M24 1HB
Tel: 0161 662 4000 www.link4life.org
Heywood Sports Complex Aquatots (Parent and Baby drop-in sessions with toys) for up to five years on Mon and Tues 12.15-1.15pm (£3.30).
Adult £2.80
West Starkey Street, Heywood OL10 4TW
Tel: 01706 367212 www.link4life.org

Under 16s swim free if you register for a pass.
Fit City Broughton Pool Closed for refurbishment until 17th May 2010. Call or check website for swim times.
Great Cheetham Street West, Salford M7 2DN
Tel: 0161 792 2375 www.leisureinsalford.info
Fit City Clarendon Parent and Baby free drop-in Weds 9.30-10.30am. Fit City run their own Parent and Baby drop-ins (with toys) on Thurs 12-1pm, cost £3.
Swim City Kids Swimming lessons for 3-4 year olds run term time £3.50 per session.
Adult £3
Liverpool Street, Salford M5 4LY
Tel: 0161 736 1494 www.salford.gov.uk
Fit City Eccles Children welcome at all times except for adult only swims. Swimming courses available for three months to five years. Contact Fit City for details.
Adults £3
Barton Lane, Eccles, Salford M30 0DD
Tel: 0161 787 7107
www.leisureinsalford.info
Fit City Irlam Pool Children welcome at all times when there aren't adult only swims. Swimming lessons for over fours.
Adult £3
Liverpool Road, Irlam M44 6BR
Tel: 0161 775 4134
www.salford.gov.uk/fitcity-ir.htm
Fit City Pendlebury Children welcome at all times when there aren't adult only swims. Swimtots lessons from three months, £21 for a six-week course.
Adult £3
Cromwell Road, Swinton, Salford M27 2SZ
Tel: 0161 793 1750
www.leisureinsalford.info

Fit City Worsley Three pools and family swims on Fri 6.30-9pm and Sun 8.30am-12pm. The small pool is available Mon-Fri 12-1pm and 3-4pm, Sun 12.30-4pm. Swimming lessons are available from three years.
Adult £3
Bridgewater Road, Walkden, Salford M28 3AB
Tel: 0161 790 2084
www.lesireinsalford.info

Avondale Leisure and Target Fitness Centre Swim play drop-in session for parents and toddlers with toys and singing. Run by an instructor. Tues 11.10-11.40am and Sat 10.45am-11.15am (£2.95). Family swim (with toys) Sun 10am-12noon.
Swimming lessons available from four years upwards.
Adult £2.85, under 16 £1.60, under threes free. Café.
Heathbank Road, Stockport SK3 0UP
Tel: 0161 477 4242
www.sportinstockport.com
Grand Central Pools
Swimtots Weds 9.30-10am, Swimplay Wed 10-10.30am with songs, games and toys. Swimming lessons from three and a half years. £4.20 per lesson.
Mon-Fri 6.30am-10pm, Sat 7am-4.30pm, Sun 7am-10pm.
12 Grand Central Square, Wellington Road South, Stockport SK1 3TA
Adult: £2.80, Child £1.60, under threes free
Tel: 0161 474 7766 www.stockport.gov.uk
Hazel Grove Pools and Target Fitness Centre Swim play drop-in session for parents and toddlers with toys and singing. Run by a teacher but is not structured apart from a short singalong at the end. Mon 1.15-1.45pm; Thurs 10-10.30am, 10.30-11.30am, 1.15-1.45pm; Fri 1-1.30pm. Cost £3.15.
After attending swim play the under fives progress to swim start and then swim link. These courses cost £4.20 per lesson. Classes available Mon and Thurs.
Family fun sessions in the small pool with toys are Sun 1.30-3.30pm.
Adult £2.80, under 16 £1.60, under threes free.
The centre sells swim nappies at reception.
Jackson Lane, Hazel Grove SK7 5JW
Tel: 0161 439 5221
www.sportinstockport.com
Marple Swimming Pool Swim play drop-in session for parents and toddlers with toys and singing £2.95. Mon 1.15-1.45pm and Tues 2-2.30pm. Cost £2.50.
After attending swim play the under fives progress to swim start and then swim link. A 10-week course costs £42. Classes available Mon, Tues and Sat.
Public swimming weekends 7.30-11am.
Adult £2.80, under 16 £1.60, under threes free.
Stockport Road, Marple, Stockport SK6 6AA
Tel: 0161 427 7070
www.sportinstockport.com

Target Fitness Cheadle Swim play drop-in session for parents and toddlers with toys and singing. Run by a teacher it's not structured apart from a short singalong at the end. Mon 9.15-9.45am, Tues and Thurs 12-12.30pm, Weds 10.15-11.15am and Sun 4-4.30pm. Cost £3.15. After attending swim play the under fives progress to swim start and then swim link.
Fun sessions (with inflatables and floats) in main and small pool on Sat 1.30-2.45pm.
Adult £2.80, under 16 £1.60, under threes free. Café area.
Soft play area in reception (£2 per child).
Shiers Drive, Cheadle, Stockport SK8 1JR
Tel: 0161 428 3216
www.sportinstockport.com
Target Fitness Romiley Two pools. Swim play drop-in session for parents and toddlers with toys and singing. Run by a teacher it costs £3.15. Mon 10.50-11.20am; Tues 9.45-10.15am, 10.15-10.45am, 10.45-11.15am; Thurs 12-12.30pm; and Sat 12.45-1.15pm.
After attending swim play the under fives progress to swim start and then swim link. Payable per term it costs £4.20 per lesson. Classes available Tues, Thurs and Sat.
Adult £2.80, under 16 £1.60, under threes go free.
Hole House Fold, Romiley, Stockport SK6 4BD
Tel: 0161 430 3437
www.sportinstockport.com

Altrincham Leisure Centre Parent and Toddler drop-in session with toys in the small pool. Tues 12.30-1.15pm and Thurs 11.15am-12.15pm. Costs £3.30.
Swim well swimming lessons available for three to four and a half year olds. A 12-week course costs £45.96. Parents are also in the pool.
Small pool open Weds 2.30-7.45pm; Sat 2-5pm and Sun 9am-12.30pm and 2-5pm. Children are welcome in the main pool at other times apart from adult only swim times.
Adult £3, Under 16 £1.50, Under fives 50p.
Oakfield Road, Altrincham, Cheshire WA15 8EW
Tel: 0161 926 3255
www.traffordleisure.co.uk
Partington Sports Village One main pool. Parent and Toddler drop-in sessions on Mon 10.30-11.30am, Thurs 9.30-10.30am for up to five year olds, with a swimming teacher. Cost £2.80.
Dinkys class swimming lessons available from two and a half to three and a half years old. A 13-week course costs £49.79, classes available Mon and Fri 3.30pm. Parents are in the pool too.
Swim well lessons available for three to four and a half year olds. A 13-week course costs £49.79.
Family fun swim sessions weekends 2-3pm.
Adult £3, under 16 £1.50, under fives 50p.
Chapel Lane, Partington, Manchester M31 4ES
Tel: 0161 777 4222
www.traffordleisure.co.uk

Sale Leisure Centre Swimming lessons available from six months, with parents in the pool. Waterbabies, parent and Toddler drop-in session (no instructor) on Thurs 9.30-11am and Fri 11am-12.45pm. Family fun swim Mon 3.30-5.15pm. Ducklings swimming lessons available from three and a half. A 13-week course costs £49.76, classes Mon-Weds and Fri.
Adult £2.90, Under 16 £1.50, Under fives 50p. Café.
Broad Road, Sale, Manchester M33 2AL
Tel: 0161 905 5588 www.traffordleisure.co.uk
Stretford Leisure Centre Parent and Toddler drop-in sessions, Tues 2-3.30pm, Thurs 10-11.30am term time only (£3.30). Also have drop-in dry play sessions called Tiny Ted upstairs Tues, Thurs and Fri 10-11.30am. These sessions cost £2.20 and include access to the soft play area there and are held all year round.
Swim well swimming lessons available from four years old. A 13-week course costs £49.79.
Adult £3, under 16 £1.50, under fives 50p. Café available.
Greatstone Road, Stretford, Manchester M32 0ZS Tel: 0161 875 1414
www.traffordleisure.co.uk
Urmston Leisure Centre Parent and Toddler drop-in sessions for under fives. Mon 2-3.45pm, Fri 10.30am-12.30pm, cost £3.30. Swimming lessons start from four and a half years old.
Family fun swim Sat 2-3pm and Sun 9am-12noon.
Adult £3, Under 16 £1.50, Under fives 50p.
Bowfell Road, Urmston, Manchester M41 5RR
Tel: 0161 749 2570
www.traffordleisure.co.uk

TAMESIDE

Leisure pass costs £3 and results in cheaper admission.
Ashton Pools Two pools. Parent and Child 'Ducklings' sessions held Mon, Weds and Fri 12-1pm. Designed to help introduce pre-school children to the water during semi-formal sessions with play, music and rhymes. Children achieve badges to mark their progress. Swimming lessons start from age five.
Adult £3.60, Under 16 £1.80, Under fives 90p, Family ticket £7.50.
Water Street, Ashton-under-Lyne OL6 7AN
Tel: 0161 330 1179
www.tamesidesporttrust.com
The Copley Centre Two pools on site. Parent and Child 'Ducklings' sessions Tues and Thurs 12.15-1.15pm and Sat 1-2pm. Duckling sessions help introduce pre-school children to the water during semi-formal sessions with play, music and rhymes. Children achieve badges to mark progress.
Adult £3.60, Under 16 £1.80, Under fives 90p. Family ticket (two adults and three children) £7.50.
Huddersfield Road, Stalybridge SK15 3ET
Tel: 0161 303 8118
www.tamesidesporttrust.com

Denton Pools Two pools. Parent and Child (pre-schoolers) 'Two in a Tub' sessions Thurs 12-1pm and Tues (during term time) from 11.15am-12noon. Sat 12.15pm-1.15pm family fun sessions with inflatables, floats and other equipment. Swimming lessons start from age five.
Adult £3.60, Under 16 £1.80, Under fives 90p. Family ticket (two adults three children) £7.50.
Victoria Street, Denton M34 9GU
Tel: 0161 336 1900
www.tamesidesporttrust.com
Medlock Leisure Centre One main new pool. Parent and Tot drop-in sessions with toys for under fives Fri 11.15am-12noon (term time) and Sun 12-1pm (£3.60 for adults, 90p for tots). Swimming lessons start from four and a half. Aquanatal sessions Tues 10-11am (term time) where a midwife is on hand.
Adult £3.60, Under 16 £1.80, Under fives 90p. Family ticket (two adults three children) £7.50.
Garden Fold Way, Droylsden, Tameside M43 7XU
Tel: 0161 370 3070
www.tamesidesporttrust.com
Hyde Leisure Pool Waves, bubbles, geysers, flume, lazy river plus more. Hyde is a free form pool where you can walk into the water from a gentle sloping beach-like approach, which is fantastic for toddlers. The centre is home to Wally Walrus. Wally sessions are exclusively for those with pre-school children under five. The emphasis is on basic water skills whilst playing games and having a singalong. Sessions (term time) Tues 1-2.30pm, Fri 10-11.15am. Ducklings Wed 6-7pm £4. Wally's Saturday Club is 9.15-10.45am. Cost £4 (one adult and one child), under fives £1.10.
Adult £5, under 19 £2.70, under fives £1.10. Family ticket (two adults three children) £12.90.
Walker Lane, Hyde, Tameside SK14 5PL
Tel: 0161 368 4057
www.tamesidesporttrust.com

WIGAN

Under 16s swim free if you register for a Lifestyle card.
Ashton Leisure Centre Closed for refurbishment, opening Spring 2010. Call or check website for details.
Old Road, Ashton-in-Makerfield, Wigan WN4 9TP
Tel: 01942 720826 www.wlct.org
Hindley Pool Surestart runs drop-in Parent and Toddler sessions Tues 1-1.30pm and Fri 9.15-9.45am. Cost £1.55.
Swimming lessons available from age four. A 10-week course costs £37.
Adult £2.95
Borsdane Road, Hindley WN2 3QN
Tel: 01942 255401 www.wlct.org
Howe Bridge Sports Centre Two pools. Parent and Toddler session Thurs 9am-12noon and Fri 1.15-3.15pm. Cost £3.10. Swimming lessons from age four (10-week course £39).
Adult £3.10
Eckersley Fold Lane, Atherton, Manchester M46 0PJ Tel: 01942 870403 www.wlct.org
Leigh Indoor Sports Centre One main pool. Parent and Toddler sessions Tues and Thurs 1.30-2.30pm. Swimming lessons available from age five (10-week course £39).

Ivy Bank Swimming School, Prestwich

Privately owned and managed, and looking from the outside like a bungalow with a conservatory attached, Ivy Bank is a small pool (7m by 3.5m) that can be hired out for parties or simply by a group of parents who want a pool to themselves. There is also a comprehensive schedule of swimming lessons from three years old that cost £42 for seven lessons (run daily after school and at weekends 9.30am-12noon). Also Aquanauts runs kiddie classes from birth upwards at Ivy Bank Mon and Fri (www.aquanauts.uk.com).

If you would like to hire out the pool privately it costs around £6 for two adults and one child. For two adults and two children it's £7.50 – there is no lifeguard.

If you want to hire the pool for a party it's around £40 for one hour with a lifeguard and inflatables. There are two changing cubicles by the side of the pool (with a toilet in each) but there is no baby-changing facility so you will need to bring your own mats.

The diary for bookings is kept just one week in advance so plenty of scope to get a slot! Parents who've been really rave about it, saying it's absolutely perfect for toddlers.

A great place to book all year round but a real treat in the summer months! Vending machine available.
31 Grosvenor Street, Prestwich, Manchester M25 1ES
Tel: 0161 773 2629

Adult £3.05
Sale Way, Leigh Sports Village, Leigh, Lancashire WN7 4JY
Tel: 01942 487800 www.wlct.org
Tyldesley Pool One main pool. Parent and Toddler sessions Tues and Thurs 16-10.30am (£1.65). Swimming available from two years old (a 10-week course costs £39). Parents are in the water.
Adult £3.05
Castle Street, Tyldesley, Manchester M29 8EG
Tel: 01942 882722 www.wlct.org

Shopping directory

Taking the stress out of shopping, here's a guide to the best places to go in and around the city.

Shopping for toddlers

Antz In Yer Pantz
Designerwear including Emile et Rose, Sarah Louise and Ben Sherman. There is a play area to keep children entertained.
38 High Street, Northwich, Cheshire CW9 5BE
Tel:01606 45555 www.antzinyerpantz.co.uk

Bambini
Collection includes Lili Gaufrette, Mayoral and Monnalisa, as well as stocking suits, ties and shirts for boys and a variety of accessories including hats and scarves.
51a Leicester Road, Salford M7 4AS
Tel: 0161 792 2233

Bee Bee's
Kids continental designer fashion clothing and footwear from newborn babies to toddlers to teens including Cocobrillo, Cakewalk, Lily Rio, Me Too and Ning Nang.
54 North John Street, St Helens WA10 2JT
Tel: 01744 25515 www.beebeeskids.co.uk

Bossy Boots
A well-stocked shop with such labels as DKNY, Diesel, Pampolina, Juicy Couture and Miss Sixty. There is a small table and chairs set for children to play at with more entertainment planned in the future.
364 Chorley Old Road, Bolton BL1 6AG
Tel: 01204 494 749
www.bossybootskidz.com

Bimbi Pazzi
Sells Italian designer children's clothing for 0-10 year olds as well as gifts for special occasions such as christenings and birthdays.
Unit 4 The Paddock, Wilmslow Road, Handforth, Cheshire SK9 3HQ
Tel: 01625 529 231 www.bimbipazzi.co.uk

Button Nose
Designer childrenswear from newborns to 14 years. Labels include Catitimini, Scotch&Soda, Monnalisa, Jottum and Ollie.
10 The Bramhall Centre, Stockport, Cheshire SK7 1AW
Tel: 0161 440 7667 www.buttonnose.co.uk

Cheeky Chums Premature Baby Clothes Store
A neonatal specialist superstore, providing everyday clothing and other necessities such as nappies for babies weighing as little as 1lb.
46 Broadway, Hindley, Wigan WN2 4JP
Tel: 01942 254 259
www.cheekychumsonline.co.uk

Em & Ted
A clothing agency constantly stocking new items, including childrenswear and toys from the Diddle range.
63 Market Street, Chapel-en-le-Frith, Derbyshire SK23 0HP
Tel: 01298 814 479 www.emandted.co.uk

Growing Trendz
This fantastic and friendly shop has an amazing amount of choice of designerwear from Alex and Oh Baby London to Coco, Marese, Sarah Louise and much more. Stock is constantly updated and the website is both easy to use and efficient.
As well as clothes and dancewear, Growing Trendz also specialises in beautiful christening and communion wear by designer Angels and Fishes. Worth a mention is that it stocks my personal favourite babyshoe brand – Robeez – the cutest fur-trimmed boot you'll find!
■ **Check out Growing Trendz's 10% discount offer exclusive to Babies in the City readers on page 15.**
1 Wilmslow Road, Cheadle, Cheshire SK8 1DW Tel: 0161 428 6482
www.growingtrendz.co.uk

Hansel and Gretal
Located in Bolton town centre, Hansel and Gretal stocks fine children's clothing for ages 0-12 years by designers Christian Dior, Monnalisa, Elle, Bench Kids, Armani, D&G and Cavalli.
Unit 4 Marsden House, Marsden Road, Bolton BL12JT Tel: 01204 373 888
www.hgclothing.co.uk

HoneyBeez Childrenswear
A spacious, bright and colourful shop with a central play area that includes books, toys and a TV. Stock includes a broad range of designerwear as well as gifts and accessories for newborns and children. There is also a small selection of 'earth friendly, natural personal care products' for both babies and mums.
728-730 Oldham Road, Failsworth, Manchester M35 9FD
Tel: 0161 688 9444 www.hbkidz.com

JoJo Maman Bebe
One of the finest children's shops out there, JoJo Maman Bebe never fails to deliver high quality goods – from quirky and adorable babywear to nursery

Junior Originals: designerwear with styles and prices to suit everyone.

Growing Trendz: junior designerwear.

essentials, beautiful children's clothes and imaginative bedroom collections, as well as lots more.

Personal favourites this season are the polarfleece all-in-ones, the classic Breton striped dresses and the really cute denim collection. If you're after a gift or just the basics like pyjamas and wellies – look no further. JoJo Maman in Hale is a joy to shop in and the website is first class.

■ **JoJo Maman Bebe has teamed up with Babies in the City to offer readers 15% discount. See page 19.**
180-182 Ashley Road, Hale, Altrincham WA15 9SF Tel: 0161 926 8450
www.jojomamanbebe.co.uk
Also in Knutsford

Junior Originals

Offers a stunning collection of designerwear with DKNY, Jean Bourget, Pampolina and Berlingot to name a few. There are styles and prices to suit everyone, with friendly staff on hand to help. There is also giftware and pre-walking shoes by Pediped.

Quite uniquely, upstairs you'll find the cafe 'Retro Lounge' providing coffee, cakes and light bites. Shopping and lunch combined in perfect harmony! Ample free parking close by.

■ **See page 81 for a fantastic 10% off at Junior Originals.**
5 Holcombe Mews, Bolton Road West (A676), Bury BL0 9RN Tel: 01204 885888
www.juniororiginals.com

BOOK SHOPS

Badger Books
22 Keirby Walk, Burnley,
Lancashire BB11 2DG
Tel: 01282 421 334
www.badger-books.co.uk

Bay Tree Books
96 High Street, Glossop, Derbyshire
SK13 8BB Tel: 01457 862 512
www.baytreeglossop.com

Chorlton Bookshop
506 Wilbraham Road, Chorlton,
Manchester M21 9AW
Tel: 0161 881 6374

Colne Bookshop
4 Market Street, Colne, Lancashire
BB8 0HR Tel: 01282 871 440
www.bookshopcolne.co.uk

Corner Bookshop
Thomas's Court, Garstang, Lancashire
PR3 1LL Tel: 01995 602 910

Curiosity Bookshop
52 High Street, Runcorn, Cheshire
WA7 1AW Tel: 01928 575956
www.curiositybookshop.co.uk

E J Morten (Booksellers)
6 Warburton Street, Didsbury,
Manchester M20 6WA
Tel: 0161 445 7629

Forget-Me-Not Bookshop
Unit 8, CPS Centre, Culcheth,
Glazebury, Warrington, Cheshire
WE3 3EH Tel: 01925 765187

George Kelsall
The Bookshop, 22 Church Street,
Littleborough, Greater Manchester
OL15 9AA
Tel: 01706 370244

George Street Books
14-16 George Street, Glossop,
Derbyshire SK13 8AY
Tel: 01457 853 413
www.georgestreetbooks.co.uk

Hale Book Shop
193 Ashley Road, Hale
Tel: 0161 928 1494
www.halebookshop.co.uk

Nantwich Bookshop
46 High Street, Nantwich, Cheshire
CW5 5AS Tel: 01270 611665
www.nantwichbookshop.co.uk

Pam's Bookend
67 Queen Street, Great Harwood,
Lancashire BB6 7QP
Tel: 01254 882477

Razma Reads
794 Wilmslow Road, Didsbury,
Manchester M20 6UH
Tel: 0161 438 6811
www.razmareads.com

Simply Books
228 Moss Lane, Bramhall,
Cheshire SK7 1BD
Tel: 0161 439 1436
www.simplybooks.info

Sweetens Bookshop
86 Deansgate, Bolton, Lancashire
BL1 1BD Tel: 01204 528 457

Thackeray's Books
48-50 Manchester Road, Denton,
Manchester M34 3LE
Tel: 0161 320 4220

The Bookshop (Marple) Ltd
70 Stockport Road, Marple
SK6 6AB Tel: 0161 427 4921

Waterstones
On the second floor of this centrally located book shop there are baby-changing facilities next to Costa Coffee. Costa will also supply hot water for heating up baby food and there are both highchairs and lift access.
91 Deansgate, Manchester M3 2BW
Tel: 0161 837 3000
www.waterstones.com
Also at Manchester Arndale, Altrincham, Bolton, Bury, Knutsford, Oldham, Stockport Merseyway, The Trafford Centre, Wilmslow and Wigan.
See your local Waterstones for Mummy Mornings – regular informal talks or discussions by childcare experts.

Shopping directory

Just Kids
Designerwear for 0-10 years plus footwear and fitting, including Mayoral, Barbara Farder, Lelli Kelly shoes and Hush Puppies. There is a set of table and chairs for children and changing rooms.
8 Church Street, Frodsham, Cheshire WA6 7EB Tel: 01928 735 550

Kids Couture
A small, friendly shop for 0-12 years with great collections from Catimini, Little Darlings, Confetti and Magilla, amongst others.
28 Church Street, Littleborough OL15 0RD Tel: 01706 838448 www.kids-couture.co.uk

Kids Exchange Agency
Selling little used designer clothing that is still in excellent condition. Kids Exchange also holds everything else you could need for your baby and child from used Bugaboos through to stairgates. A veritable treasure trove!
26 Manchester Road, Wilmslow, Cheshire SK9 1BG Tel: 01625 537664 www.kids-exchange.co.uk

Lily's Wardrobe
A children's boutique buying and selling new and recycled designer clothing, shoes, toys, nursery equipment, furniture, customised gifts and more. Fully kitted out to make shopping with little ones bearable – buggy friendly layout, baby changing facilities, a fantastic play area decorated with a circus mural with ball pool and a television to watch movies.
1A Kingsway South, Latchford Village, Warrington WA4 1LT Tel: 01925 638140 www.lilyswardrobe.co.uk

Little Trendies
This shop is child friendly, with a dedicated play area for children to relax and entertain themselves in. Designers include Emile et Rose, Pampolina, Deux Par Deux, Quiksilver, Ollie and Brum.
14 High Street, Standish, Wigan WN6 0HL Tel: 01257 472 700 www.littletrendies.co.uk

Mamas & Papas
You'll probably already be familiar with this brand's products from when you were getting ready to have your baby, but M&P is worth re-visiting as it has a very good children's clothing range and well-designed educational toys with great walkers and push-alongs. It also offers a useful car-seat fitting service.
Mamas & Papas, Manchester Fort Shopping Park, Cheetham Hill Road, Manchester M8 8EP Tel: 0845 268 2000 www.mamasandpapas.co.uk

Marwoods Baby and Childrenswear
Designerwear for 0-8 years plus clothing for christenings and other special occasions. Established for 25 years.
Market Hall, Albion Street, Oldham OL1 3BG Tel: 0161 620 3979 www.marwoodschildrenswear.co.uk

Nino Kids
Designer labels for boys and girls aged 0-12 years. Collections

---

Arnouts Family Shoes
165 Fog Lane, Didsbury, Manchester M20 6FJ Tel: 0161 445 3251

Bear Feet
484a Bury Old Road, Prestwich, Manchester M25 1NL Tel: 0161 772 0600 www.bearfeet.co.uk

Charles Clinkard
25 Regent Crescent, The Trafford Centre, Manchester M17 8AR Tel: 0845 0179 062 www.charlesclinkard.co.uk

Hands
291 Buxton Road, Stockport, Cheshire SK2 7NS Tel: 0161 483 3183

Happy Feet
12 Minshull Street, Knutsford WA16 6LG Tel: 01565 652752

Little Toe Peep
42 Dale Street, Milnrow, Rochdale, Lancashire OL16 4HS Tel: 01706 868 221 www.littletoepeep.co.uk

Little Wanderers
144-146 Tonge Moor Road, Bolton BL2 2DP Tel: 01204 522533 www.littlewanderers.co.uk

0-16 Footsteps
92 Water Lane, Wilmslow, Cheshire SK9 5BB Tel: 01625 538863

Pitter Patter Children's Shoes
1 St Thomas Parade, Lees, Oldham OL4 6DA Tel: 0161 627 1506 www.pitterpattershoes.co.uk

Teejays
550 Chorley Old Road, Bolton BL1 6AB Tel: 01204 841 464

This Little Piggy
Unit 2, 289a Chester Road, Hartford, Northwich, Cheshire CW8 1QL Tel: 01606 76735

Tiger Feet Shoes
3 Bramhall Shopping Centre, Bramhall, Cheshire SK7 1AW Tel: 0161 439 4393 297 London Road, Hazel Grove, Cheshire SK7 4PS Tel: 0161 439 4393 www.tigerfeetshoes.co.uk

Tip Toes
796a Edenfield Road, Norden, Rochdale OL12 7RB Tel: 01706 750322

Whittakers The Shoemakers
Located on the main street in the town centre, Whittakers has been selling shoes to families around Bolton for

Whittakers stocks the largest collection of shoes in the north west.

generations. Stocking the largest collection of shoes in the north west, experienced and knowledgeable staff provide an expert fitting service. There's a wide selection of brands to choose from, including Clarks, Start-rite, Kickers and Lelli Kelly. The children's department downstairs is nice and big and also has lots of toys for the children to play with. Pay and display car parking is close by. Well worth a special trip.
108-110 Deansgate, Bolton, Lancashire BL1 1BD Tel: 01204 533931

SHOPPING DIRECTORY

Pixie: the place to go for a brilliant selection of designer clothes and gifts.

include Catimini, Pampolina, Timberland, DKNY, Joules, Kenzo, Room Seven, Coco and Bob & Blossom. There is a gift service and mail order available.

35 Millfield Lane, Tarporley, Cheshire CW6 0BA Tel: 01829 733 317
www.ninokids.co.uk

Petites Mode

Stock mainly includes schoolwear and specialist clothing for christenings and communions.

9 Tatton Road, Sale, Cheshire M33 7EB
Tel: 0161 973 4231

Pixie

A gorgeous designer childrenswear boutique selling favourite names such as Imps&Elfs, Toffee Moon, Miniature, I Love Gorgeous, Timberland and No Added Sugar. Pixie stocks a terrific selection of clothes from baby to 10 years. It's the perfect place to pick up a new baby gift too – cashmere blankets, hats and cute babygrows are available all year round.

For 2010, Pixie is expanding into contemporary womenswear with labels such as NoaNoa, Petit Bateau and maternitywear Seraphine. Pixie is also a stockist of Kidsmill – beautiful, hand-built nursery furniture.

■ £50 of Pixie vouchers with Kidsmill purchase. See page 11.

6 Albert Hill Street, Didsbury Village, Manchester M20 6RF Tel: 0161 445 5230
www.pixiechildrenswear.com

Plum

Exquisite boutique selling exclusive designer labels for children as well as having a comprehensive maternitywear section on the upper floor.

120 Ashley Road, Hale, Cheshire WA14 2UN
Tel: 0161 941 1818 www.plum-hale.co.uk

Precious Little Treasures

Very pretty shop selling great gifts for babies and children with leading brands such as Little Shrimp, Trousselier and Noonoo.

Swan Courtyard, Clitheroe, Lancashire BB7 2DQ Tel: 01200 426123
www.preciouslittletreasures.co.uk

Puddleducks

Established in 1994, this shop offers baby and childrenswear, accessories, gifts and toys as well as beautiful christening outfits.

125 High Street, Uppermill, Oldham OL3 6BD Tel: 01457 875 769
www.puddleduckskids.co.uk

Rachel Antoni Ltd

This shop focuses very much on the 'family product', stocking a wide range of both maternitywear and childrenswear from 0-16 years as well as nursery equipment, prams and toys.

37 Gloucester Road, Gee Cross, Hyde SK14 5JG Tel: 0161 366 0375
www.rachelantoni.co.uk

Spruced Goose

A great range of designer baby and girls' boutique clothing, along with some of the more unusual and funky designer boys clothes as well. Brands include names such as Eliane et Lena, Taille O, D'Arcy Brown and Agatha Ruiz de la Prada Baby. Spruced Goose has a very good website too.

1 Moss Lane, Whitefield, Manchester M45 6QE Tel: 0161 796 8096
www.sprucedgoose.com

Teeny Boppers

Launched in 2004 by a mum frustrated at the lack of boys' clothing available, Teeny Boppers is crammed full of designers such as IndiJo, Miniman, Berlingot and Feu Follet. It caters for birth-16 years.

53 High Street West, Glossop SK13 8AZ
Tel: 01457 863370 www.teenyboppers.biz

Ten Little Monkeys

Holds a collection of design-led childrenswear that includes Diesel, No Added Sugar, Ollie and a personal favourite of mine, Dandy Star. The product range caters for the smallest baby up to kids aged 12. Ten Little Monkeys also stocks the gorgeous BabyBloch ballerina baby shoes.

46 Parsonage Green, Wilmslow, Cheshire SK9 1HT Tel: 01625 418 782
www.tenlittlemonkeys.co.uk

Tiddleywinks

A unique shop that specialises in hand-crafted gifts, such as personalised babygrows and T-shirts (all hand embroidered), photo frames and door plaques.

Blakemere Craft Centre, Chester Road, Sandiway, Cheshire CW8 2EB
Tel: 01606 889 558 www.tiddleywinks.biz

Tillyflop's

Stock includes exclusive baby and childrenswear for 0-16 years and has a small play area in the corner of the shop.

84 Rochdale Road, Royton, Oldham OL2 6QF
Tel: 0161 785 9211 www.tillyflops.co.uk

Totos

A lovely shop with a huge stock of baby and children's designerwear for 0-14 years such as Coco, Little Darlings, Marese and Pampolina. There is also a large collection of toys including Steiff teddy bears. And a new addition coming in March 2010 – Little Legs Shoes – opening within Totos.

5 Grafton Street, Altrincham, Cheshire WA14 1DU
Tel: 0161 928 7657 www.totos.co.uk

SHOPPING DIRECTORY

Shopping directory

CITY CENTRE

Boots
There is a baby room on the first floor which includes a breastfeeding room, changing facilities and a bottle warmer. There are no customer toilets.
Boots, 32 Market Street, Manchester M1 1PL Tel: 0161 832 6533
www.boots.com

House of Fraser (Kendals)
Parking is on site – though a bit pricey. There's a child-friendly restaurant (see cafés on page 74) and the children's clothing department and toy shop situated on the 6th floor are lovely. Baby-changing is on the 3rd and 6th floor – the latter of these has three steps up to it.
House of Fraser, Deansgate, Manchester M60 3AU Tel: 0161 832 3414
www.houseoffraser.co.uk

Manchester Arndale Centre
There's plenty of baby-changing, nursing chairs and parent and toddler toilets. Bottle-warming facilities can be found in the Foodchain.
Manchester Arndale, Manchester M4 3AQ Tel: 0161 833 9851
www.manchesterarndale.com

JOHN LEWIS

John Lewis at Cheadle is fairly unbeatable. The baby-changing facilities are always spotlessly clean, there are free nappy and wipe dispensers, bottle-warming facilities and nursing chairs. The café welcomes mums and tots and the staff will help you with trays and provide bottle-warmers. Children's meals are available or a free baby jar with an adult's meal. They will even loan you a pushchair if you've forgotten yours.
John Lewis, Wilmslow Road, Cheadle, Cheshire SK8 3BZ Tel: 0161 491 4914
www.johnlewis.com

THE TRAFFORD CENTRE

The Trafford Centre is pretty good if you have to go shopping with the kids. For £2.50 an hour, you can hire a Little Tikes Car Buggy and push them round (£20 deposit). Security wristbands (free) and pushchairs to borrow (ID and a £20 cash deposit) are also available from customer services.

Near John Lewis you'll find the 'Jumping Fountain' – which shoots huge jets of water 50ft in the air. Every day at 1pm and 3pm you can see Barney Bear – a large teddy driving a red car. You'll find face painting in The Orient restaurant area, and on the ground floor, a crèche and play area. For 0-10 year olds, this includes two ball pools, two wavy slides, climbing nets, tube crawls and rope swings. The crèche is available for 2-8 year olds.

All Trafford Centre toilet areas include parent and child toilets and unisex baby-changing facilities, as well as vending machines selling nappies and a breast-feeding room. The following shops also have excellent facilities:

Boots has a dedicated baby room at the back of the shop on the ground floor. You'll find bottle-warming machines, baby-changing stations, nursing chairs and a children's toilet.
Debenhams On the first floor, there are changing facilities in the toilets. The Style Café also on the first floor has a baby food and bottle-warming station (including a microwave). They sell Cow & Gate baby jars and children's deli-boxes.
John Lewis has a dedicated parent room near the toy area on the ground floor. You'll find a bottle-warmer, screened areas for baby feeding, changing stations, a nappy dispenser (£1.50 each), a drinking fountain and a parent and child toilet.
Selfridge's Next to Paperchase on the first floor, there are two baby-changing rooms.
The Trafford Centre: Mon-Fri 10am-10pm, Sat 10am-8pm, Sun 12-6pm.
The Trafford Centre, Junction 9 or 10 off the M60, Manchester M17 8AA
Tel: 0161 749 1510 www.traffordcentre.co.uk
Crèche and play area Tel: 0161 746 9000

TOY SHOPS

Busy Bee Toy Shop, Chorlton
Britain's first toy shop cooperative with a wide range of toys suitable from birth including Playskool, Fisher Price and Viking toys. It sells the very cute Granimals range of knitted toys which make ideal new baby gifts.
517 Wilbraham Road, Manchester M21 0UF Tel: 0161 881 5838
www.busybeetoyshop.co.uk

Forget-Me-Not, Culcheth
Specialises in leading brands of traditional toys and games and best-selling books. Great toys ranging from Lego Ben 10 through to Sophie la giraffe teether toy.
CPS Centre, Culcheth, Cheshire WE3 3EH Tel: 01925 765187
www.forgetmenottoyandbookshop.co.uk

Little Nut Tree Toys, Wilmslow
The focus here is on eductional toys, spanning key stages from birth to ten. Plus a selection of party and baby gifts.
48 Parsonage Green, Wilmslow SK9 1HT Tel: 01625 525382
www.littlenuttreetoys.co.uk

Little Treasures, Ramsbottom
As well as a great range in toys, Little Treasures specialises in beautiful bespoke children's furniture made by owner Jamie, member of the Guild of Master Craftsmen.
Little Treasures, 47 Bolton Street, Ramsbottom, Lancashire BL0 9HU
Tel: 01706 828644
www.yourlittletreasures.co.uk

Monkey Puzzle, Chorlton
Stocks brands of toys sourced mainly from Europe. The shelves are crammed with puppets, wooden train sets and accessories that are compatible with the big brands, marble runs, a good selection of 'pocket money' toys, learning aids and sticker books.
Monkey Puzzle, 93 Manchester Road, Chorlton, Manchester M21 9GA
48 Parsonage Green, Wilmslow SK9 1HT
Tel 01618620100
www.monkeypuzzletoys.com

My Wendy House, Stockport

Stocks mainly toys and a wide range of accessories, including dressing-up clothes from Cuckoo, Vogue and Treasure Trove, and Phil and Ted pushchairs.

24-26 Little Underbank, Stockport, Cheshire SK1 1JT Tel: 0161 480 5783
www.mywendyhouse.com

Oklahoma, Northern Quarter, Manchester

Primarily a gift shop aimed at adults, there are also lots for little ones including wind-up donkeys, kitsch lunch boxes, Whoopee cushions and Fisher Price retro toys.

Oklahoma, 74-76 High Street, Manchester M4 1ES Tel: 0161 834 1136

Rumpus, Didsbury

A pleasure to shop in – manager Louise is always ready to help steer you in the direction of the perfect present. Rumpus stocks a really brilliant range of toys for babies up to eight years. The Whoozit range for babies make perfect presents, alongside Brio pull-alongs and the always

Rumpus: labelled a top independent retailer by The Guardian.

gorgeous wheelybugs – probably the best ride-along toy ever! There are a variety of 'pocket money' toys starting from 20p as well as kites, puzzles and games.

With brands like Playmobil, Sylvannian Family, Orchard and Pintoy you'll definitely find what you want here. There's a craft table and Brio rail set for children to play with whilst you browse. Included in The Guardian's list of top independent retailers.

Rumpus, 2 Albert Hill Street, Didsbury, Manchester M20 6RF
Tel: 0161 445 1097
www.rumpus-toys.co.uk

Toto's, Altrincham

A children's clothes shop that has a large range of toys as well, including favourites such as Steiff bears, Playmobil, Sylvanian Families and Galt.

Toto's, 5 Grafton Street, Altrincham WA14 1DH
Tel: 0161 928 7657 www.totos.co.uk

Toys & Tales, Bramhall

A fairly large shop stocking toys from birth and brands such as Playmobil, Sylvanian Families, Thomas and Steiff. There's a great collection of dressing-up clothes, books, jigsaws and musical instruments to choose from (including a very good range of guitars). There's a sofa in one area with toy tables for the children to play at. Plus beautiful art canvases and prints for children painted by owner Kaye.

Toys & Tales, 44-46 Bramhall Lane South, Bramhall, Stockport, Cheshire SK7 1AH
Tel: 0161 439 6002
www.toysandtales.com

Traditional Toys, Bolton

Specialising in timeless wooden toys, such as rocking horses, Italian hand-made rag dolls, the Paddington Bear collection, Beatrix Potter products, wooden dolls houses, trikes and trailors.

Traditional Toys, The Last Drop Village, Bolton BL7 9PZ Tel: 01204 597862
www.traditionaltoyshop.co.uk

Mums directory

It's great finding things to do with babies and toddlers, but there are lots of other elements to parenting that could use a mention as well, some essential, some educational – and some fun.

Mums directory

Buggyfit is a fun, energising outdoor exercise class designed specifically for new mums. It is an hour long and usually involves a two or three mile route. Classes start with a moderate warm-up walk, moving into a power walk or run along with exercises to strengthen and tone specific muscles.
Sessions cost from £4.50 and classes are held in Altrincham, Appleton, Chorlton, Didsbury, Northwich and Rochdale
Tel: 01844 202 081 www.buggyfit.co.uk

Bumps and Bashes Bumps and Bashes is aimed at parents of babies and children and is a brilliant course (just three hours long) that is all about helping you plan for an emergency and making sure you don't feel helpless in the event of something going wrong. I learnt how to carry out CPR, what to do with burns and scalds, about choking and poisoning and lots more.

A nice touch is that at the end of the class, you're given a paediatric first aid handbook and a laminated emergency contact sheet to take home. I think Bumps and Bashes is a great concept and wholeheartedly recommend it to any parent. Why not get together a few friends – Kate will come to your house with her manikins and teach you in-situ.
Regular courses at various locations £34 for a class; £175 for a party of six (each additional person £20, maximum eight).
Tel: 07966 315699 www.bumpsandbashes.com

Cottontails Nappy Laundry Service delivers freshly laundered pure cotton nappies to your door at the same time and on the same day each week, collecting the soiled nappies for laundering. Several local authorities allow you to try the nappy laundry service free of charge for a trial month, contact Cottontails direct to see if you qualify.
Greater Manchester, Cheshire and Lancashire. Cost is £9.25 per week/£40 per month.
Tel: 0161 708 8223 www.cottontails.co.uk

Greater Manchester Fire Service offers a free home fire risk assessment service that everyone should take up. You simply book an appointment and a week later three firemen arrive along with a fire engine to your house, you can just imagine my

little boy's face! After a few questions, the crew then inspect your house and install brand new (free) smoke alarms wherever necessary. They also advise you on an escape plan in case of a fire and the whole thing takes less than half-an-hour.
Tel: 0800 555 815 www.manchesterfire.gov.uk

Glofamily offers a unique range of pre and postnatal fitness classes and childbirth preparation courses in Manchester and Cheshire. Classes include Saturday morning Aquanatal and Postnatal Aqua; they are great fun and the postnatal is surprisingly hard! At the other end of the spectrum, 'Bikini Bootcamp' will burn calories and improve your cardiovascular fitness. It also offers an optional 'weigh in' and food diary to take home.

Glofamily also runs childbirth preparation courses – a particular favourite is the Next Time Round course. An opportunity to work out what went wrong the first time so it doesn't happen again!
Tel: 0844 800 7380 info@glofamily.com www.glofamily.com

Heaven Spa Based at the Hilton hotel in Beetham Tower, central Manchester and Didsbury, Heaven

Glofamily: a range of pre and post-natal fitness classes.

Spa offers special packages for pre and post-natal luxury pampering. You can enjoy Mello Mama, Lighten Up and The Yummy Tummy. Or if your body needs some serious attention, there's treatments called Boot Camp for Bums, Tums and Boobs!
Heaven Spa, 115 Lapwing Lane, Didsbury M20 6UR Tel: 0161 448 8786
Heaven Spa, 2nd Floor, Hilton Manchester, Deansgate M3 4LQ Tel: 0161 870 1789
www.heaven-spa.co.uk

MumStuff Run by a small team of mums and dedicated to all things 'Mum', this is a wonderful website company specialising in gifts and essentials for mums-to-be and new mums. Take a look at the Mama Bijoux disque bracelets, which can be personalised on both sides with anything you wish such as a name and birth date.
Tel: 0845 0090607 www.mumstuff.co.uk

The National Childbirth Trust provides expert information and trusted practical and emotional support through a fantastic network of groups run by volunteer mums and dads. Each local branch has a busy social calendar for parents with babies of all ages; from days out with other families to Bumps and Babies Groups, Cheeky Monkeys Tea Parties and Nearly New Sales. The NCT also has a pregnancy, birth and breastfeeding helpline which you do not need to be a member to call.
Tel: 0300 33 00 770 www.nct.org.uk

Pink Spaghetti is a home PA Service that is designed to help busy parents by giving them back time. They do the jobs you just don't have time for, such as researching, booking, suggesting, shopping, planning, and reminding.
Tel: 0844 504 7465 www.pink-spaghetti.co.uk

Pramactive The slogan claims 'a workout for you…and baby comes too'. Pramactive is a fun, sociable and effective outdoor postnatal exercise class that incorporates an aerobic workout using the pram as well as park equipment such as benches, railings and hills plus resistance bands, hand weights and boxing gloves!

The sessions have a strong emphasis on mums working at their own pace but having the opportunity to chat, make new friends and have fun.
Chorlton £4.50 per lesson.
Tel Claire Currie on 0771 3183522 www.pramactive.co.uk

Riverford When expecting child number three and with the prospect of doing another edition of Babies in the City, I had to get fit, healthy and more organised. I started getting Riverford food boxes just after my youngest was born and they are great. Knowing that a fresh veggie box is arriving at the end of the week means at least one job is done. Riverford reckons its boxes are 19 per cent cheaper than the supermarkets and that doesn't include the free delivery! The quality of food is exceptional and you can change your order online up to 24 hours before delivery. Ted's already four months old and with weening on the horizon, they will be perfect for all that pureeing.
Tel: 0845 6002311 www.riverford.co.uk/stockley

SureStart is based in children's centres throughout Manchester. Families can source local information and have access to free services including early education and childcare, advice on parenting, local childcare options, health screening, health visitor services, breast-feeding support and help with getting back to work. For your nearest SureStart centre please check the website.
www.direct.gov.uk/surestart

The well-equipped crèche at Virgin Active.

VIRGIN ACTIVE

Virgin Active health clubs are brilliantly geared towards families and are all about making it easy for parents using the facilities – it's great.

First and foremost is the Crèche – otherwise known as Club V. There's a separate room for the under threes (they can start at six weeks) – it's all quite newly refurbished so it's very clean and bright with carpeted floors, plenty of toys, activity gyms, cots and bouncy chairs. The staff ratio is 3:1 and the maximum amount of time you can leave your baby is two hours.

The larger room at Club V is given over to those aged three and over. Again it's a stimulating environment with plenty of games, a kitchen corner, train table, art and craft table and three wall-mounted plasma screens with playstation and Wii for the older kids. There's even a small room with soft play equipment in!

The classes on offer are too many to name but to give you a flavour: for the younger members there's 'Funky Monkey Dribblers' – a session taken by FA coaches where kids learn the basics of ball control and dribbling; 'Funky Monkey Mess' – arts and crafts sessions; and 'Funky Monkey Movers' – where little ones dance along to songs like 'Ring a Ring o' Roses' and 'Incy Wincey Spider'. For older kids there are classes such as 'Barmy Army' assault course, Cheerleading, Lacrosse and Spanish Club. These are included within the membership fee and take place all week.

A final mention should be about the swimming facilities – there are two pools at Virgin, one especially for the kids with inflatables and floats to play with. After all the activity, you can hang out at V-Café, which is fully equipped with a kids' menu, comfy sofas, television, computers and a few toys as well. All told, Virgin Active is very impressive!
Crèche prices (you do need to be a member of Virgin Active): 1hr £4.25, 1 1/2 hrs £6.40, 2hrs £8.50, 10hr pass £35. For members' children under 3, a one-off yearly payment of £5 entitles them to unlimited swimming. For children over 3, £15 per month entitles them to 2hrs free childcare per day, a 1hr class per day and unlimited swimming.
■ **Quote Babies in the City when you join Virgin Active for a special discount on your membership**
Virgin Active, Unit 8, Parrswood Entertainment Centre, Wilmslow Road, Manchester M20 5PG
Tel: 0161 249 5600 www.virginactive.co.uk

Riverford: healthy food boxes delivered to your door.

USEFUL INFORMATION

Public transport

Greater Manchester has one of the friendliest public transport networks in the country. If you're daunted by the idea of taking young children on buses, trains or trams then hopefully the following provided by GMPTE will get you on the buses!

Travelling in and around Greater Manchester

On weekdays we recommend that you start your journey after the morning rush hour – after 9.30am – when services are less busy and there is more space to carry a pushchair. Train and Metrolink tram tickets cost less at 'off-peak' times which are after 9.30am on weekdays and all day on Saturday, Sunday and public holidays. Children under five travel free and if you're over 60 and taking the grandchildren on a day trip, it doesn't get cheaper than this.

BUSES

Buses are particularly handy because there's probably a route and a stop near where you live. Modern buses are child-friendly with wide doors and space to store your buggy. If the bus is busy you might need to fold your buggy.

On newer buses, the driver can lower the bus to pavement level to let you get on and off easily. Accessible buses are shown in bus timetables with a wheelchair symbol.

When you arrive in Manchester city centre there are two main bus stations – at Piccadilly Gardens and Shudehill Interchange. There are also plenty of bus stops convenient for other parts of the city.

As well as single tickets many bus companies offer returns and day tickets that can be used on all the services run by that company – so check with the driver.

TRAINS

Local trains are a great way to travel with many well-located stations in Manchester and other local town centres. Trains are spacious, comfortable and most have toilets and plenty of luggage space.

There are five train stations in the centre of Manchester. Piccadilly and Victoria are the main stations and Oxford Road, Deansgate and Salford Central are served by many local routes. All main stations have baby-changing facilities.

Stations vary in their design and many have ramps for your buggy. Some still have steps plus there is usually a step up onto the train. The rail map on page 122 shows the routes and the stations that have parking and step-free access.

If you don't live near a station, and have to drive, many have free parking. Often the price of a ticket will be less than petrol used to get to both your destination and parking.

If you buy a rail ticket to Manchester centre from a Greater Manchester rail station (see rail map) you can use it to travel free on Metrolink trams in Manchester city centre.

All single and return train tickets cost less at off-peak times. At off-peak times you can also buy a Rail Ranger ticket that lets you travel anywhere in Greater Manchester. An Evening Ranger ticket allows the same travel after 6.30pm. Buy your ticket from the ticket office or from the conductor on the train if this is closed.

Tip – if you already have a rail season ticket between two Greater Manchester rail stations you can use it to travel anywhere in Greater Manchester at weekends and public holidays!
National Rail Enquiries 08457 48 49 50 www.nationalrail.co.uk

METROLINK TRAMS

Greater Manchester's Metrolink trams provide links between Bury, Altrincham or Salford Quays and Eccles to Manchester city centre.

Metrolink was specially designed with easy access so there is no gap between the platform edge and the tram itself and all stops have either a ramp, lift or escalator access. The central section of the tram is an area specifically designed for wheelchairs and prams. The sign on the platform (disabled access) will tell you where to wait to board at the correct doors on the vehicle. Under fives travel free and children over five pay half fare. A Metrolink Saver ticket (previously known as

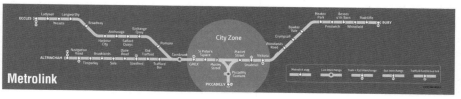

Metrolink

TO FIND OUT ABOUT BUS, TRAIN AND TRAM SERVICES TO EACH VENUE PHONE TRAVELINE ON 0871 200 22 33

USEFUL INFORMATION

Public transport

A new mum takes advantage of the low-level access on the bus and heads in to Manchester on a Saturday afternoon.

MetroMax) lets you make as many tram journeys as you like for a whole day and are available at any time. Buy your ticket from the ticket machine at the Metrolink stop before you make your journey.

Trams run frequently, generally during the day every six minutes on the Bury and Altrincham lines and every 12 minutes on the Eccles line, so there isn't a timetable – simply turn up and wait for the next one to arrive.
Metrolink Customer Services 0161 205 2000 www.metrolink.co.uk

GETTING AROUND MANCHESTER CITY CENTRE

Metroshuttle is the name of the free bus services running around Manchester's city centre streets. There are three circular routes, covering all of the main city centre areas. Metroshuttle buses are low-floor, easy access with a frequency of about every five minutes on Service 1 (orange), every 10 minutes on Service 2 (green) and every 10 minutes on Service 3 (purple).

Metroshuttle links Piccadilly, Victoria, Oxford Road and Deansgate rail stations and many bus and Metrolink tram stops. So whatever the reason for your visit, you can use Metroshuttle to get around, hopping on and off as often as you wish.

All three services run Mon-Sat 7am-7pm. Services 1 and 2 run on Sundays 10am-6pm. (No service 3 on Sundays).

YOUR TICKET TO RIDE

You can buy single or return tickets from the driver on buses, from ticket machines (before you board) on tram stops, or from ticket offices (or on board) for local trains.

COMBINED BUS, TRAIN AND TRAM JOURNEYS

DaySaver tickets let you make as many journeys as you wish at off-peak times using a combination of buses, trains and trams. The DaySaver ticket range lets you choose which combination of travel you want. Buy a DaySaver from the bus driver, station ticket office (or conductor on the train if closed) or tram stop ticket machine before you make your first trip.
Full details are available from www.gmpte.com, GMPTE Travelshops or by phoning Traveline on 0871 200 22 33.

FINDING OUT MORE FROM GMPTE

There are GMPTE Travelshops at all major bus stations in Greater Manchester. Travelshop staff can help you plan your journey for buses, trains and trams; and can provide free timetables, maps and other leaflets you may need. They will also give you independent advice about the best tickets available for your journey.

Information is displayed at most bus stops and tram stops, and at bus and train stations. www.gmpte.com also has all the information you need, complete with a journey planner, maps of the area and timetables for individual services to download.
You can also phone Traveline on 0871 200 22 33 for information and advice about all the services available. The lines are open between 7am and 8pm weekdays and from 8am on weekends and public holidays.

Metroshuttle

MANCHESTER
CITY CENTRE

0   100   200 yards
0   100   200 metres

●●● Road with bus route/bus stop
▬▬▬ Road without bus route
▬▬▬ Motorway
→ One way street
▬◉▬ Train line & station
▬○▬ Metrolink tram line & stop
ℹ Information centre
≈ Bridge
Pedestrianised area or road
Featured building
Park or garden
»»» Water, lock & towpath
Footpath

METROSHUTTLE:
Free buses linking all parts
of the city centre

▬① Route 1 and bus stop
▦① Route 1 peak time only
▬② Route 2 and bus stop
▬③ Route 3 and bus stop

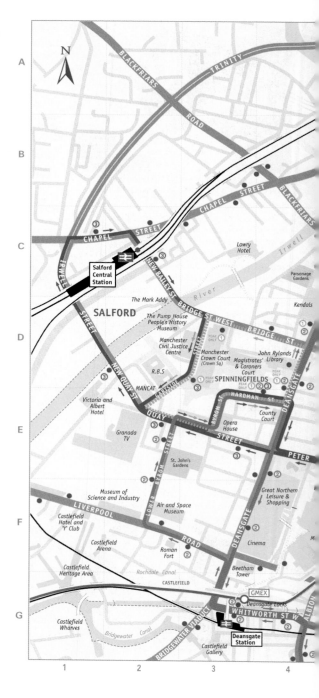

Greater Manchester Rail Network

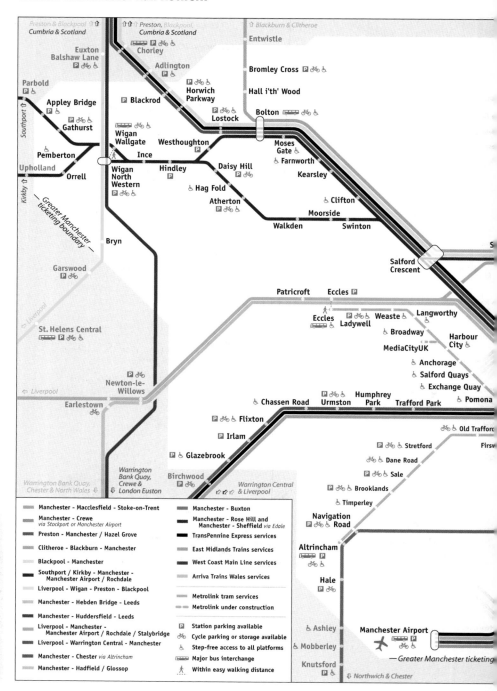

Legend:

- Manchester - Macclesfield - Stoke-on-Trent
- Manchester - Crewe *via Stockport or Manchester Airport*
- Preston - Manchester / Hazel Grove
- Clitheroe - Blackburn - Manchester
- Blackpool - Manchester
- Southport / Kirkby - Manchester - Manchester Airport / Rochdale
- Liverpool - Wigan - Preston - Blackpool
- Manchester - Hebden Bridge - Leeds
- Manchester - Huddersfield - Leeds
- Liverpool - Manchester - Manchester Airport / Rochdale / Stalybridge
- Liverpool - Warrington Central - Manchester
- Manchester - Chester *via Altrincham*
- Manchester - Hadfield / Glossop

- Manchester - Buxton
- Manchester - Rose Hill and Manchester - Sheffield *via Edale*
- TransPennine Express services
- East Midlands Trains services
- West Coast Main Line services
- Arriva Trains Wales services

- Metrolink tram services
- Metrolink under construction

- 🅿 Station parking available
- 🚲 Cycle parking or storage available
- ♿ Step-free access to all platforms
- 🚌 Major bus interchange
- 🚶 Within easy walking distance

TO FIND OUT ABOUT BUS, TRAIN AND TRAM SERVICES TO EACH VENUE PHONE TRAVELINE ON 0871 200 22 33

USEFUL INFORMATION

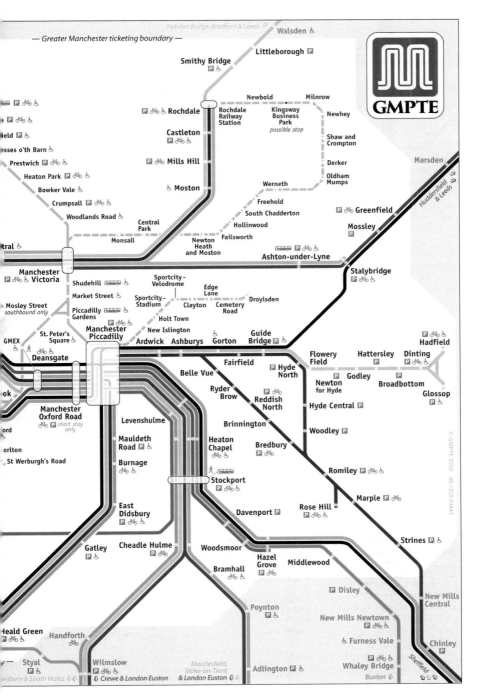

Air travel

Manchester Airport has recently undergone an £80 million facelift and children's areas have definitely improved. To make things easier allow yourself plenty of time for absolutely everything!

Jetting off with the kids

GETTING THERE

Manchester Airport is supported by excellent road and rail links and the train station is connected to Terminal 1 by a walkway. Buses and trains run 24/7.

If you're driving to the airport, pre-book a car park as it's considerably better value. The new Jet Parks has rates starting from as little as £2.99 a day. Either call or book online. The better value parking options can be further away from the terminals with a bus transfer. Premier Park is a 5/10 minute transfer and the Long Stay car park is a 5 minute transfer. Alternatively you can pay extra and park in the Short Stay car park and walk into the terminal. For complete indulgence there is also Valet Parking. Based directly next to the Terminals it is just a few minutes walk to the check-in desks. If you can splash out it makes it a much less stressful start to your trip, especially if you're travelling with children.

■ **Take a look at the inside cover of Babies in the City for a fantastic deal on Valet Parking at Manchester Airport**

IN THE TERMINAL

You can take your buggy all the way to the gate and there are new pushchair friendly channels leading through to security making things a little easier.

If you are taking baby food or milk, it must be in a re-sealable container and you will have to taste it before going through security. These can be any size.

Any liquids or creams must be 100ml or less if you're carrying it in your hand luggage. Boots is located after security in all terminals so you can purchase items such as milk cartons and baby jars to carry-on with you.

Baby changing facilities in Terminal 1 have been upgraded and now include a bottle warmer and a breastfeeding area. In Terminals 2 and 3 baby changing is inside or by the ladies toilet. There is a children's play area in The Food Village in Terminal 2. There are art desks in most eating areas where your children can colour in and play. For older children there are games rooms available throughout the airport. Terminal 1's Real Food Company also offers a kids' play area with a TV showing the latest cartoons, a puzzle-mania table and colouring sets.

For Summer 2010, the Airport hopes to open another child's play facility airside within Terminal 2. It will be open 24 hours and suitable for children between 3 and 12 years.

If you want a bit of luxury, there are lounges that allow children; the Bollin Lounge in Terminal 1 and the Styal Lounge in Terminal 2. They offer complimentary drinks, snacks, newspapers and magazines. The Bollin costs £17.95 per person and you have to pay full price for children of any age. The Styal lounge has a £20 policy per person, £10 per child aged up to 6 years. Children under 6 years are welcome by airline invitation only.

Available throughout the airport and in most café areas are hot spots for laptops.

EATING

The Real Food Company in Terminals 1 and 2 offer a 'Globetrotters' meal for just £1.99 that includes a range of options, including half jacket potatoes with a filling or beans on toast, and a soft drink. There is also a Globetrotters 'pick n mix' where younger passengers choose from five products including a ham or cheese sandwich, fruit jelly, a piece of fruit, crisps and chocolate bar as well as a cold drink.

FINALLY

It's worth contacting your airline before you travel, to see what they provide on board for children, such as sky cots, baby food, toddler meals and any children's entertainment. If you're travelling on your own with small children, also enquire to see what extra help they can offer.

Manchester Airport, Manchester M90 1QX
Tel: 08712 710 711 www.manchesterairport.co.uk
Car Park Mon-Sun 7am-10pm Tel: 0871 310 2200
Executive Lounge Tel: 0870 787 6877 www.executivelounges.com

USEFUL INFORMATION

Index

Index